FALL OF MAN

PLANET OF THE APES

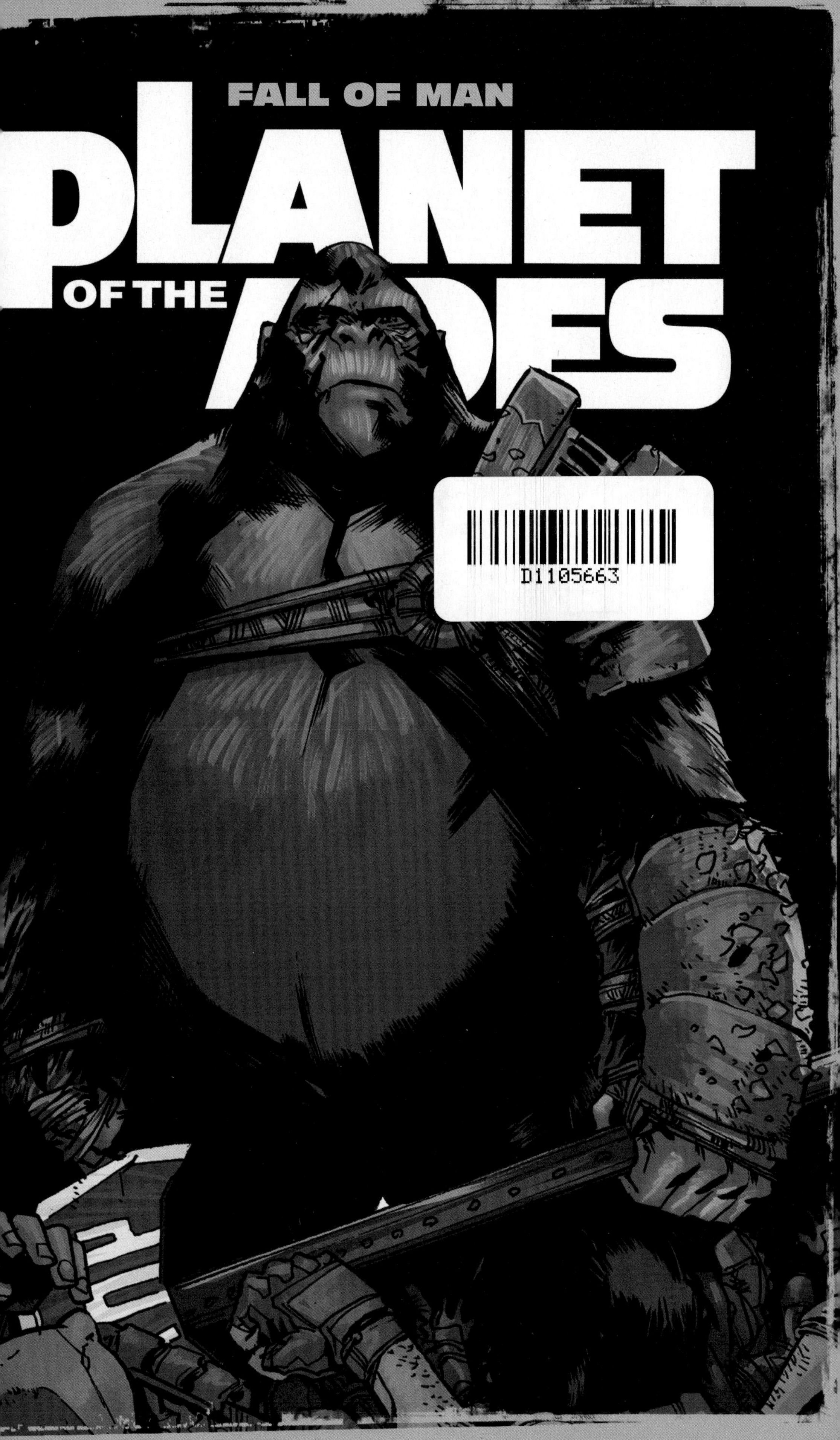

Collection Editor **Jennifer Grünwald**

Assistant Editor **Daniel Kirchhoffer**

Associate Manager, Talent Relations **Lisa Montalbano**

VP Production & Special Projects **Jeff Youngquist**

Book Designer **Jay Bowen**

Manager & Senior Designer **Adam Del Re**

SVP Print, Sales & Marketing **David Gabriel**

Editor in Chief **C.B. Cebulski**

PLANET OF THE APES: FALL OF MAN. Contains material originally published in magazine form as PLANET OF THE APES (2023) #1-5. First printing 2023. ISBN 978-1-302-95086-6. Published by MARVEL WORLDWIDE, INC., a subsidiary of MARVEL ENTERTAINMENT, LLC. OFFICE OF PUBLICATION: 1290 Avenue of the Americas, New York, NY 10104. © 2023 20th Century Studios. No similarity between any of the names, characters, persons, and/or institutions in this book with those of any living or dead person or institution is intended, and any such similarity which may exist is purely coincidental. Marvel and its logos are TM Marvel Characters, Inc. **Printed in Canada.** KEVIN FEIGE, Chief Creative Officer; DAN BUCKLEY, President, Marvel Entertainment; DAVID BOGART, Associate Publisher & SVP of Talent Affairs; TOM BREVOORT, VP, Executive Editor; NICK LOWE, Executive Editor, VP of Content, Digital Publishing; DAVID GABRIEL, VP of Print & Digital Publishing; SVEN LARSEN, VP of Licensed Publishing; MARK ANNUNZIATO, VP of Planning & Forecasting; JEFF YOUNGQUIST, VP of Production & Special Projects; ALEX MORALES, Director of Publishing Operations; DAN EDINGTON, Director of Editorial Operations; RICKEY PURDIN, Director of Talent Relations; JENNIFER GRÜNWALD, Director of Production & Special Projects; SUSAN CRESPI, Production Manager; STAN LEE, Chairman Emeritus. For information regarding advertising in Marvel Comics or on Marvel.com, please contact Vit DeBellis, Custom Solutions & Integrated Advertising Manager, at vdebellis@marvel.com. For Marvel subscription inquiries, please call 888-511-5480. **Manufactured between 8/25/2023 and 9/26/2023 by SOLISCO PRINTERS, SCOTT, QC, CANADA.**

10 9 8 7 6 5 4 3 2 1

MARVEL COMICS PRESENTS

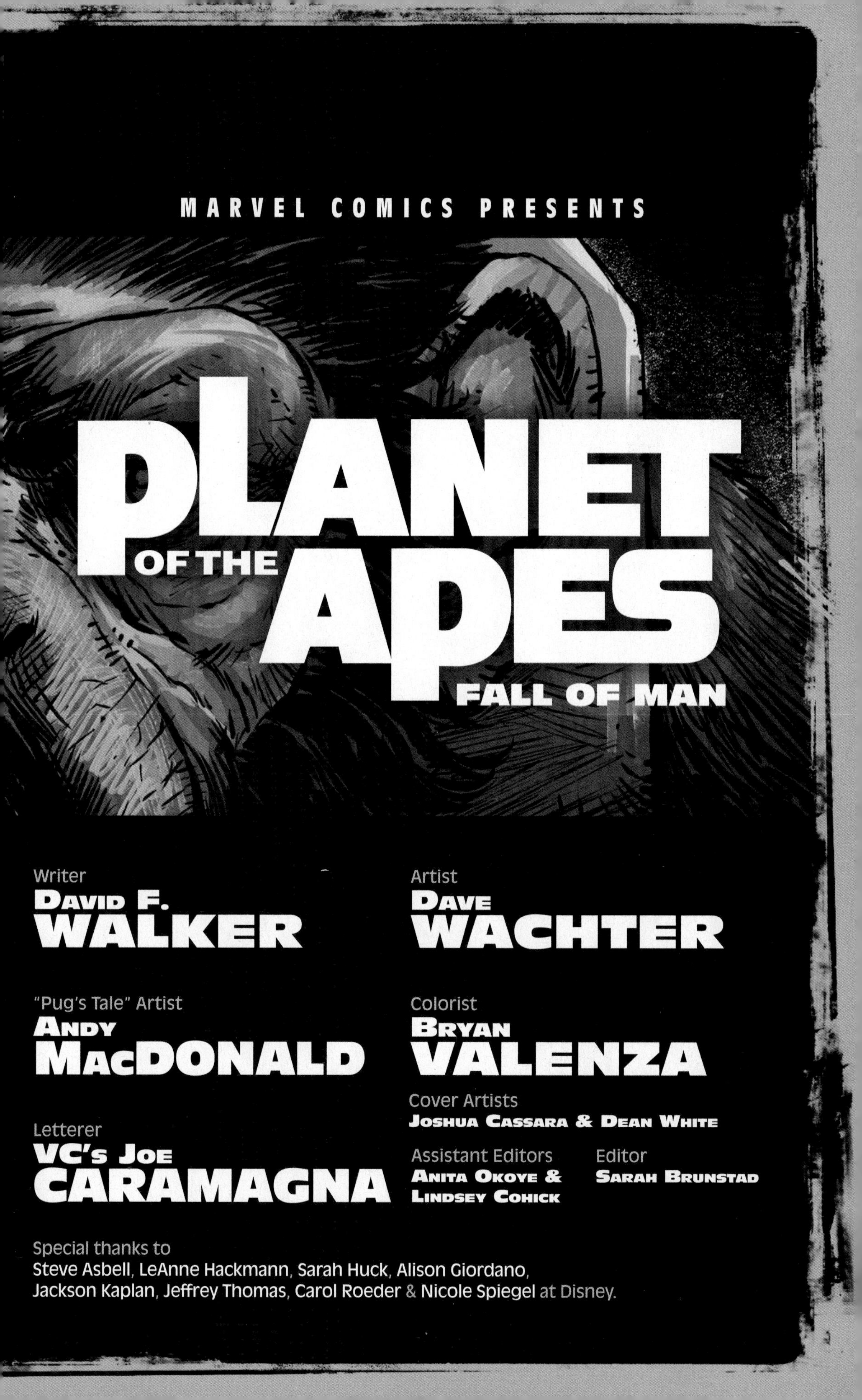

PLANET OF THE APES
FALL OF MAN

Writer
DAVID F. WALKER

Artist
DAVE WACHTER

"Pug's Tale" Artist
ANDY MACDONALD

Colorist
BRYAN VALENZA

Cover Artists
JOSHUA CASSARA & DEAN WHITE

Letterer
VC's JOE CARAMAGNA

Assistant Editors
ANITA OKOYE & LINDSEY COHICK

Editor
SARAH BRUNSTAD

Special thanks to
Steve Asbell, LeAnne Hackmann, Sarah Huck, Alison Giordano,
Jackson Kaplan, Jeffrey Thomas, Carol Roeder & Nicole Spiegel at Disney.

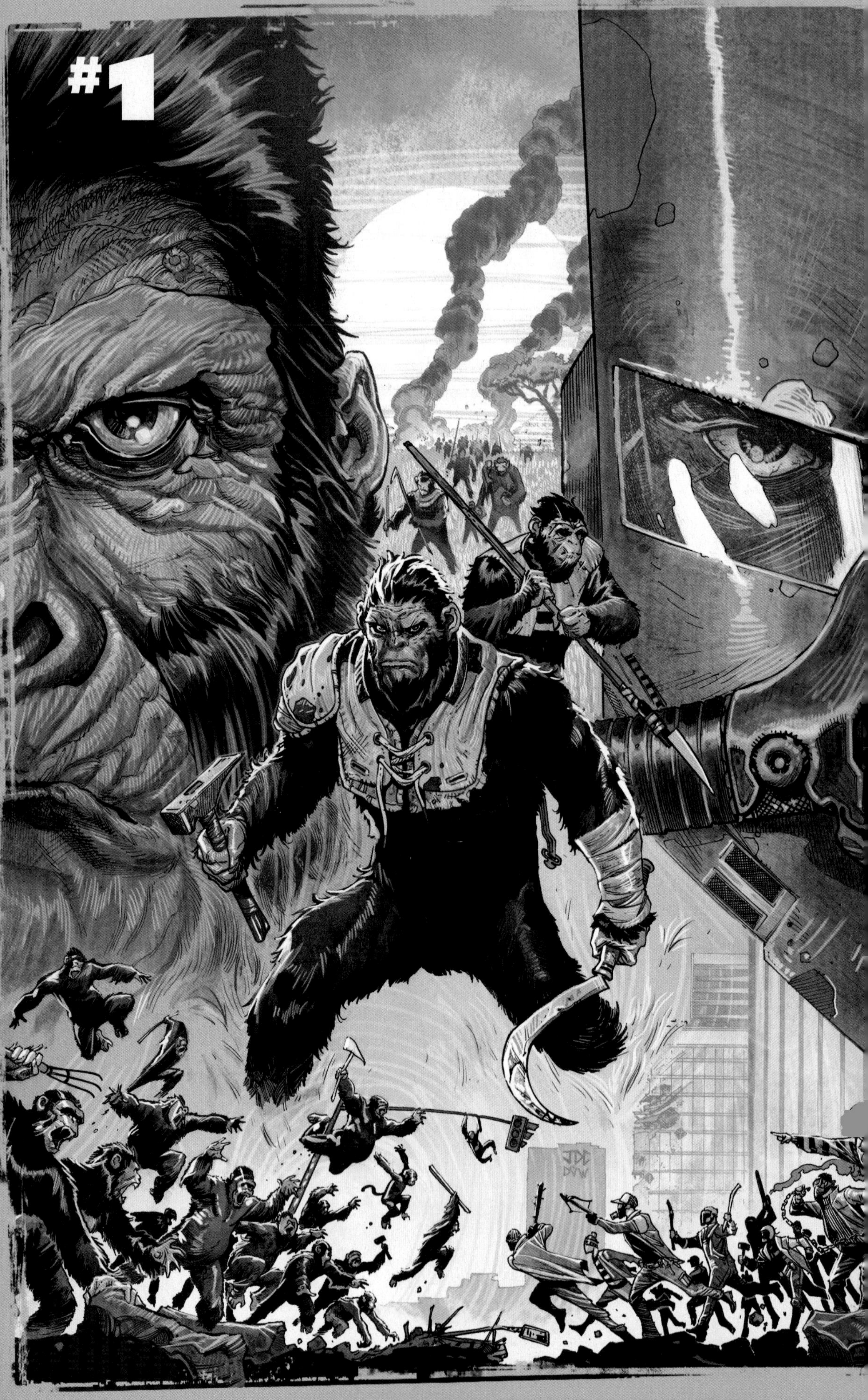
#1

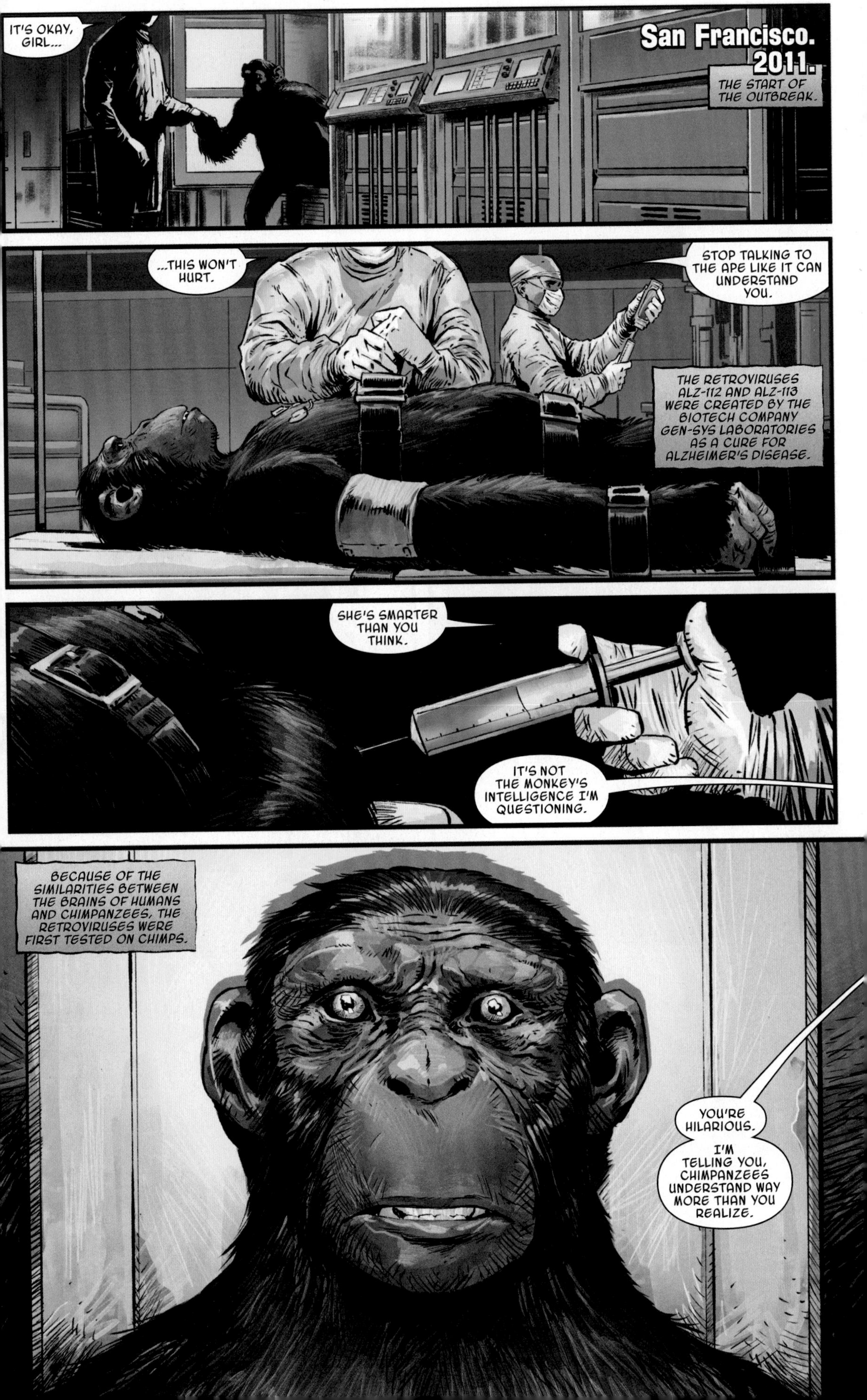

IT'S OKAY, GIRL...
San Francisco. 2011.
THE START OF THE OUTBREAK.
...THIS WON'T HURT.
STOP TALKING TO THE APE LIKE IT CAN UNDERSTAND YOU.
THE RETROVIRUSES ALZ-112 AND ALZ-113 WERE CREATED BY THE BIOTECH COMPANY GEN-SYS LABORATORIES AS A CURE FOR ALZHEIMER'S DISEASE.
SHE'S SMARTER THAN YOU THINK.
IT'S NOT THE MONKEY'S INTELLIGENCE I'M QUESTIONING.
BECAUSE OF THE SIMILARITIES BETWEEN THE BRAINS OF HUMANS AND CHIMPANZEES, THE RETROVIRUSES WERE FIRST TESTED ON CHIMPS.
YOU'RE HILARIOUS.
I'M TELLING YOU, CHIMPANZEES UNDERSTAND WAY MORE THAN YOU REALIZE.

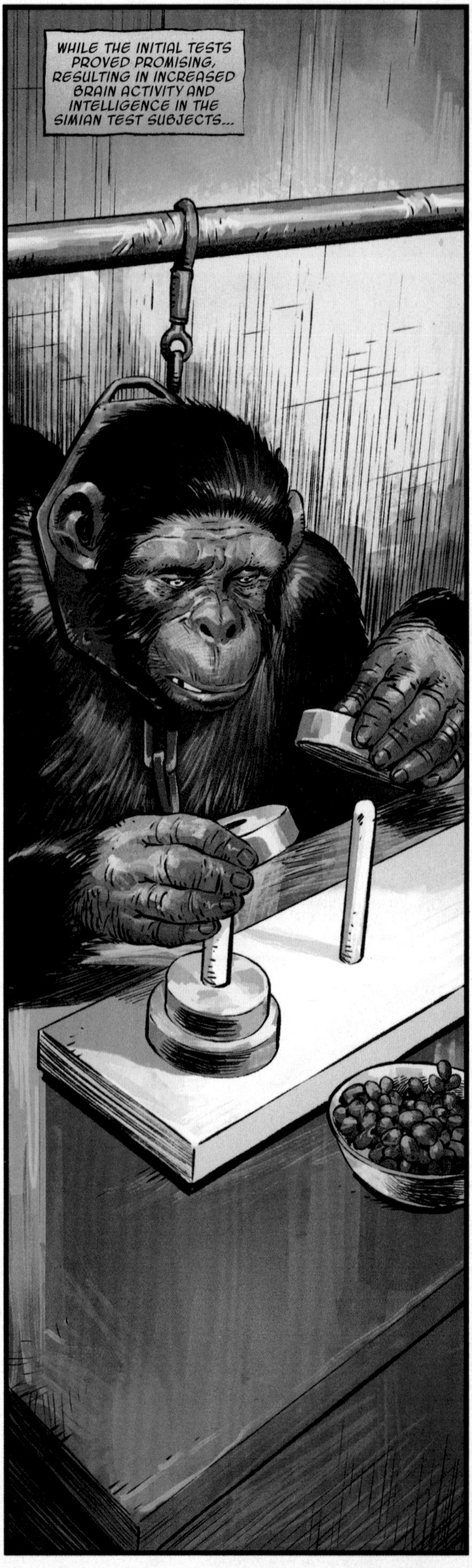
WHILE THE INITIAL TESTS PROVED PROMISING, RESULTING IN INCREASED BRAIN ACTIVITY AND INTELLIGENCE IN THE SIMIAN TEST SUBJECTS...

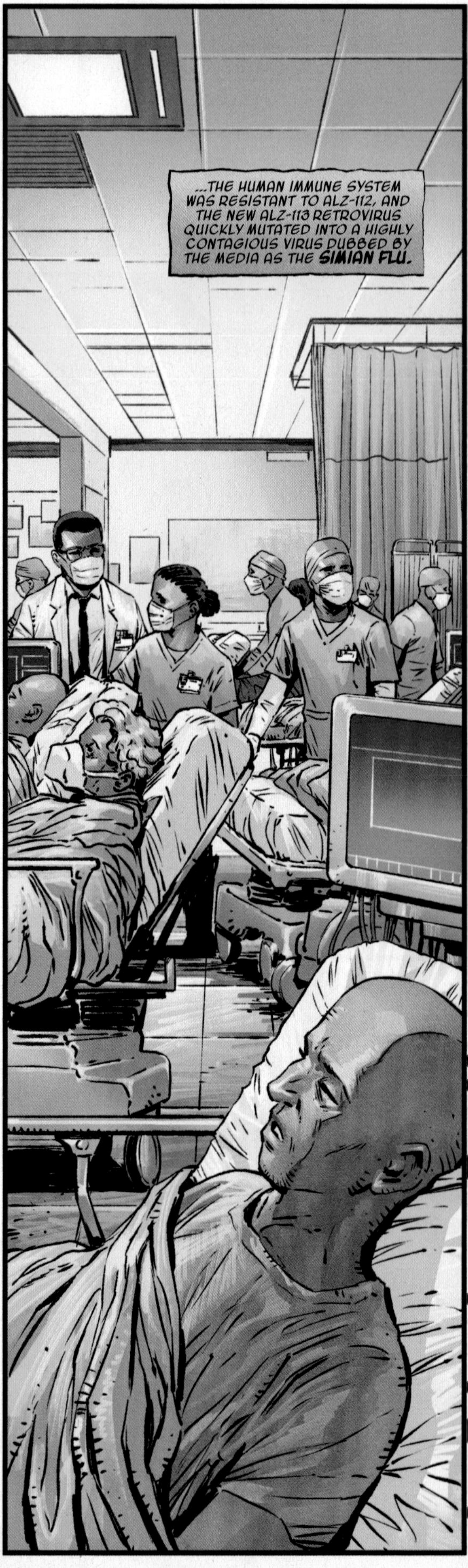
...THE HUMAN IMMUNE SYSTEM WAS RESISTANT TO ALZ-112, AND THE NEW ALZ-113 RETROVIRUS QUICKLY MUTATED INTO A HIGHLY CONTAGIOUS VIRUS DUBBED BY THE MEDIA AS THE SIMIAN FLU.

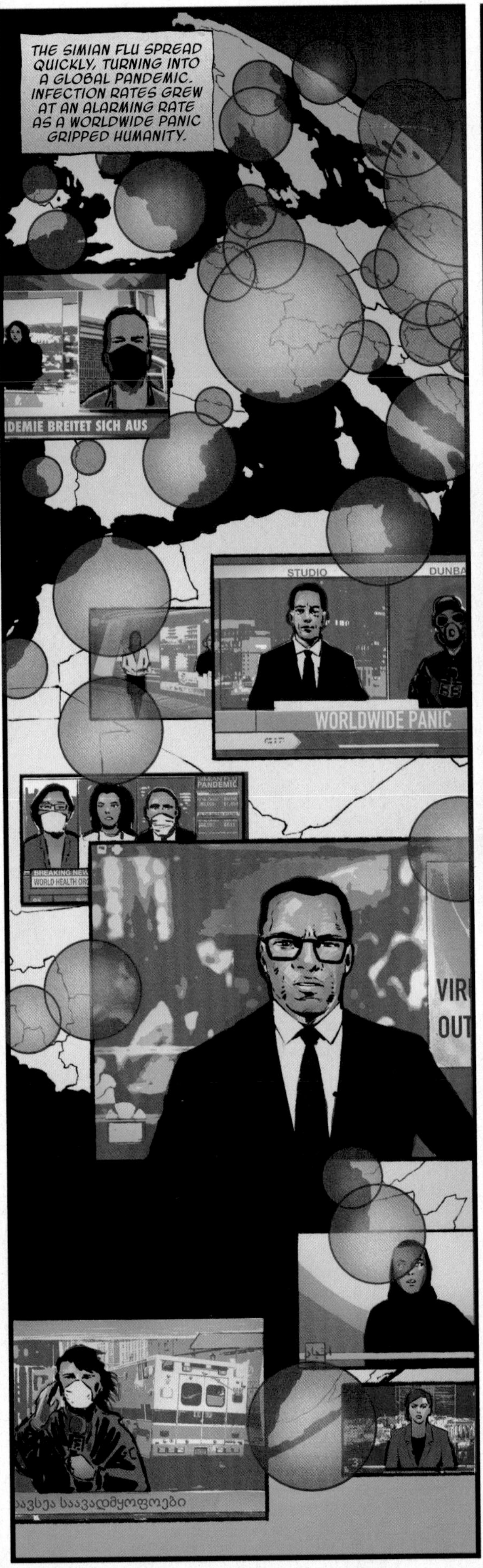
THE SIMIAN FLU SPREAD QUICKLY, TURNING INTO A GLOBAL PANDEMIC. INFECTION RATES GREW AT AN ALARMING RATE AS A WORLDWIDE PANIC GRIPPED HUMANITY.
DEMIE BREITET SICH AUS
STUDIO
DUNBA
WORLDWIDE PANIC
SIMIAN FLU PANDEMIC
BREAKING NEW
WORLD HEALTH ORG
VIR
OUT

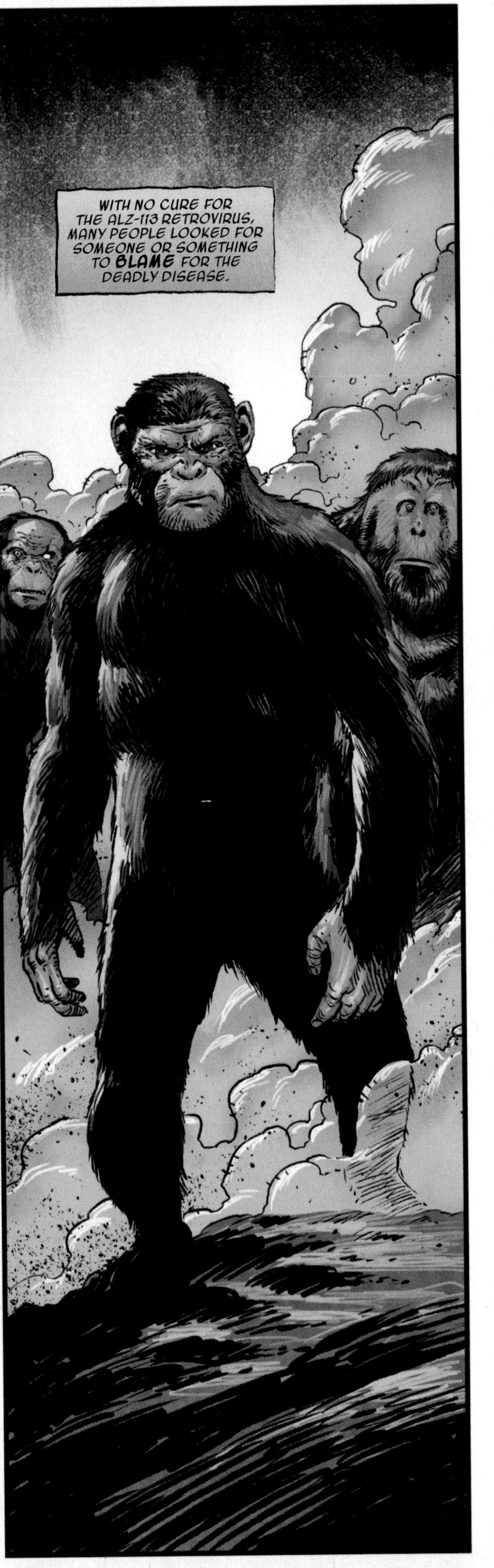
WITH NO CURE FOR THE ALZ-113 RETROVIRUS, MANY PEOPLE LOOKED FOR SOMEONE OR SOMETHING TO **BLAME** FOR THE DEADLY DISEASE.

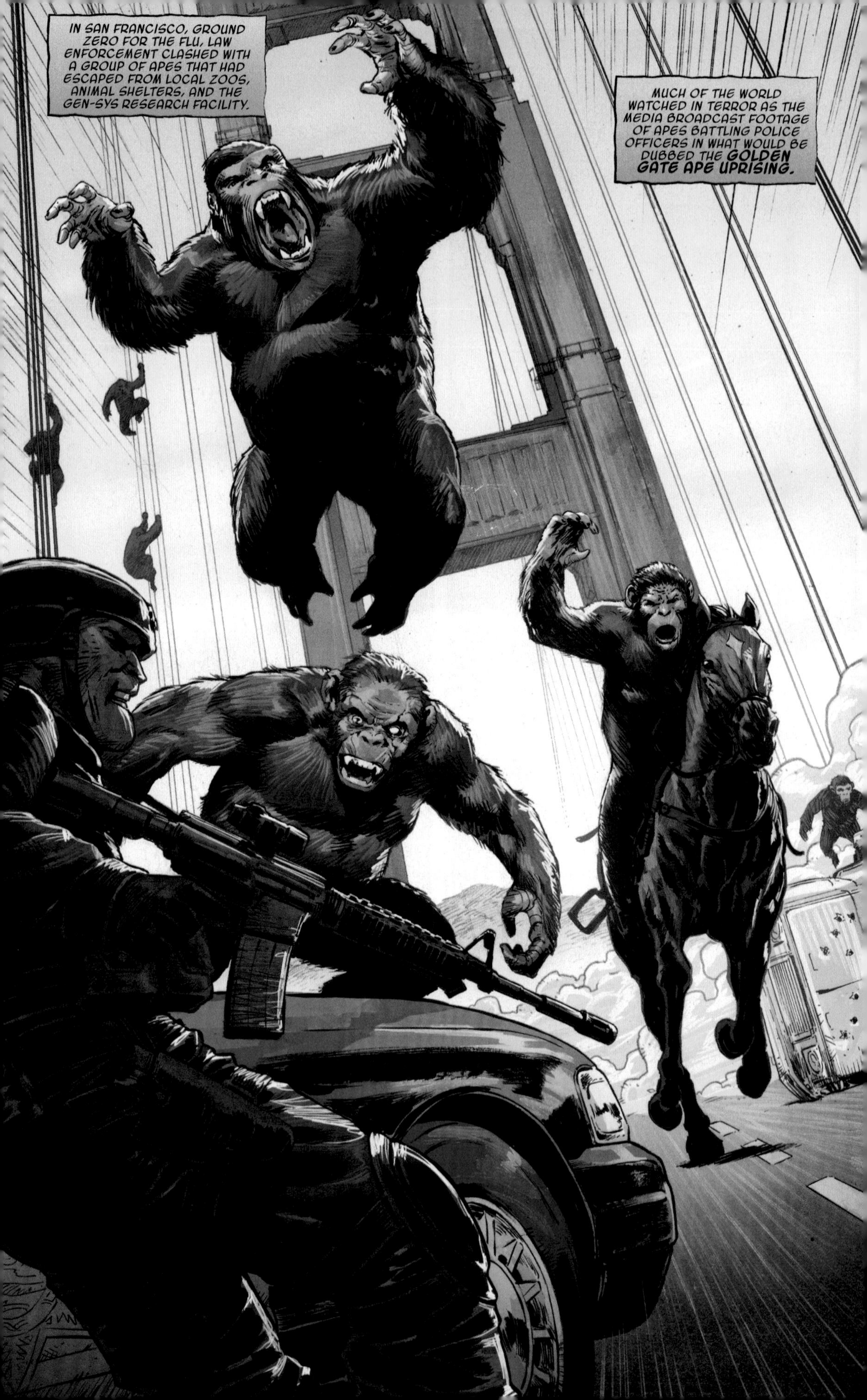
IN SAN FRANCISCO, GROUND ZERO FOR THE FLU, LAW ENFORCEMENT CLASHED WITH A GROUP OF APES THAT HAD ESCAPED FROM LOCAL ZOOS, ANIMAL SHELTERS, AND THE GEN-SYS RESEARCH FACILITY.
MUCH OF THE WORLD WATCHED IN TERROR AS THE MEDIA BROADCAST FOOTAGE OF APES BATTLING POLICE OFFICERS IN WHAT WOULD BE DUBBED THE **GOLDEN GATE APE UPRISING.**

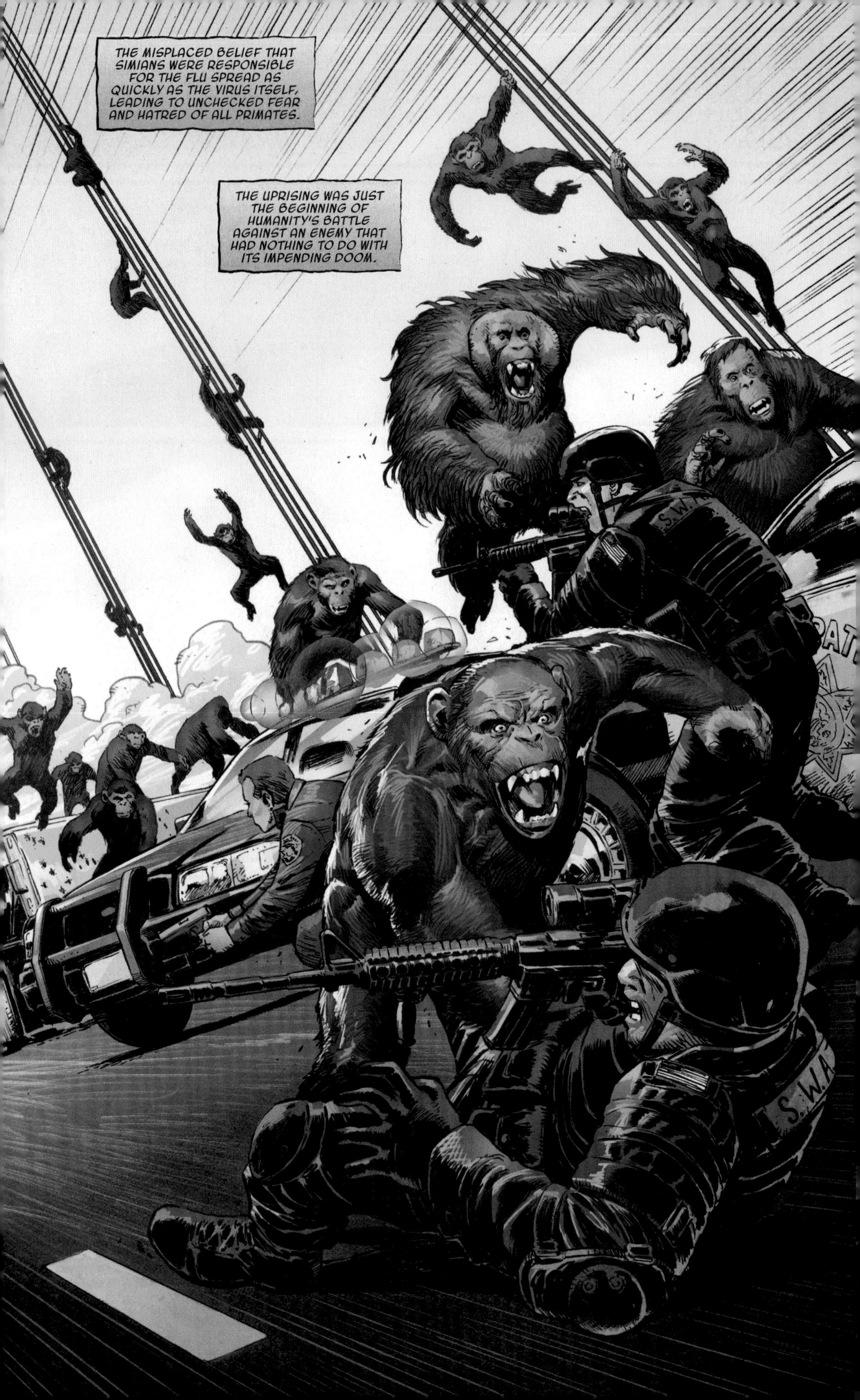
THE MISPLACED BELIEF THAT SIMIANS WERE RESPONSIBLE FOR THE FLU SPREAD AS QUICKLY AS THE VIRUS ITSELF, LEADING TO UNCHECKED FEAR AND HATRED OF ALL PRIMATES.
THE UPRISING WAS JUST THE BEGINNING OF HUMANITY'S BATTLE AGAINST AN ENEMY THAT HAD NOTHING TO DO WITH ITS IMPENDING DOOM.

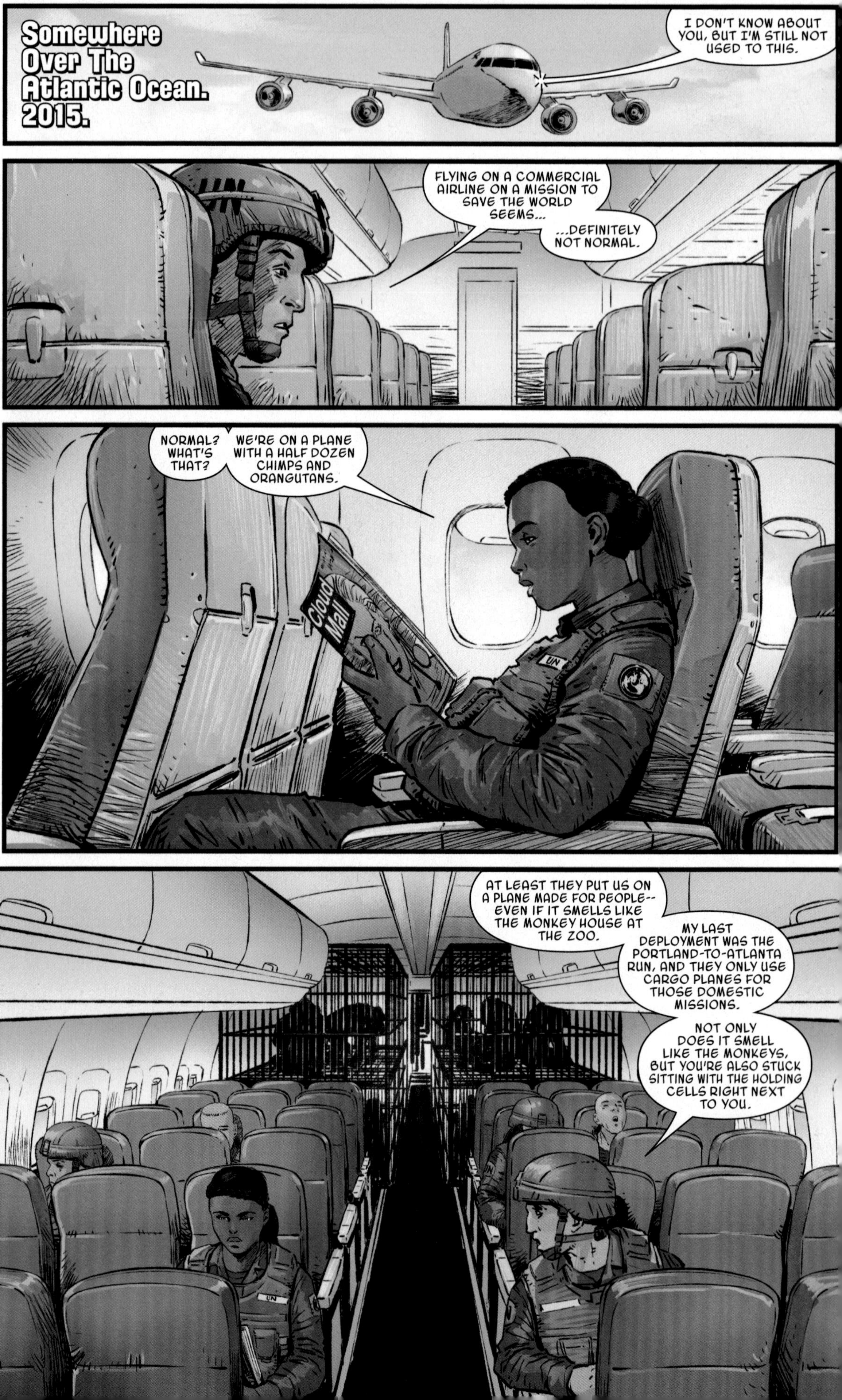
Somewhere Over The Atlantic Ocean. 2015.
I DON'T KNOW ABOUT YOU, BUT I'M STILL NOT USED TO THIS.
FLYING ON A COMMERCIAL AIRLINE ON A MISSION TO SAVE THE WORLD SEEMS...
...DEFINITELY NOT NORMAL.
NORMAL? WHAT'S THAT?
WE'RE ON A PLANE WITH A HALF DOZEN CHIMPS AND ORANGUTANS.
Cloud Mall
AT LEAST THEY PUT US ON A PLANE MADE FOR PEOPLE-- EVEN IF IT SMELLS LIKE THE MONKEY HOUSE AT THE ZOO.
MY LAST DEPLOYMENT WAS THE PORTLAND-TO-ATLANTA RUN, AND THEY ONLY USE CARGO PLANES FOR THOSE DOMESTIC MISSIONS.
NOT ONLY DOES IT SMELL LIKE THE MONKEYS, BUT YOU'RE ALSO STUCK SITTING WITH THE HOLDING CELLS RIGHT NEXT TO YOU.

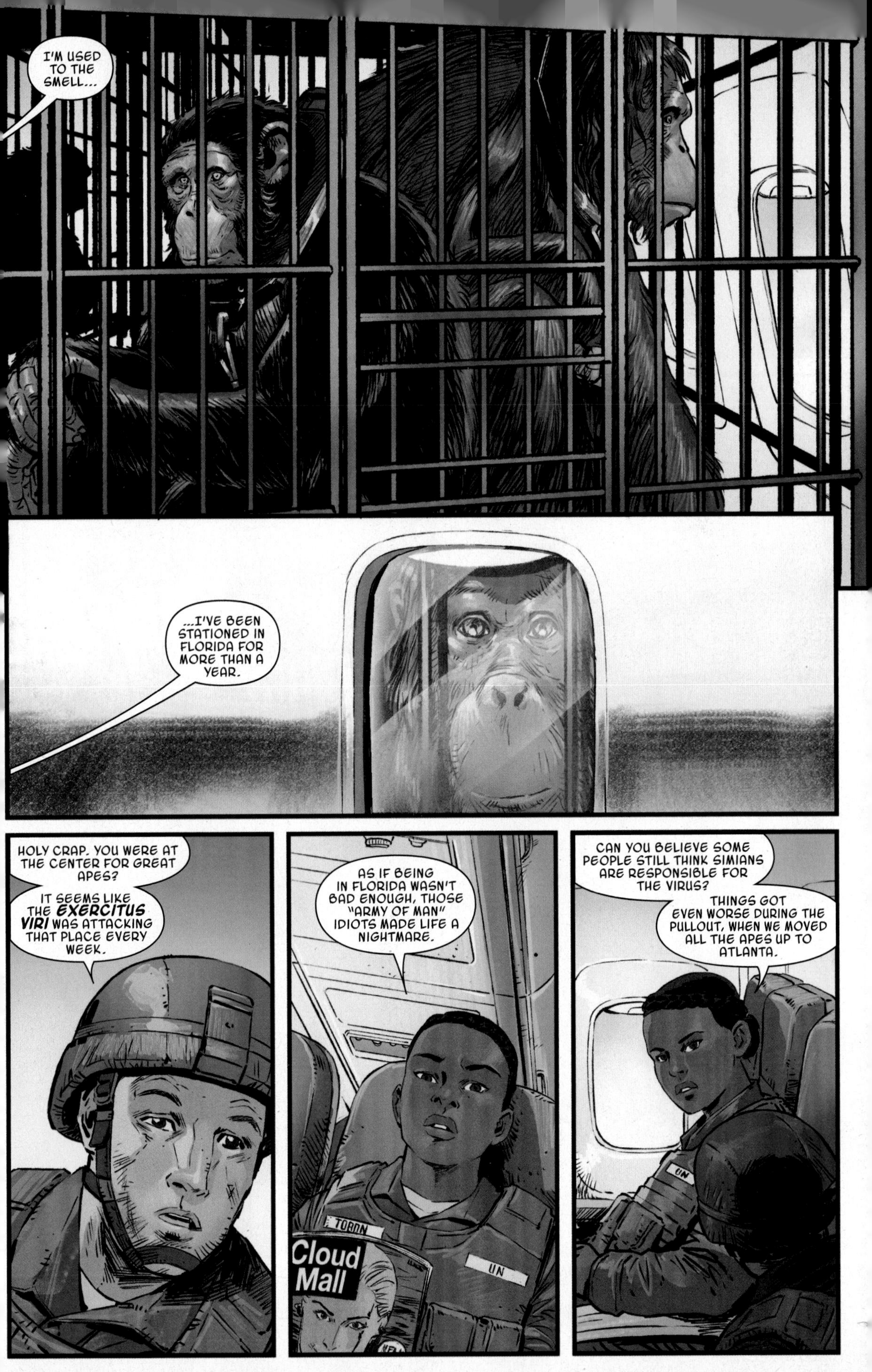
I'M USED TO THE SMELL...
...I'VE BEEN STATIONED IN FLORIDA FOR MORE THAN A YEAR.
HOLY CRAP. YOU WERE AT THE CENTER FOR GREAT APES?
IT SEEMS LIKE THE EXERCITUS VIRI WAS ATTACKING THAT PLACE EVERY WEEK.
AS IF BEING IN FLORIDA WASN'T BAD ENOUGH, THOSE "ARMY OF MAN" IDIOTS MADE LIFE A NIGHTMARE.
TORNN
UN
Cloud Mall
CAN YOU BELIEVE SOME PEOPLE STILL THINK SIMIANS ARE RESPONSIBLE FOR THE VIRUS?
THINGS GOT EVEN WORSE DURING THE PULLOUT, WHEN WE MOVED ALL THE APES UP TO ATLANTA.
UN

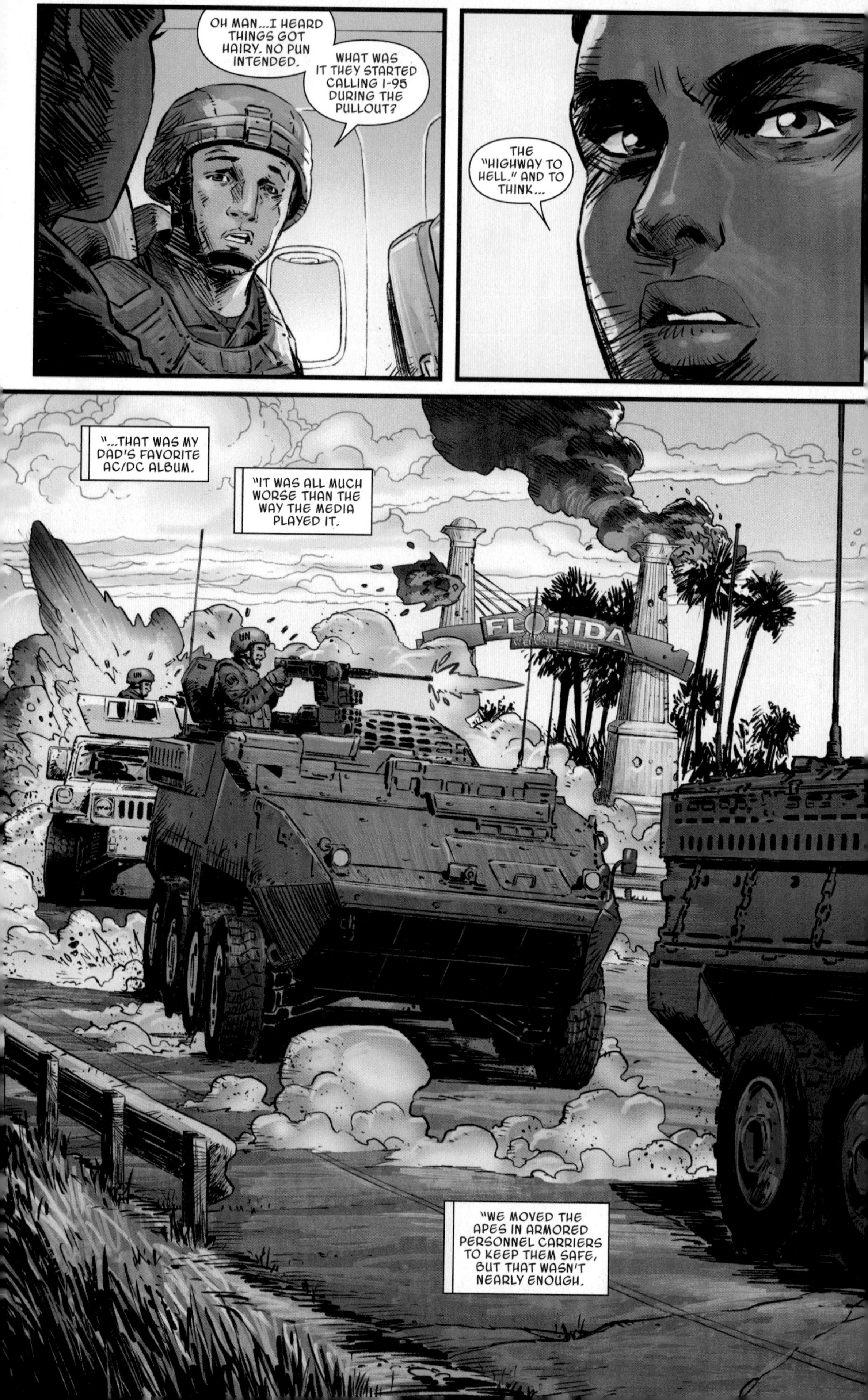
OH MAN...I HEARD THINGS GOT HAIRY. NO PUN INTENDED.
WHAT WAS IT THEY STARTED CALLING I-95 DURING THE PULLOUT?
THE "HIGHWAY TO HELL," AND TO THINK...
"...THAT WAS MY DAD'S FAVORITE AC/DC ALBUM.
"IT WAS ALL MUCH WORSE THAN THE WAY THE MEDIA PLAYED IT.
FLORIDA
"WE MOVED THE APES IN ARMORED PERSONNEL CARRIERS TO KEEP THEM SAFE, BUT THAT WASN'T NEARLY ENOUGH.

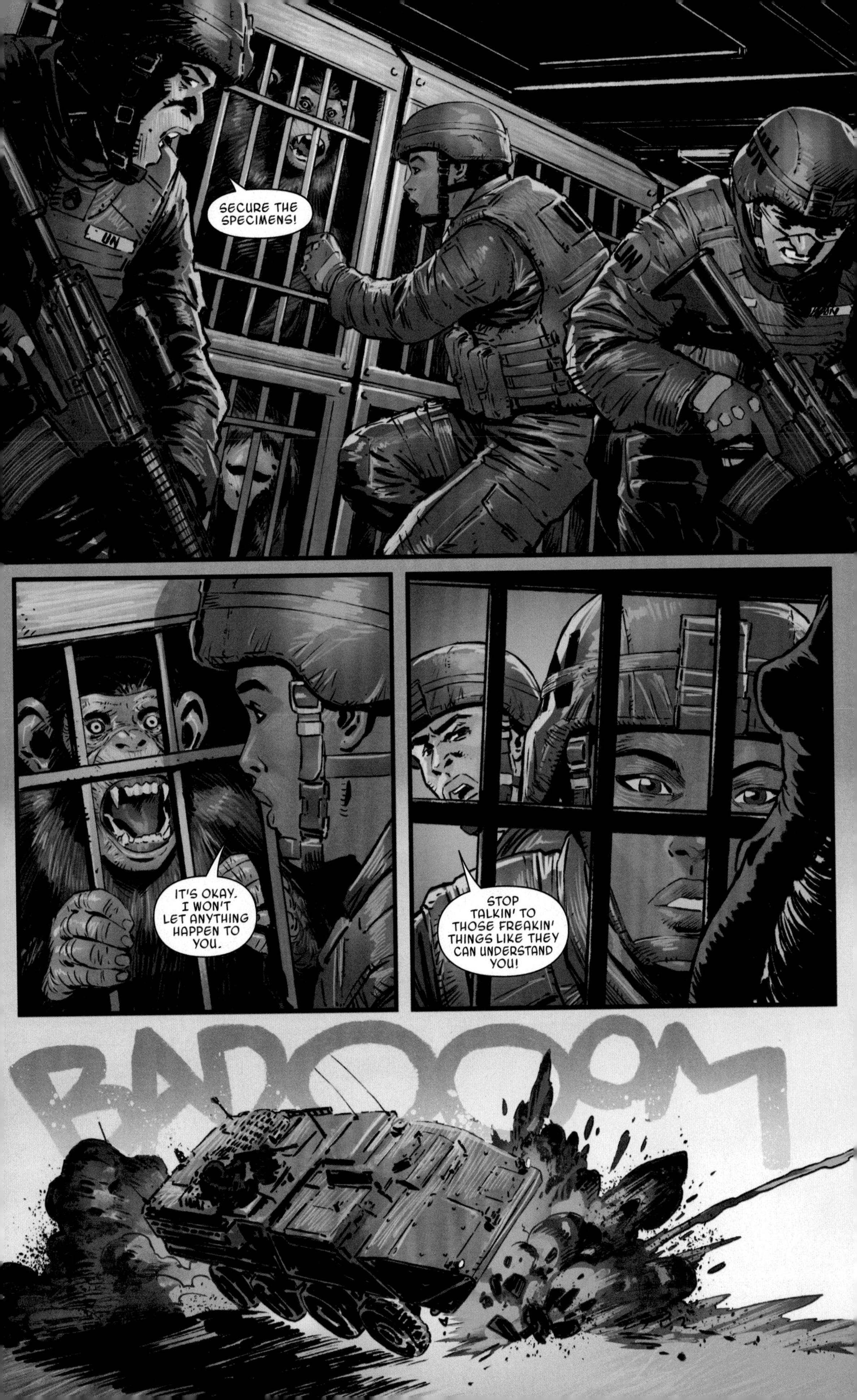
SECURE THE SPECIMENS!
IT'S OKAY. I WON'T LET ANYTHING HAPPEN TO YOU.
STOP TALKIN' TO THOSE FREAKIN' THINGS LIKE THEY CAN UNDERSTAND YOU!
BADOOOM

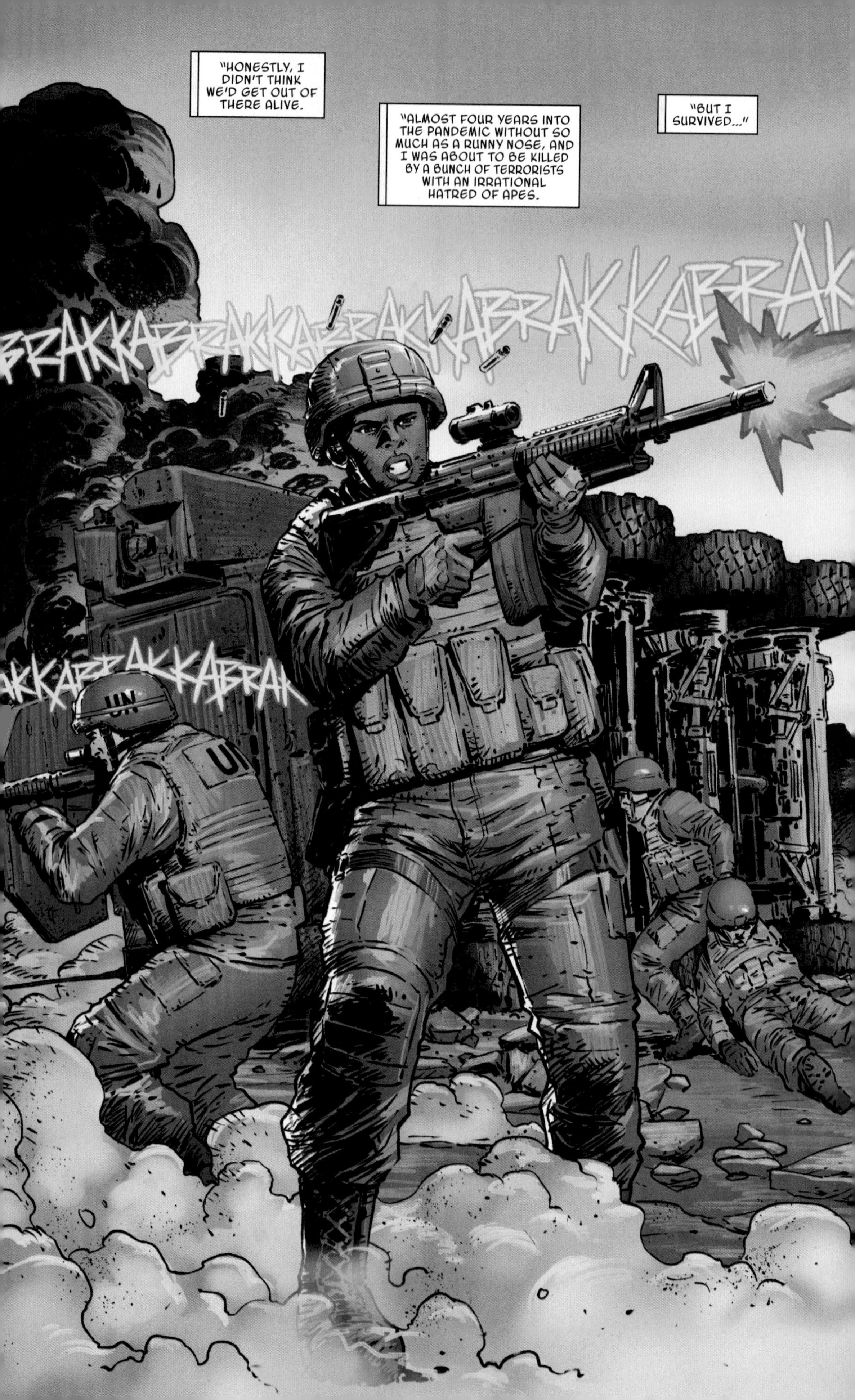
"HONESTLY, I DIDN'T THINK WE'D GET OUT OF THERE ALIVE.
"ALMOST FOUR YEARS INTO THE PANDEMIC WITHOUT SO MUCH AS A RUNNY NOSE, AND I WAS ABOUT TO BE KILLED BY A BUNCH OF TERRORISTS WITH AN IRRATIONAL HATRED OF APES.
"BUT I SURVIVED..."
BRAKKABRAKKABRAKKABRAKKABRAK
KABRAKKABRAK
UN

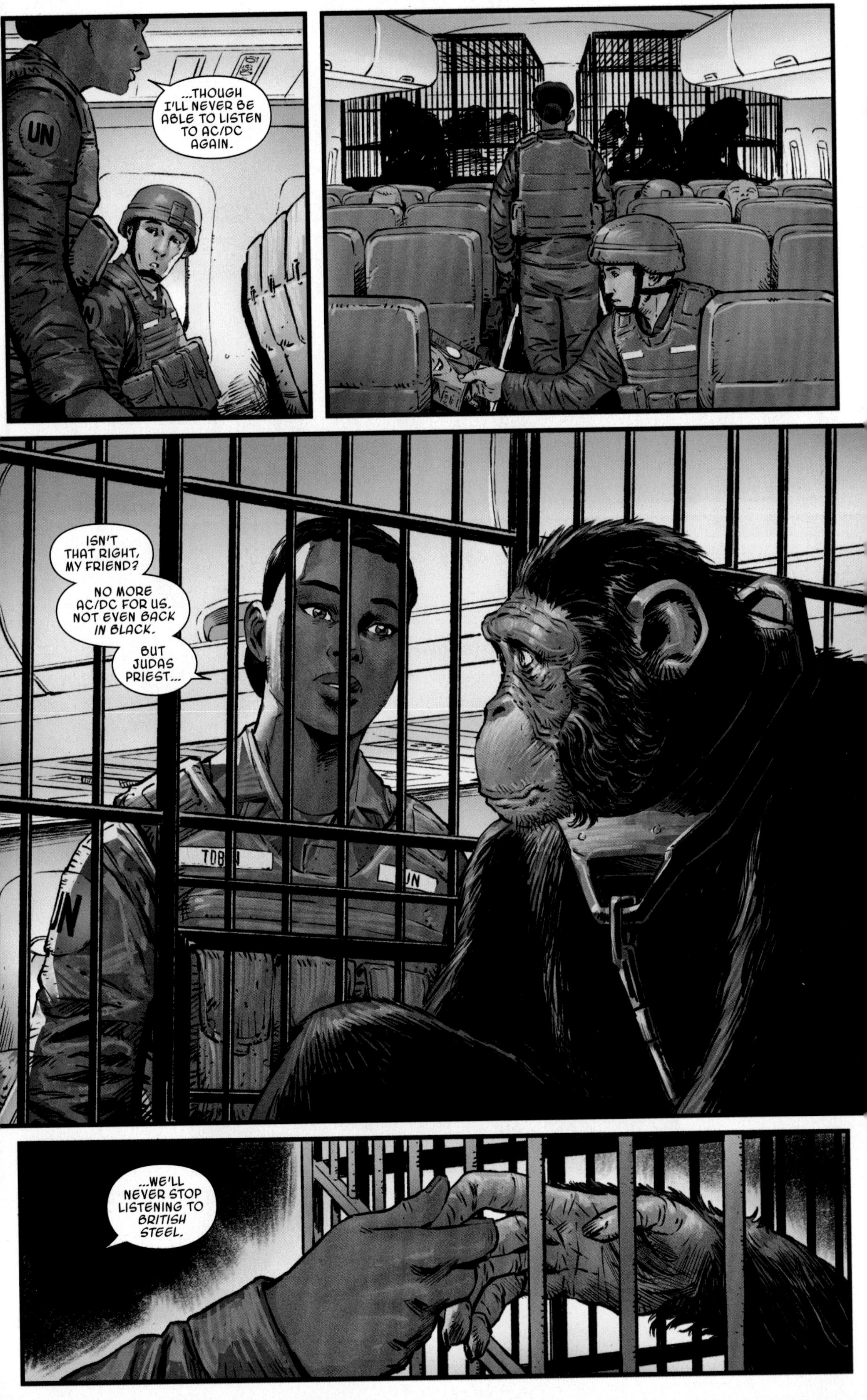
...THOUGH I'LL NEVER BE ABLE TO LISTEN TO AC/DC AGAIN.
ISN'T THAT RIGHT, MY FRIEND?
NO MORE AC/DC FOR US. NOT EVEN BACK IN BLACK.
BUT JUDAS PRIEST...
...WE'LL NEVER STOP LISTENING TO BRITISH STEEL.

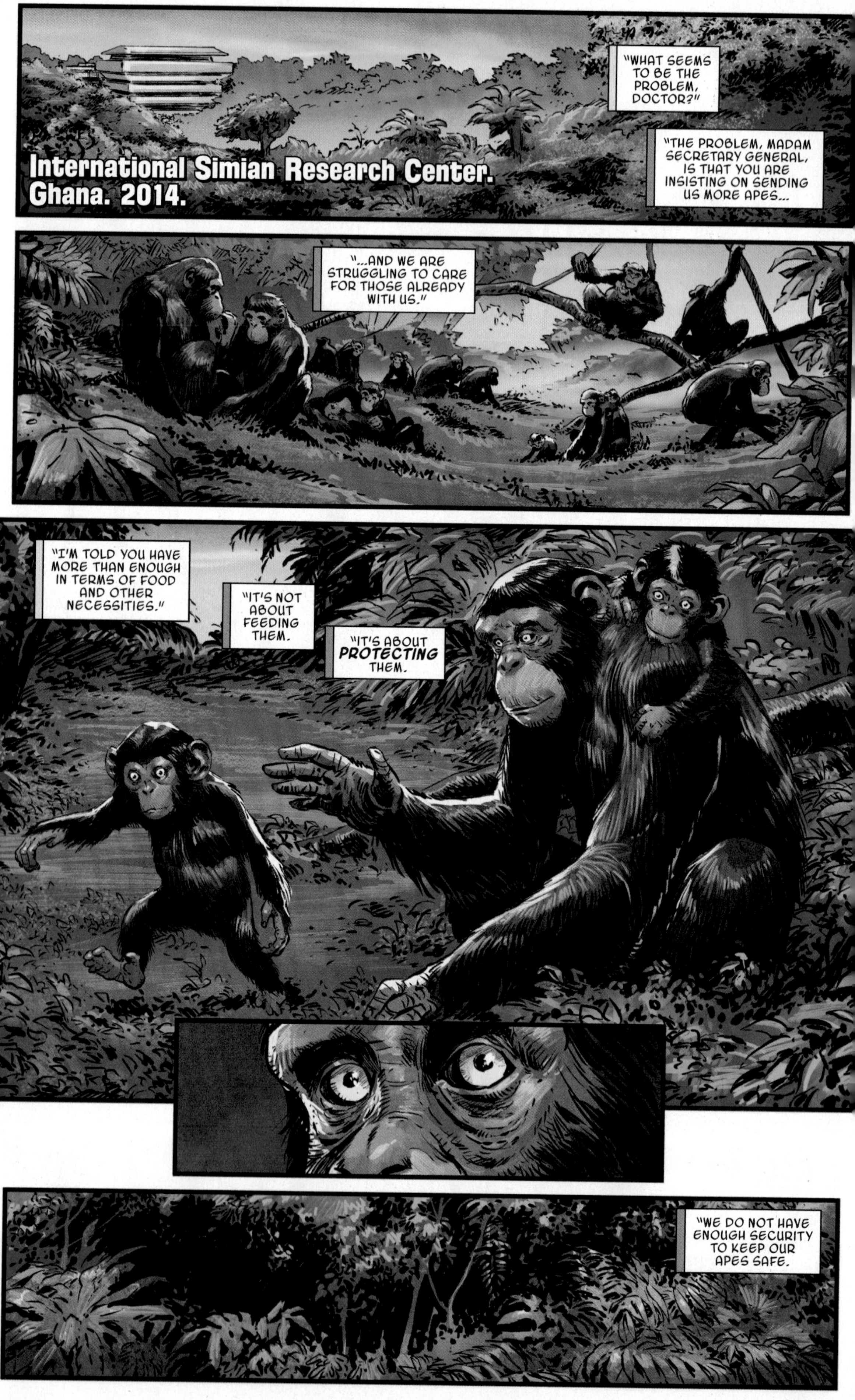
International Simian Research Center. Ghana. 2014.
"WHAT SEEMS TO BE THE PROBLEM, DOCTOR?"
"THE PROBLEM, MADAM SECRETARY GENERAL, IS THAT YOU ARE INSISTING ON SENDING US MORE APES...
"...AND WE ARE STRUGGLING TO CARE FOR THOSE ALREADY WITH US."
"I'M TOLD YOU HAVE MORE THAN ENOUGH IN TERMS OF FOOD AND OTHER NECESSITIES."
"IT'S NOT ABOUT FEEDING THEM.
"IT'S ABOUT PROTECTING THEM.
"WE DO NOT HAVE ENOUGH SECURITY TO KEEP OUR APES SAFE.

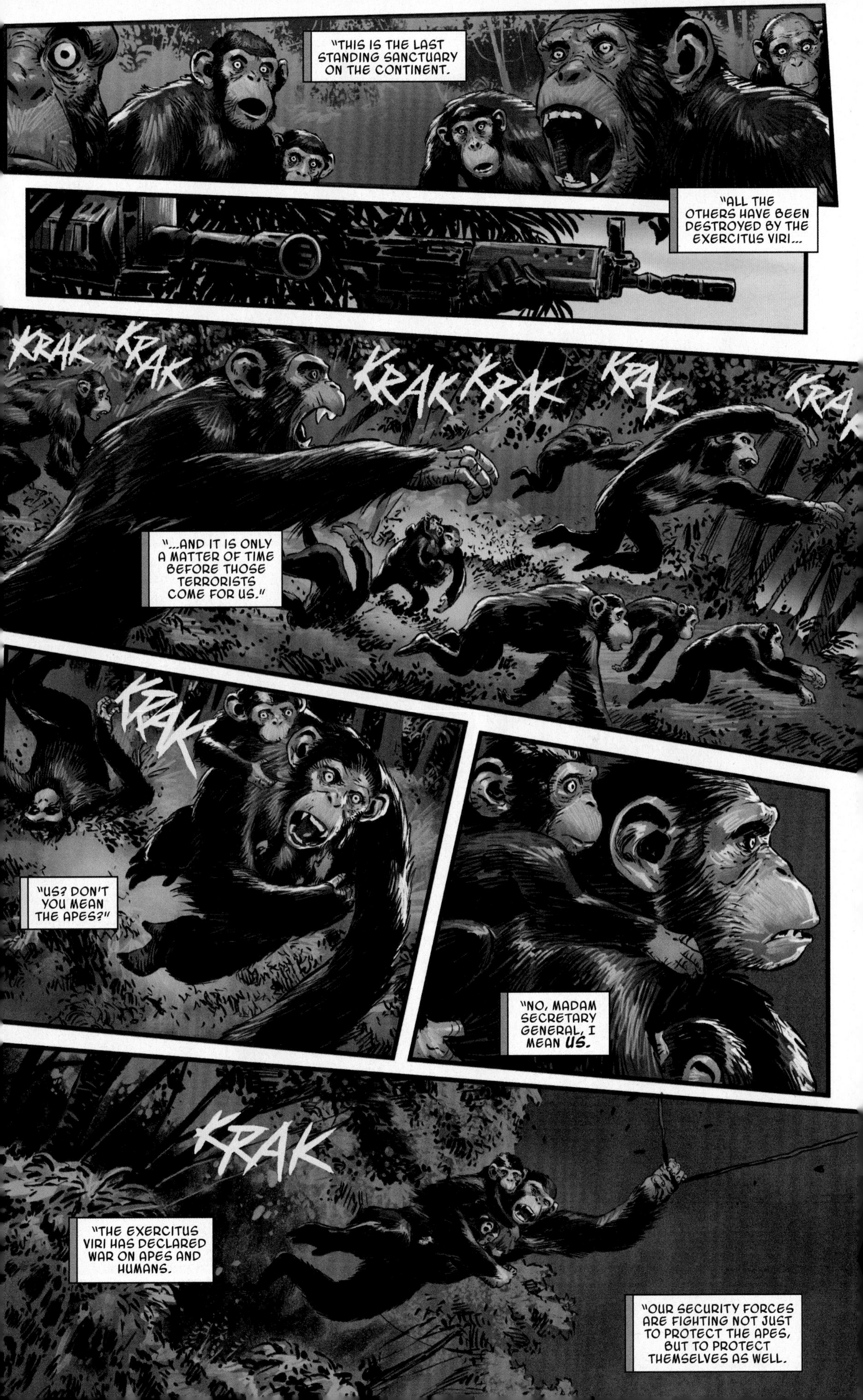
"THIS IS THE LAST STANDING SANCTUARY ON THE CONTINENT.
"ALL THE OTHERS HAVE BEEN DESTROYED BY THE EXERCITUS VIRI...
KRAK KRAK KRAK KRAK KRAK
"...AND IT IS ONLY A MATTER OF TIME BEFORE THOSE TERRORISTS COME FOR US."
KRAK
"US? DON'T YOU MEAN THE APES?"
"NO, MADAM SECRETARY GENERAL, I MEAN US.
KRAK
"THE EXERCITUS VIRI HAS DECLARED WAR ON APES AND HUMANS.
"OUR SECURITY FORCES ARE FIGHTING NOT JUST TO PROTECT THE APES, BUT TO PROTECT THEMSELVES AS WELL.

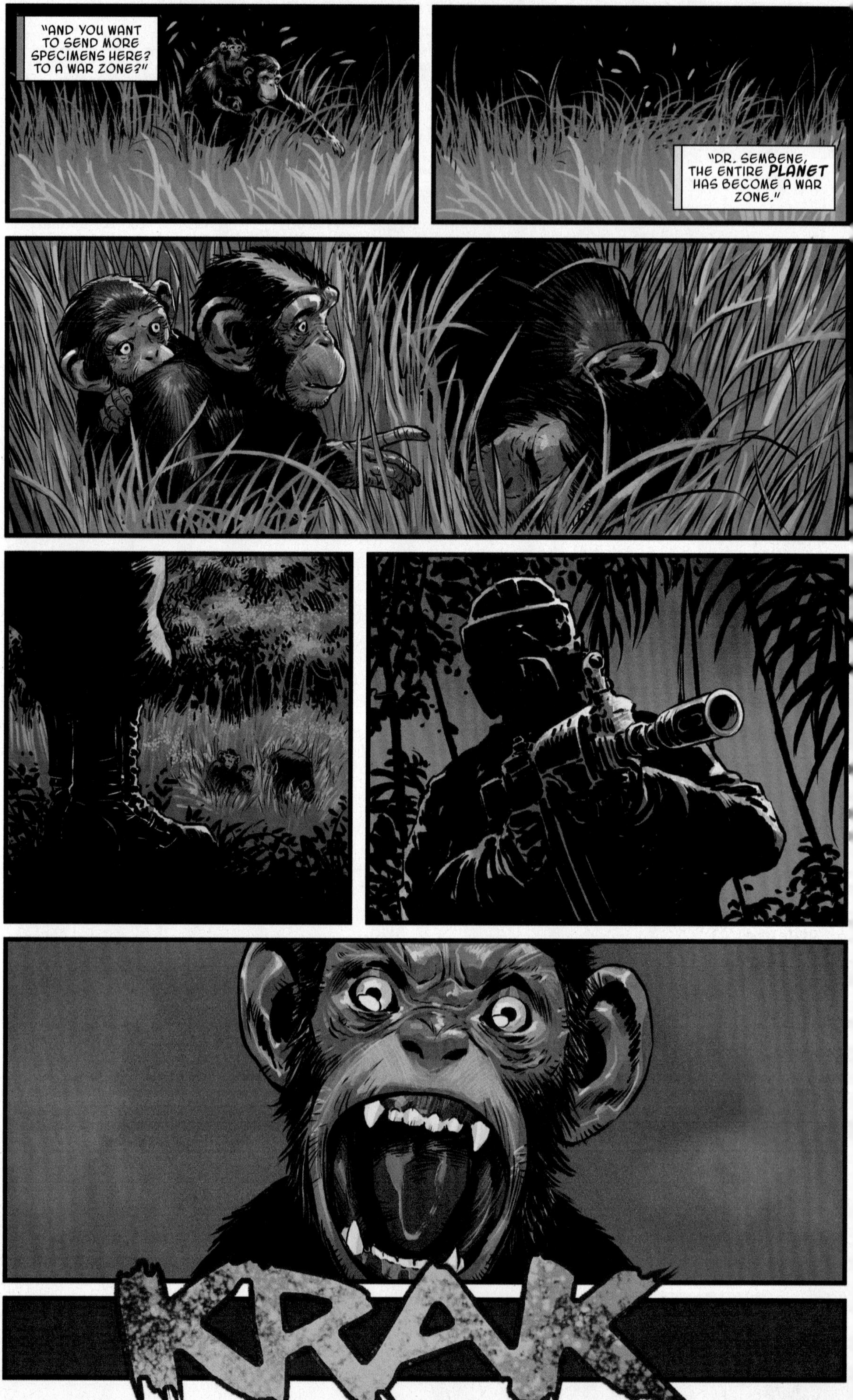
"AND YOU WANT TO SEND MORE SPECIMENS HERE? TO A WAR ZONE?"
"DR. SEMBENE, THE ENTIRE PLANET HAS BECOME A WAR ZONE."
KRAK

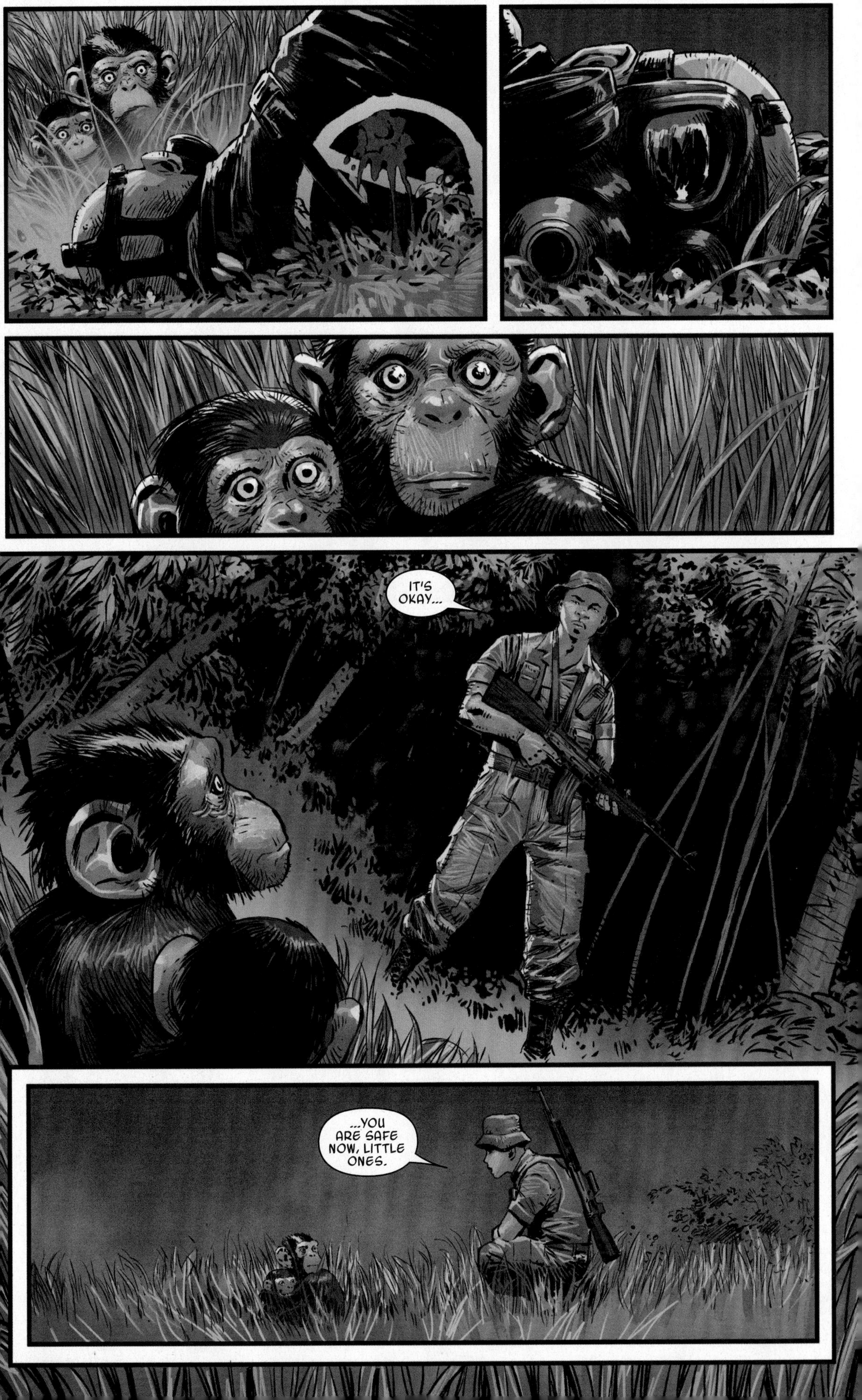
IT'S OKAY...
...YOU ARE SAFE NOW, LITTLE ONES.

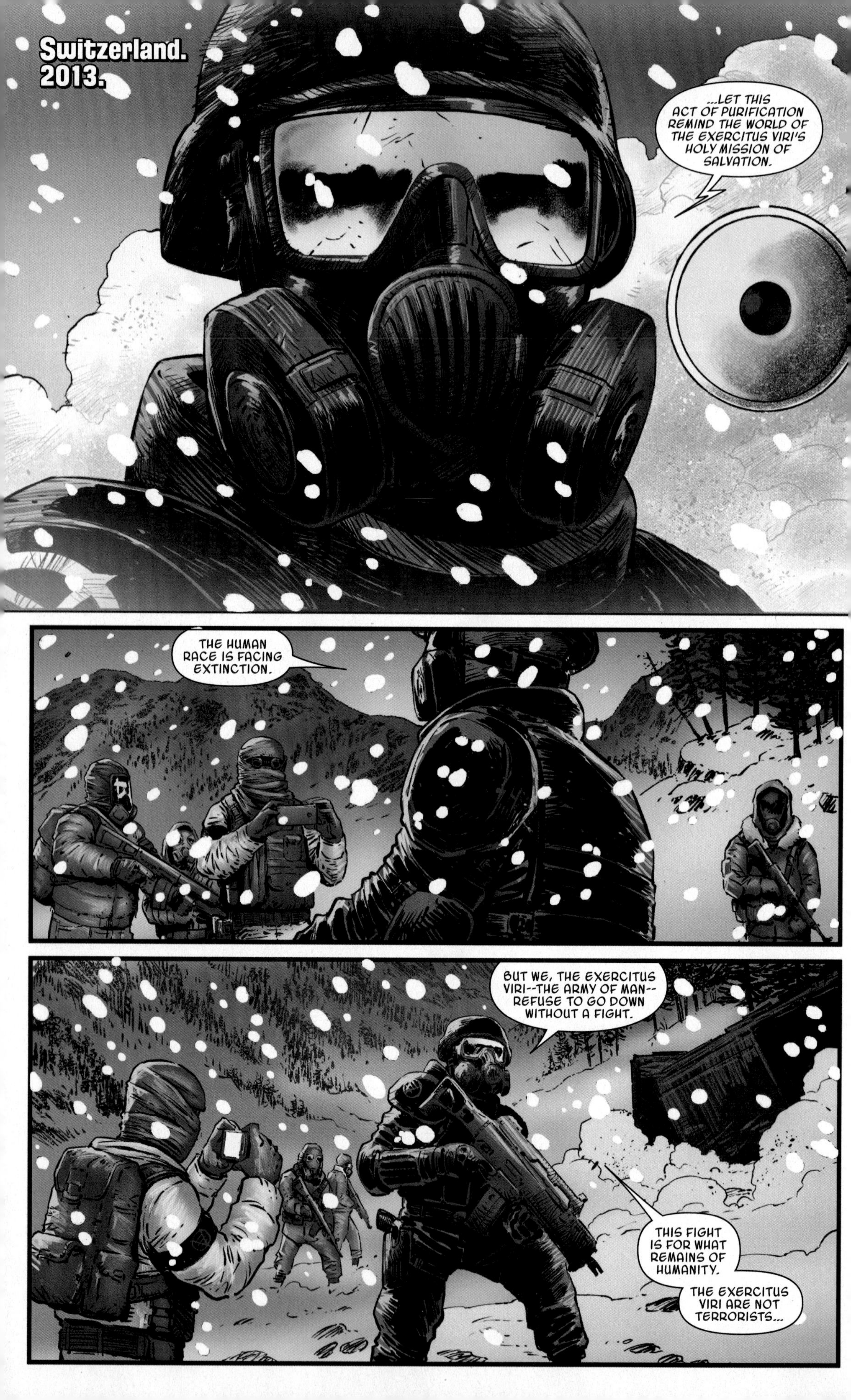
Switzerland.
2013.
...LET THIS ACT OF PURIFICATION REMIND THE WORLD OF THE EXERCITUS VIRI'S HOLY MISSION OF SALVATION.
THE HUMAN RACE IS FACING EXTINCTION.
BUT WE, THE EXERCITUS VIRI--THE ARMY OF MAN--REFUSE TO GO DOWN WITHOUT A FIGHT.
THIS FIGHT IS FOR WHAT REMAINS OF HUMANITY.
THE EXERCITUS VIRI ARE NOT TERRORISTS...

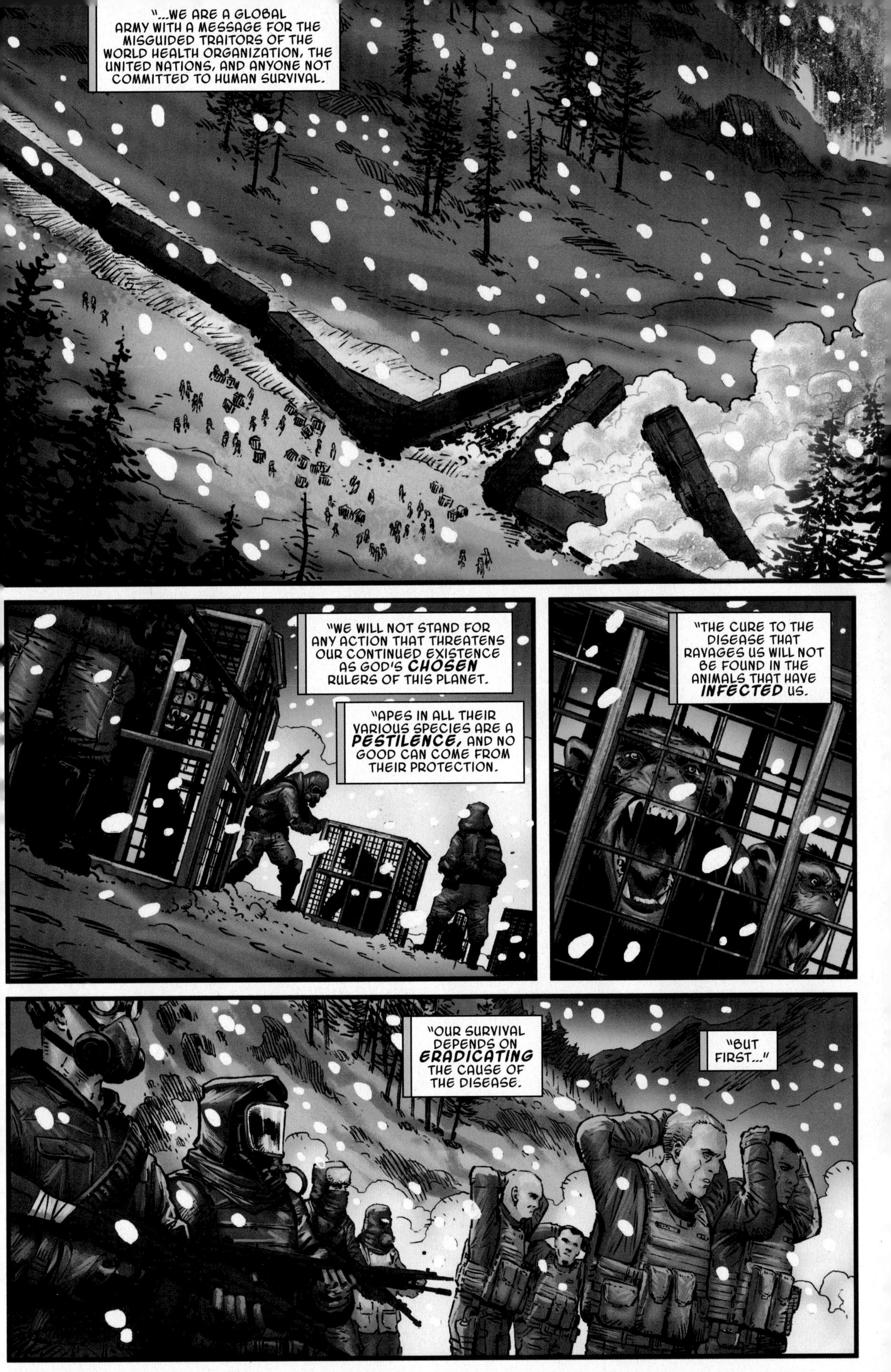
"...WE ARE A GLOBAL ARMY WITH A MESSAGE FOR THE MISGUIDED TRAITORS OF THE WORLD HEALTH ORGANIZATION, THE UNITED NATIONS, AND ANYONE NOT COMMITTED TO HUMAN SURVIVAL.
"WE WILL NOT STAND FOR ANY ACTION THAT THREATENS OUR CONTINUED EXISTENCE AS GOD'S CHOSEN RULERS OF THIS PLANET.
"APES IN ALL THEIR VARIOUS SPECIES ARE A PESTILENCE, AND NO GOOD CAN COME FROM THEIR PROTECTION.
"THE CURE TO THE DISEASE THAT RAVAGES US WILL NOT BE FOUND IN THE ANIMALS THAT HAVE INFECTED US.
"OUR SURVIVAL DEPENDS ON ERADICATING THE CAUSE OF THE DISEASE.
"BUT FIRST..."

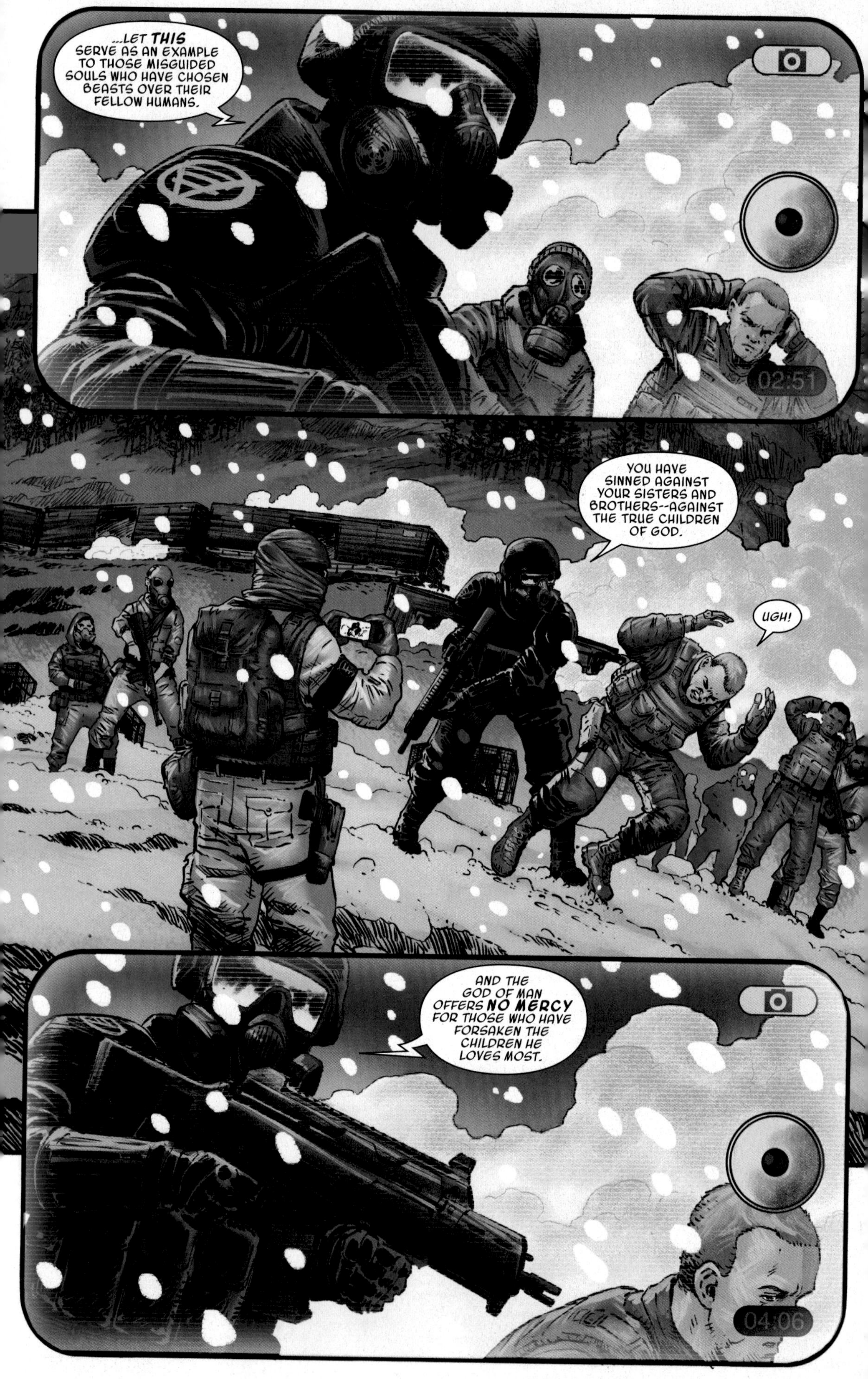
...LET THIS SERVE AS AN EXAMPLE TO THOSE MISGUIDED SOULS WHO HAVE CHOSEN BEASTS OVER THEIR FELLOW HUMANS.
02:51
YOU HAVE SINNED AGAINST YOUR SISTERS AND BROTHERS--AGAINST THE TRUE CHILDREN OF GOD.
UGH!
AND THE GOD OF MAN OFFERS NO MERCY FOR THOSE WHO HAVE FORSAKEN THE CHILDREN HE LOVES MOST.
04:06

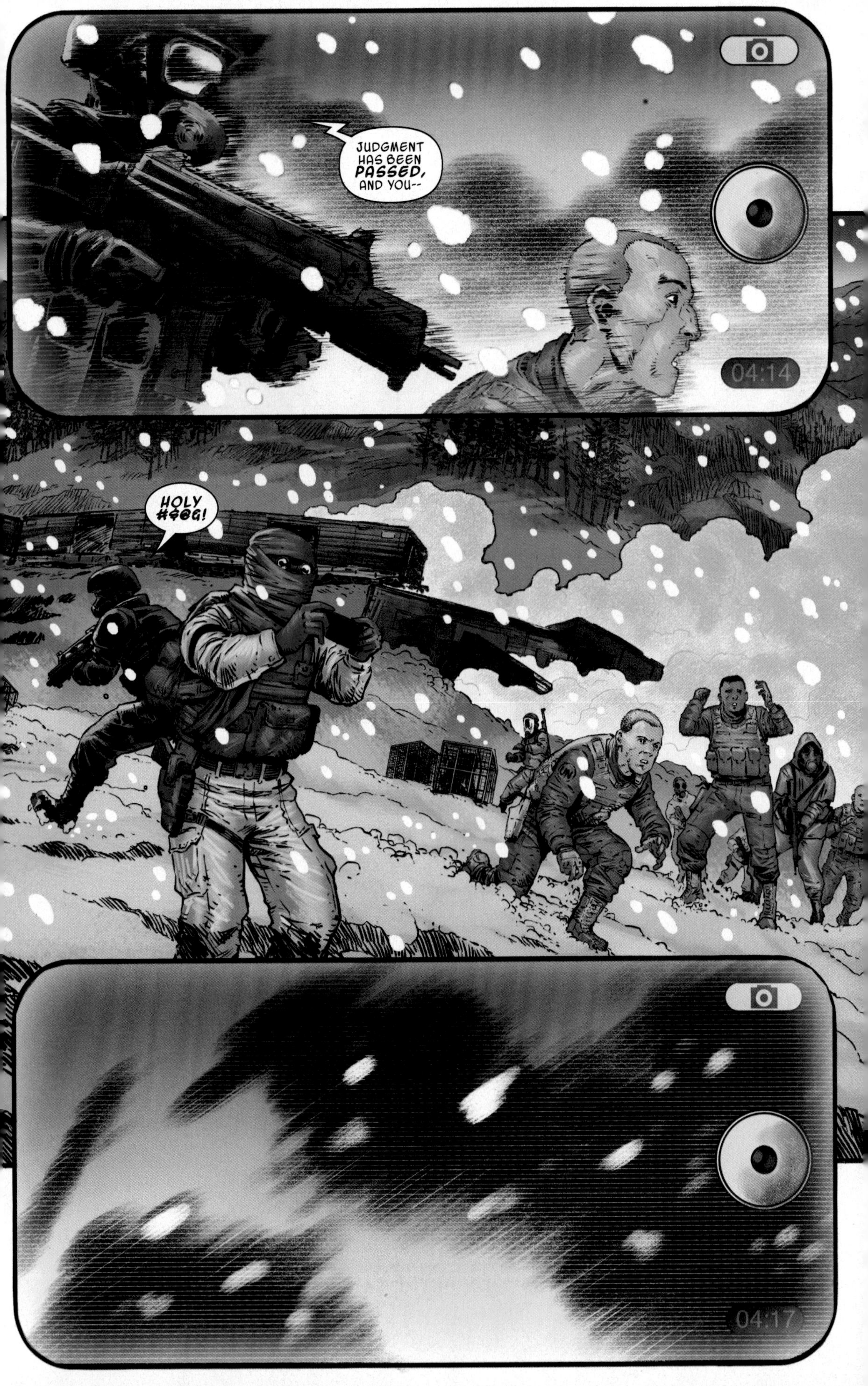
JUDGMENT HAS BEEN PASSED, AND YOU--
04:14
HOLY #$@G!
04:17

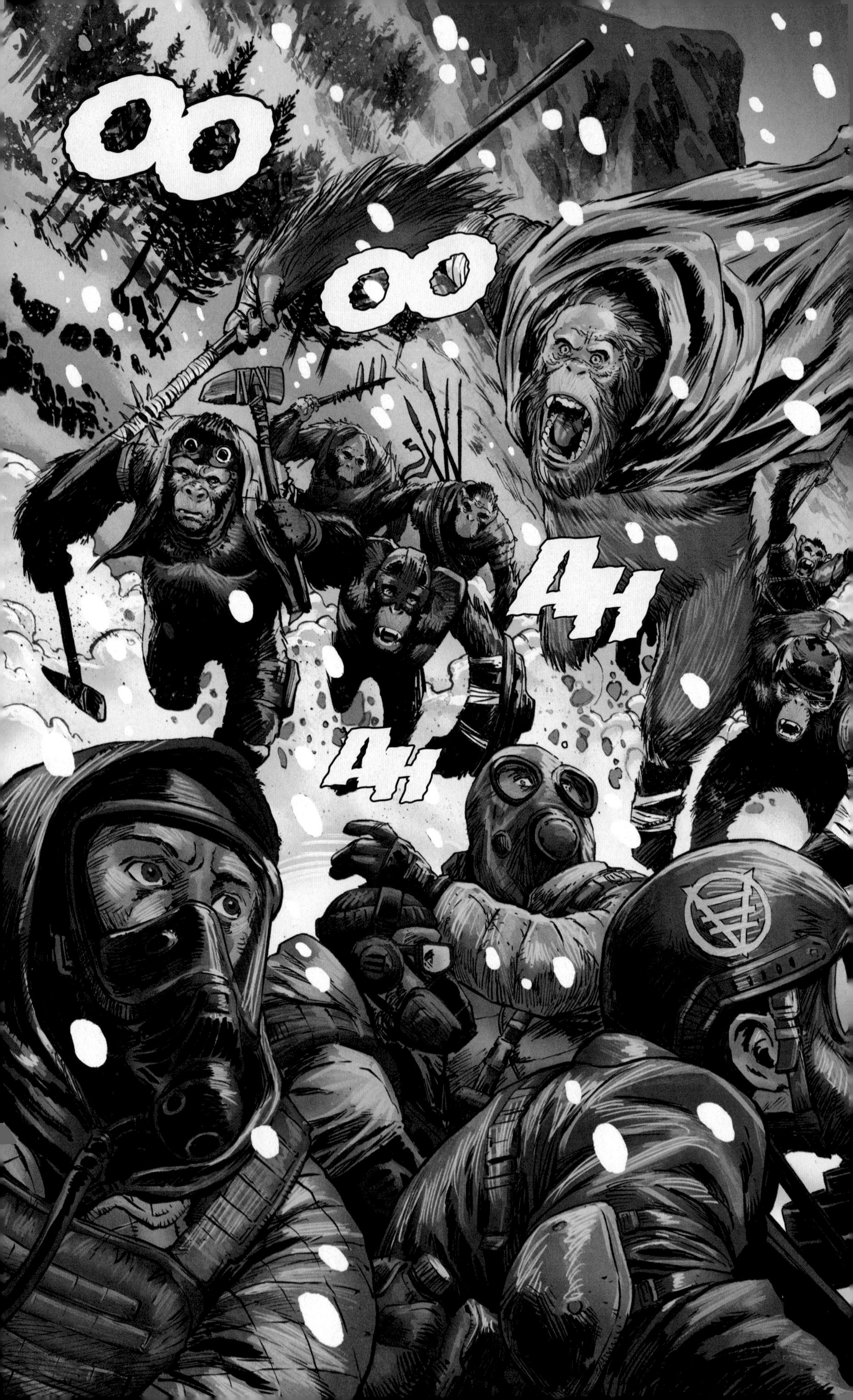
OO
OO
AH
AH

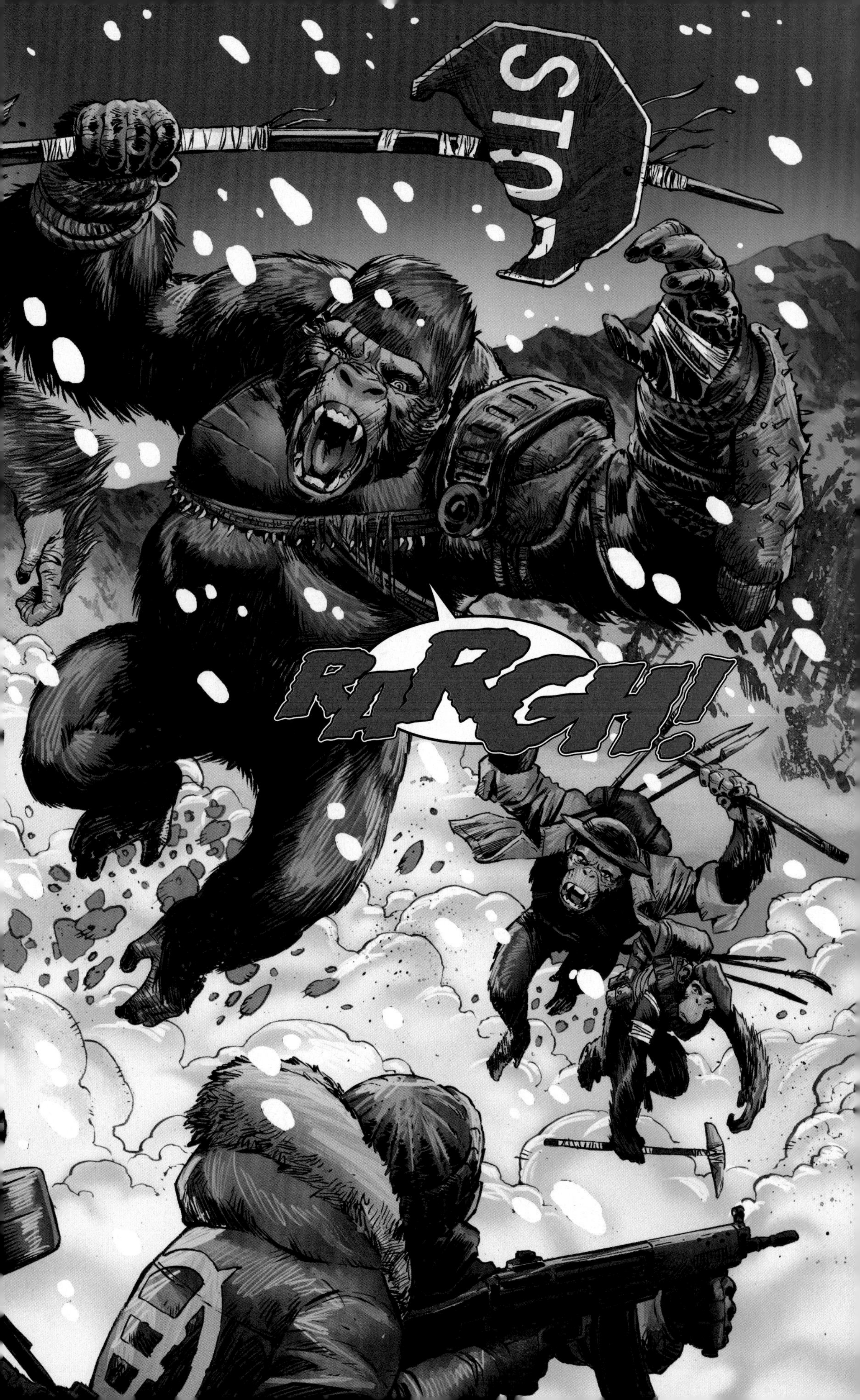
STO
RARGH!

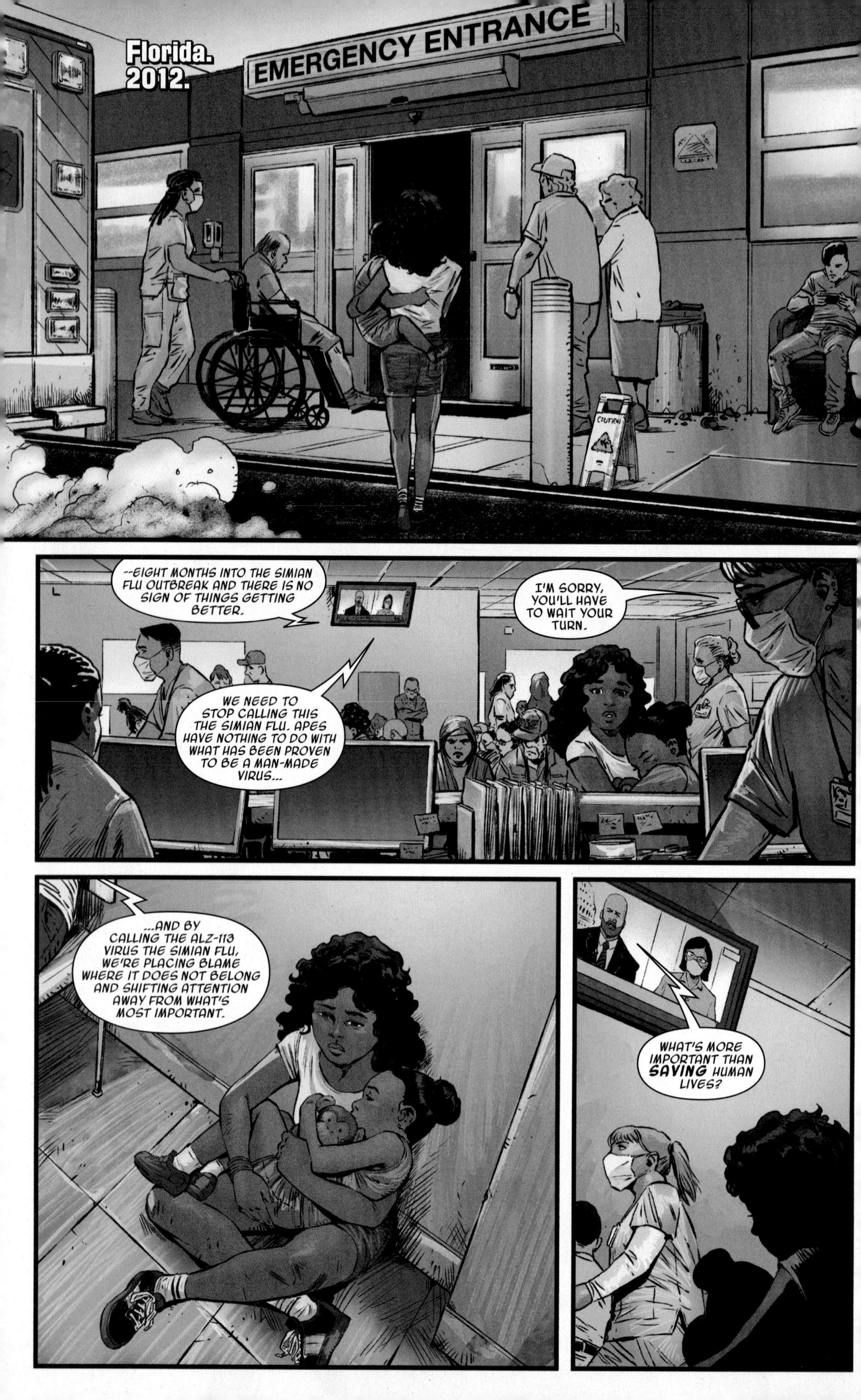
Florida. 2012.
EMERGENCY ENTRANCE
CAUTION
--EIGHT MONTHS INTO THE SIMIAN FLU OUTBREAK AND THERE IS NO SIGN OF THINGS GETTING BETTER.
I'M SORRY, YOU'LL HAVE TO WAIT YOUR TURN.
WE NEED TO STOP CALLING THIS THE SIMIAN FLU. APES HAVE NOTHING TO DO WITH WHAT HAS BEEN PROVEN TO BE A MAN-MADE VIRUS...
...AND BY CALLING THE ALZ-113 VIRUS THE SIMIAN FLU, WE'RE PLACING BLAME WHERE IT DOES NOT BELONG AND SHIFTING ATTENTION AWAY FROM WHAT'S MOST IMPORTANT.
WHAT'S MORE IMPORTANT THAN SAVING HUMAN LIVES?

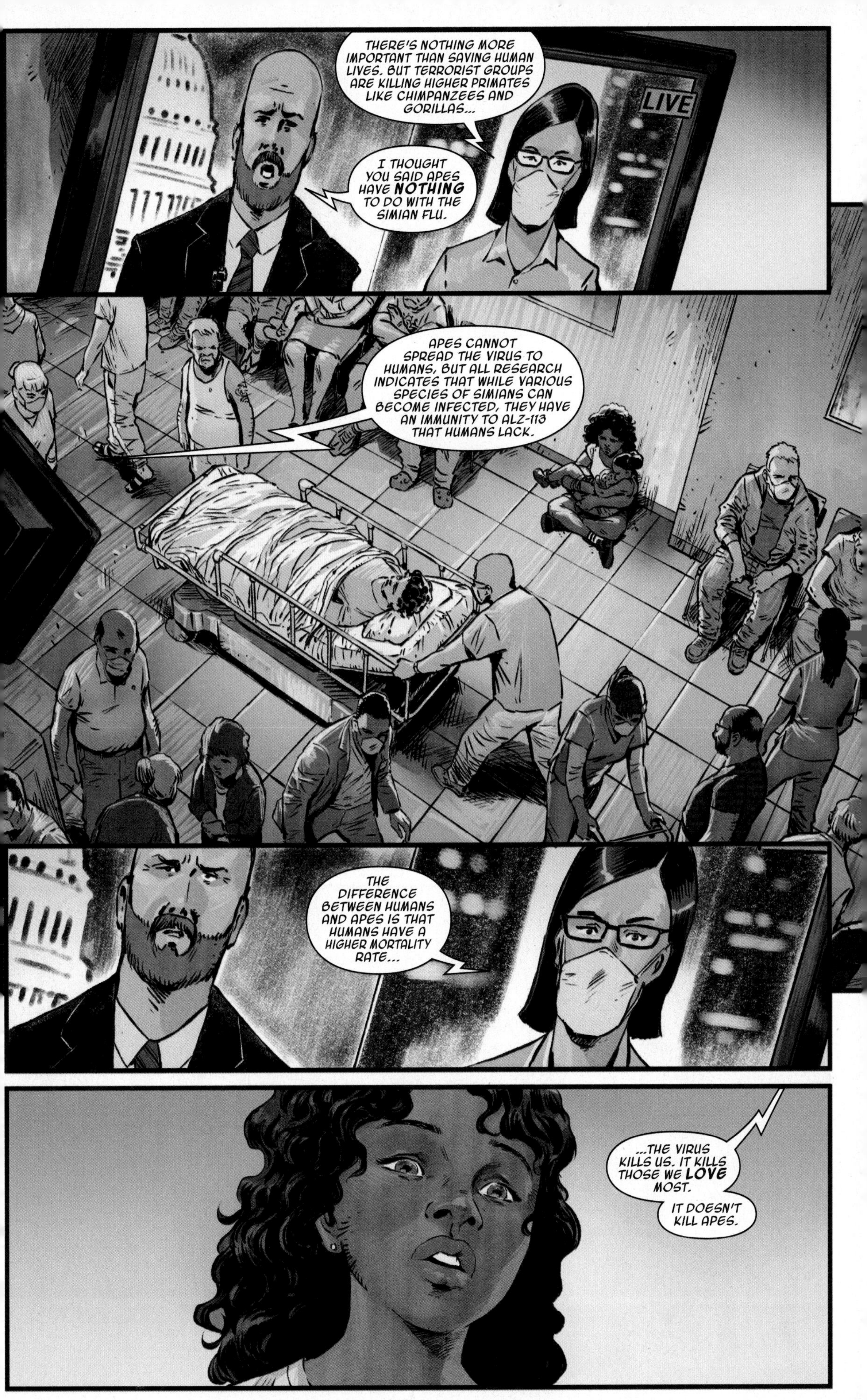
THERE'S NOTHING MORE IMPORTANT THAN SAVING HUMAN LIVES. BUT TERRORIST GROUPS ARE KILLING HIGHER PRIMATES LIKE CHIMPANZEES AND GORILLAS...
LIVE
I THOUGHT YOU SAID APES HAVE **NOTHING** TO DO WITH THE SIMIAN FLU.
APES CANNOT SPREAD THE VIRUS TO HUMANS, BUT ALL RESEARCH INDICATES THAT WHILE VARIOUS SPECIES OF SIMIANS CAN BECOME INFECTED, THEY HAVE AN IMMUNITY TO ALZ-113 THAT HUMANS LACK.
THE DIFFERENCE BETWEEN HUMANS AND APES IS THAT HUMANS HAVE A HIGHER MORTALITY RATE...
...THE VIRUS KILLS US. IT KILLS THOSE WE **LOVE** MOST.
IT DOESN'T KILL APES.

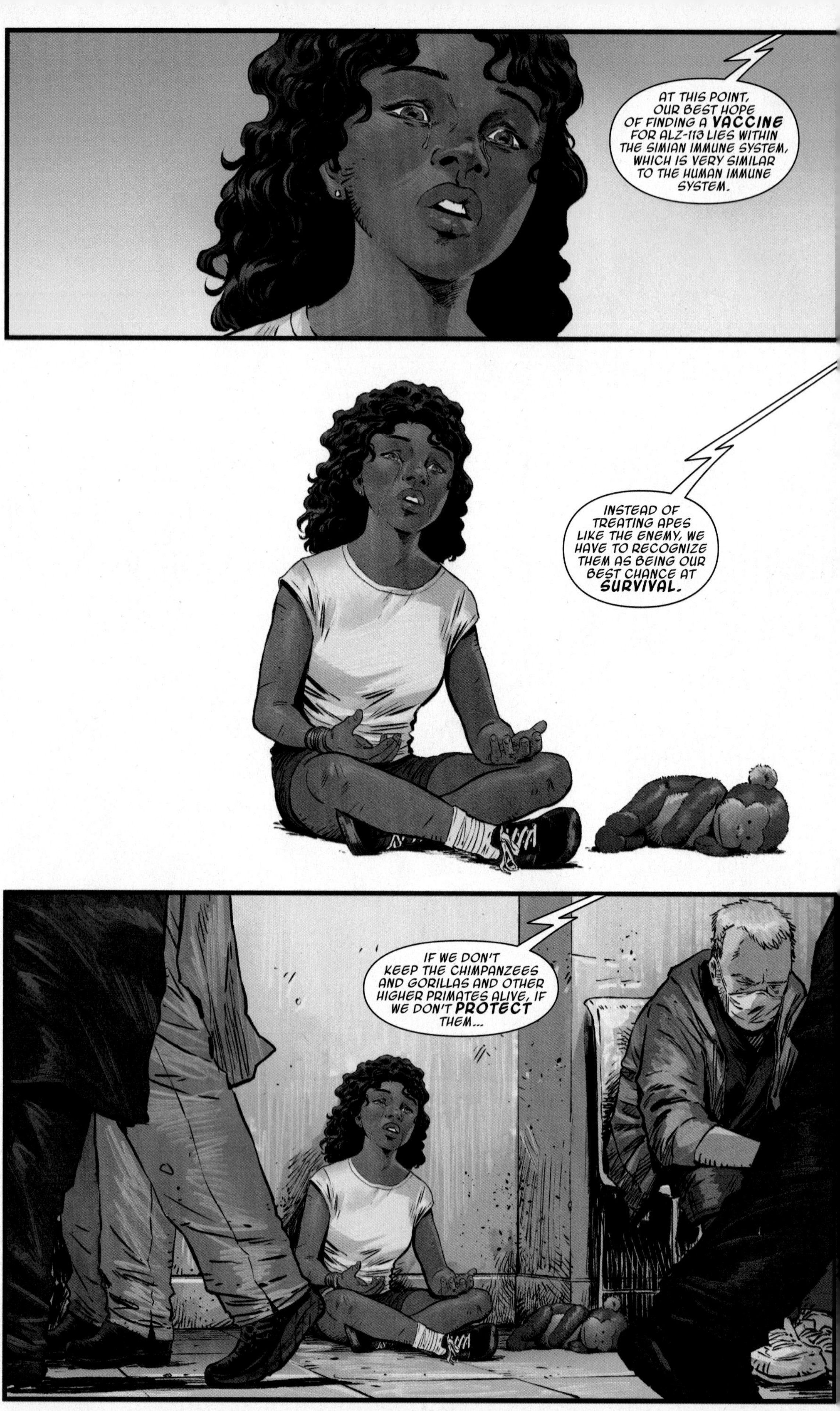
AT THIS POINT, OUR BEST HOPE OF FINDING A VACCINE FOR ALZ-113 LIES WITHIN THE SIMIAN IMMUNE SYSTEM, WHICH IS VERY SIMILAR TO THE HUMAN IMMUNE SYSTEM.
INSTEAD OF TREATING APES LIKE THE ENEMY, WE HAVE TO RECOGNIZE THEM AS BEING OUR BEST CHANCE AT SURVIVAL.
IF WE DON'T KEEP THE CHIMPANZEES AND GORILLAS AND OTHER HIGHER PRIMATES ALIVE, IF WE DON'T PROTECT THEM...

...THEN WE'VE SIGNED OUR OWN DEATH WARRANTS.

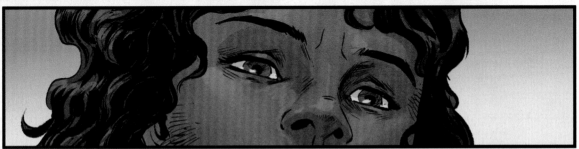

2015.

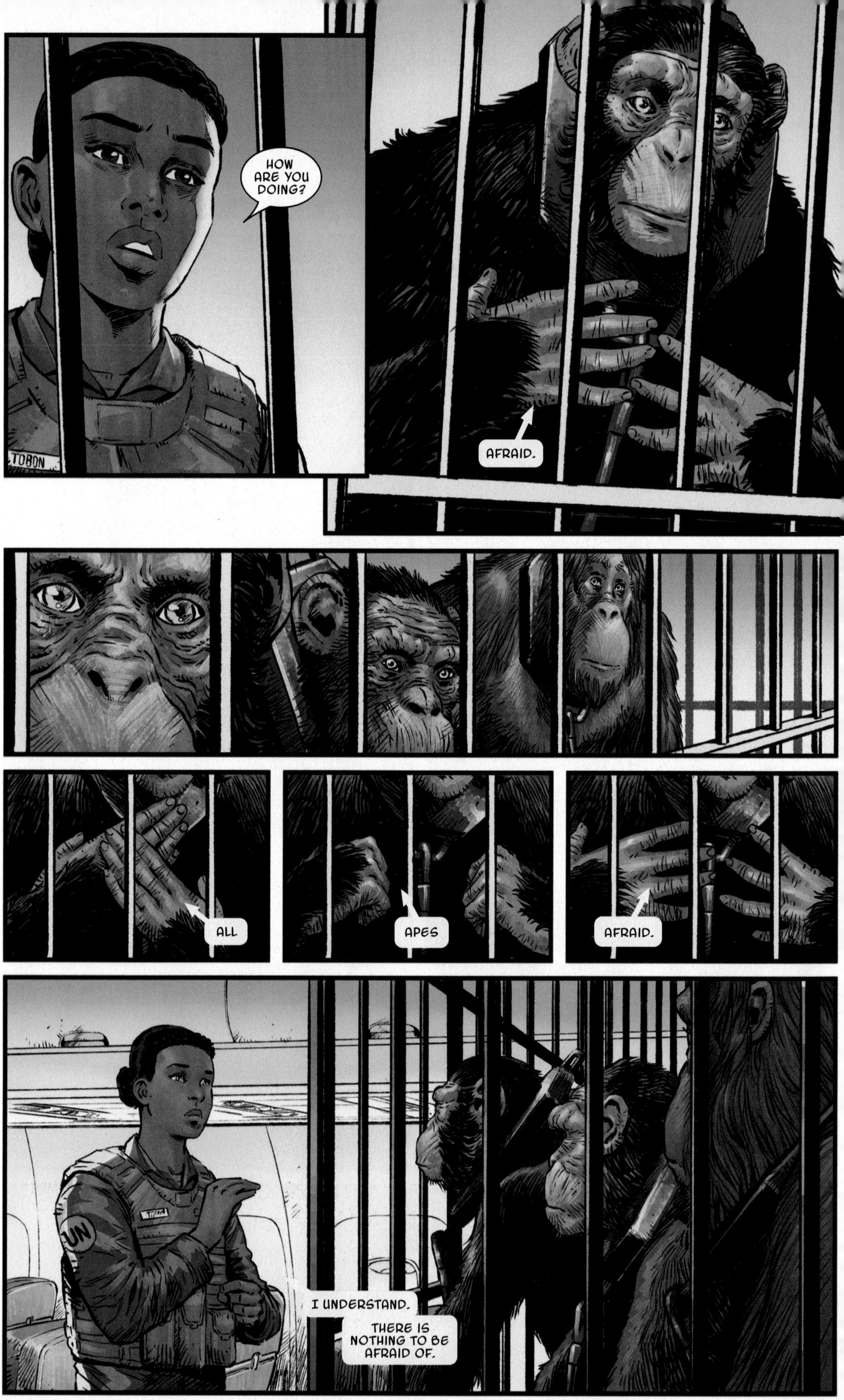
HOW ARE YOU DOING?
AFRAID.
ALL
APES
AFRAID.
I UNDERSTAND.
THERE IS NOTHING TO BE AFRAID OF.

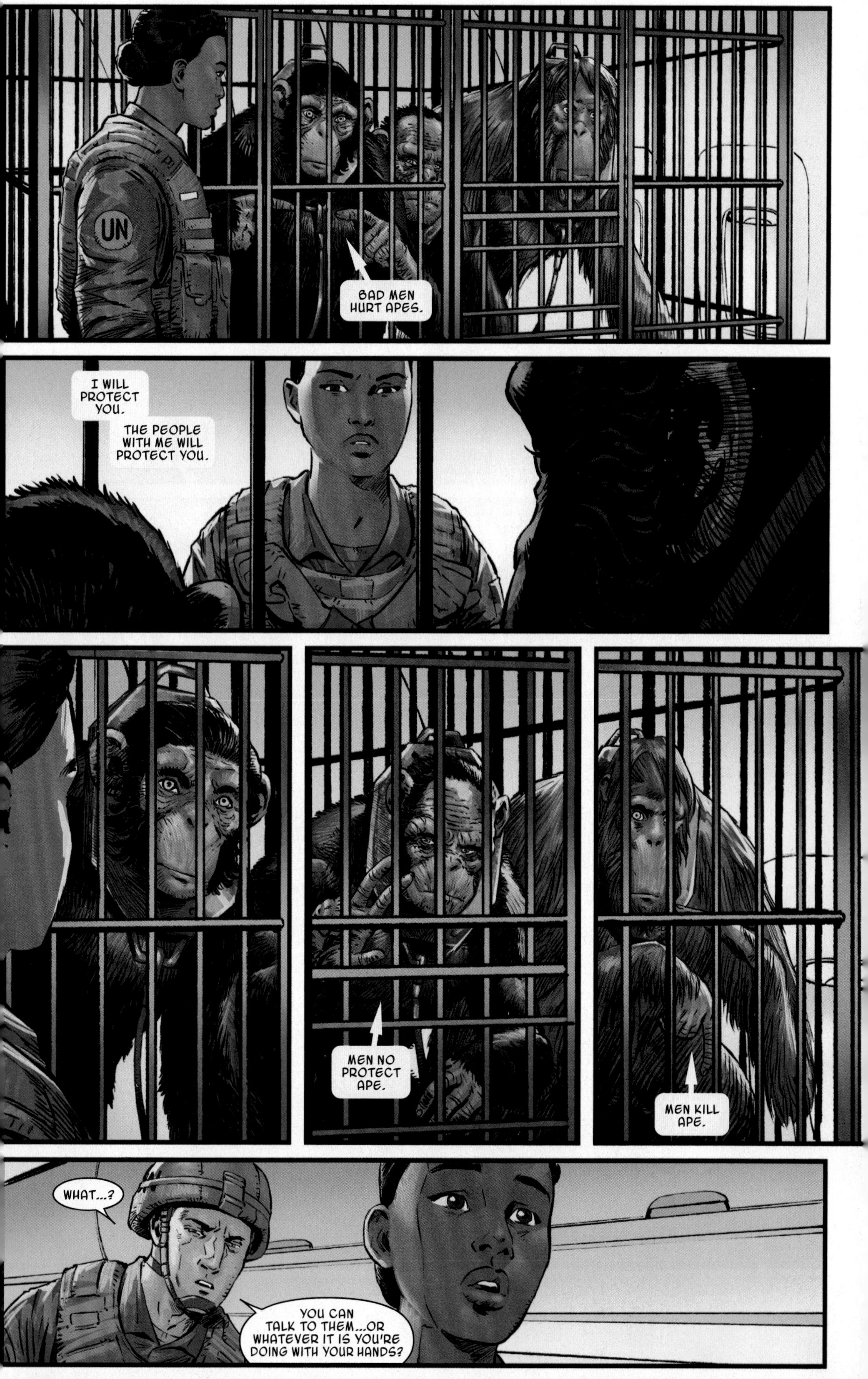
BAD MEN HURT APES.
I WILL PROTECT YOU.
THE PEOPLE WITH ME WILL PROTECT YOU.
MEN NO PROTECT APE.
MEN KILL APE.
WHAT...?
YOU CAN TALK TO THEM...OR WHATEVER IT IS YOU'RE DOING WITH YOUR HANDS?

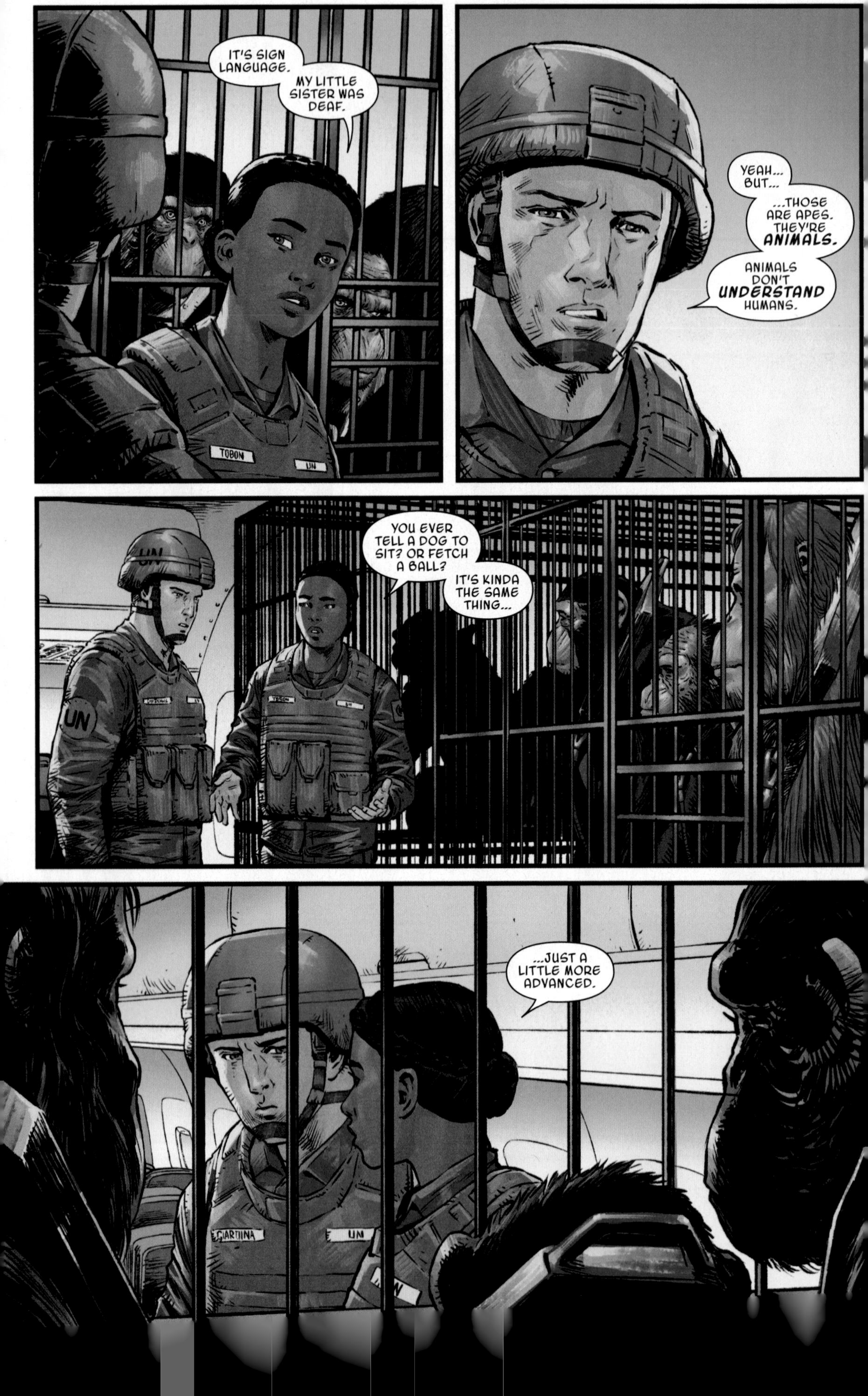
IT'S SIGN LANGUAGE.
MY LITTLE SISTER WAS DEAF.
TOBON
UN
YEAH... BUT...
...THOSE ARE APES. THEY'RE ANIMALS.
ANIMALS DON'T UNDERSTAND HUMANS.
UN
UN
YOU EVER TELL A DOG TO SIT? OR FETCH A BALL?
IT'S KINDA THE SAME THING...
...JUST A LITTLE MORE ADVANCED.
GIARDINA
UN

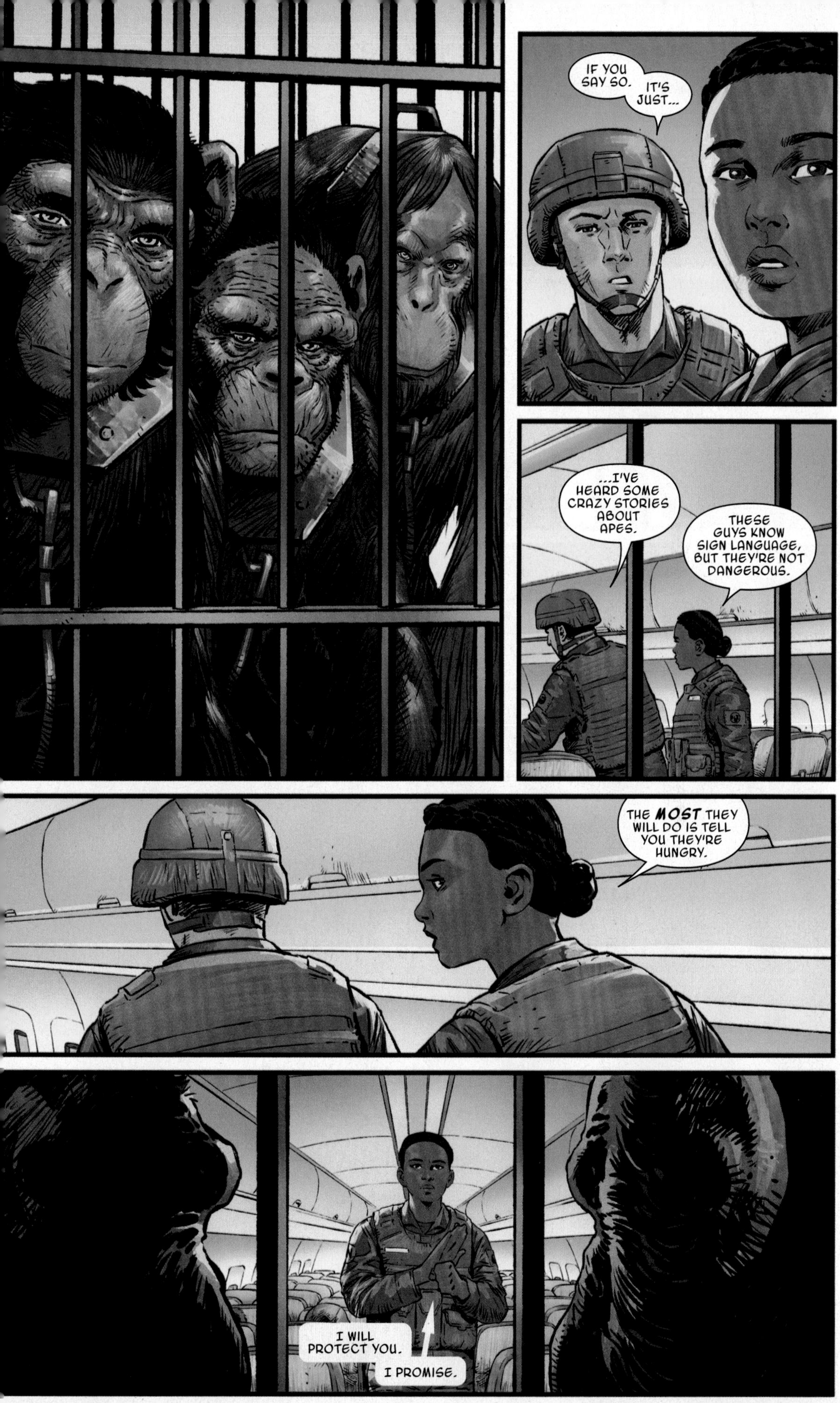
IF YOU SAY SO.
IT'S JUST...
...I'VE HEARD SOME CRAZY STORIES ABOUT APES.
THESE GUYS KNOW SIGN LANGUAGE, BUT THEY'RE NOT DANGEROUS.
THE MOST THEY WILL DO IS TELL YOU THEY'RE HUNGRY.
I WILL PROTECT YOU.
I PROMISE.

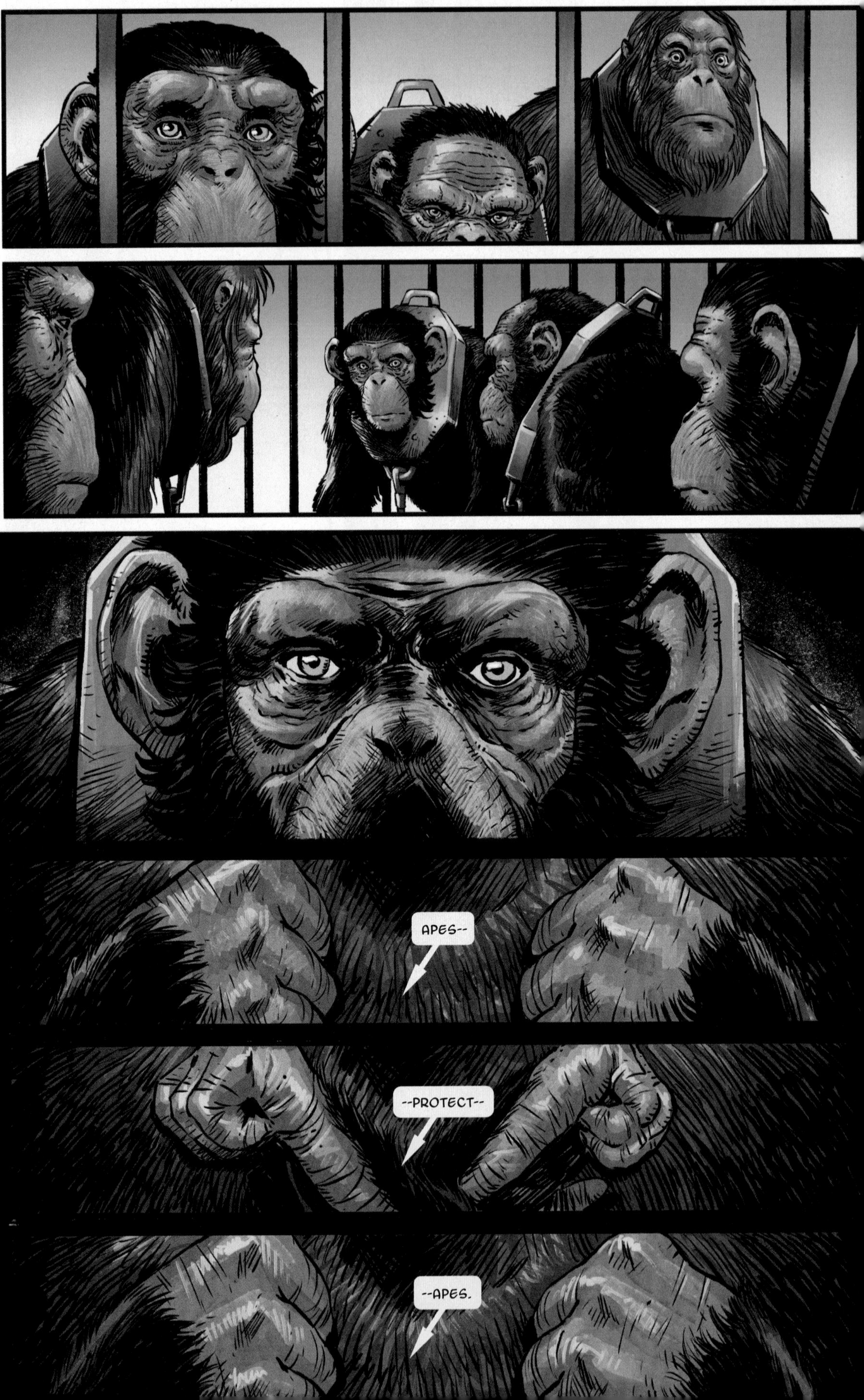
APES--
--PROTECT--
--APES.

YANICK PAQUETTE & **ALEJANDRO SÁNCHEZ**

#1 Variant

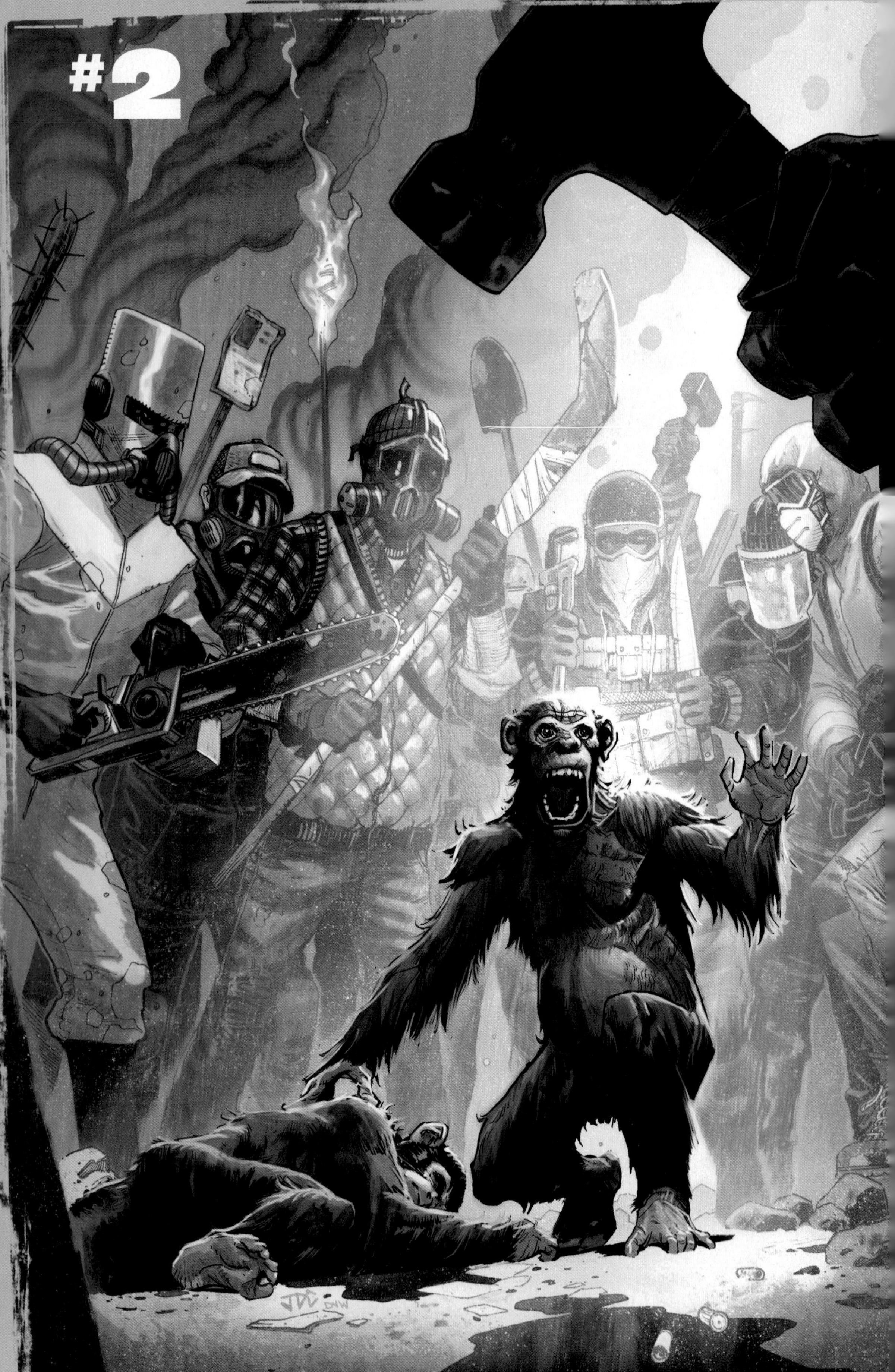
#2

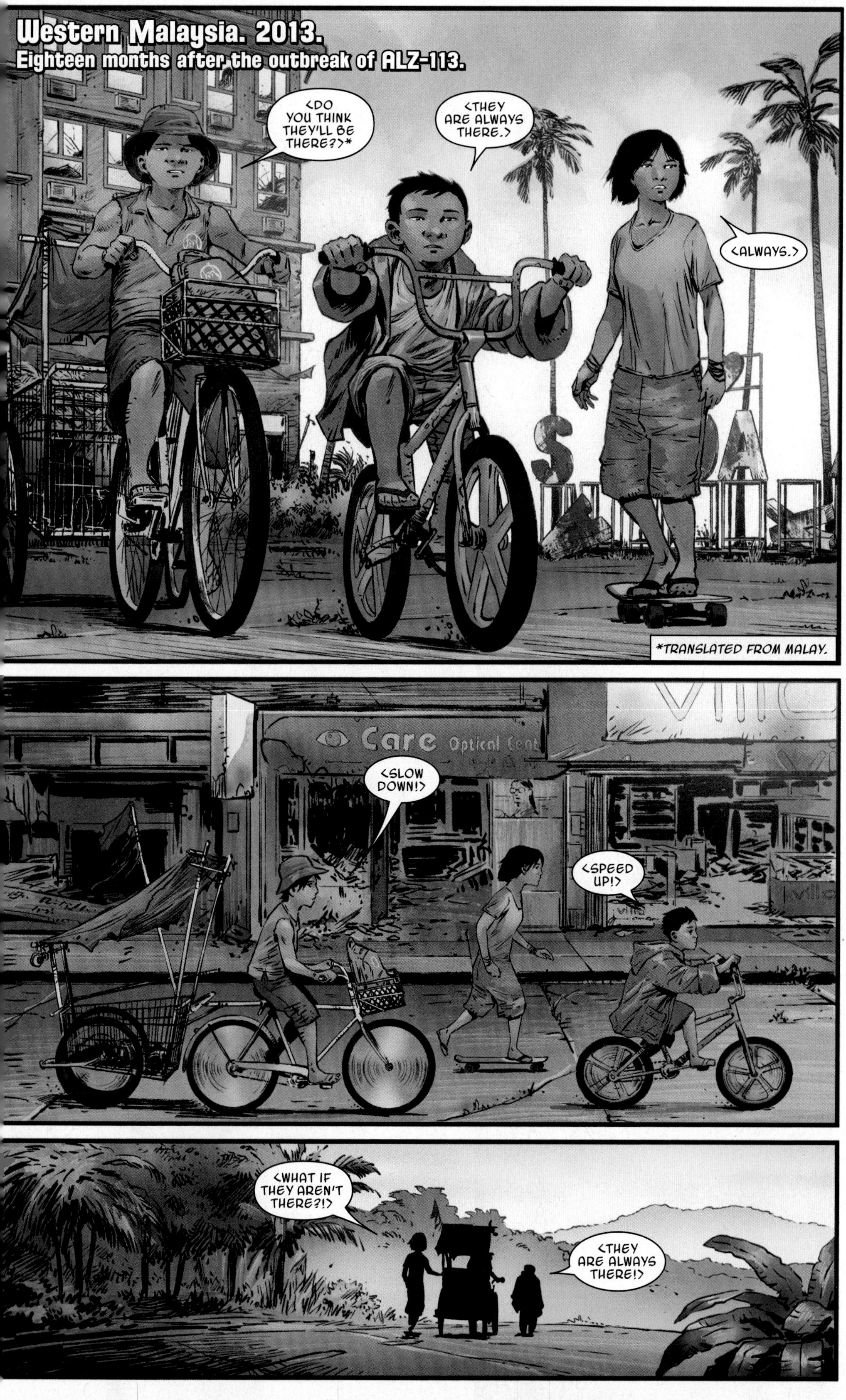
Western Malaysia. 2013.
Eighteen months after the outbreak of ALZ-113.
<DO YOU THINK THEY'LL BE THERE?>*
<THEY ARE ALWAYS THERE.>
<ALWAYS.>
*TRANSLATED FROM MALAY.
Care Optical Cent
<SLOW DOWN!>
<SPEED UP!>
<WHAT IF THEY AREN'T THERE?!>
<THEY ARE ALWAYS THERE!>

WELCOME

SALMAT DATANG

BORNEO
ORANGUTAN REHABILITATION CENTRE
PUSAT PEMULIHAN ORANGUTAN

<I TOLD YOU.>

<ALL OF THIS...>

<...IS THIS ALL FOR US?!>

<WHO ELSE WOULD IT BE FOR?>

<ALL FOR US.>

<I DON'T THINK HE BELIEVED ME.>

<DID YOU BRING THE ONE I TOLD YOU TO BRING?>

<LOOK!>

<WE BROUGHT YOU GIFTS!>

WHERE THE ANIMALS ROAM

STORY AND ART BY CLIVE MELDAHOLM

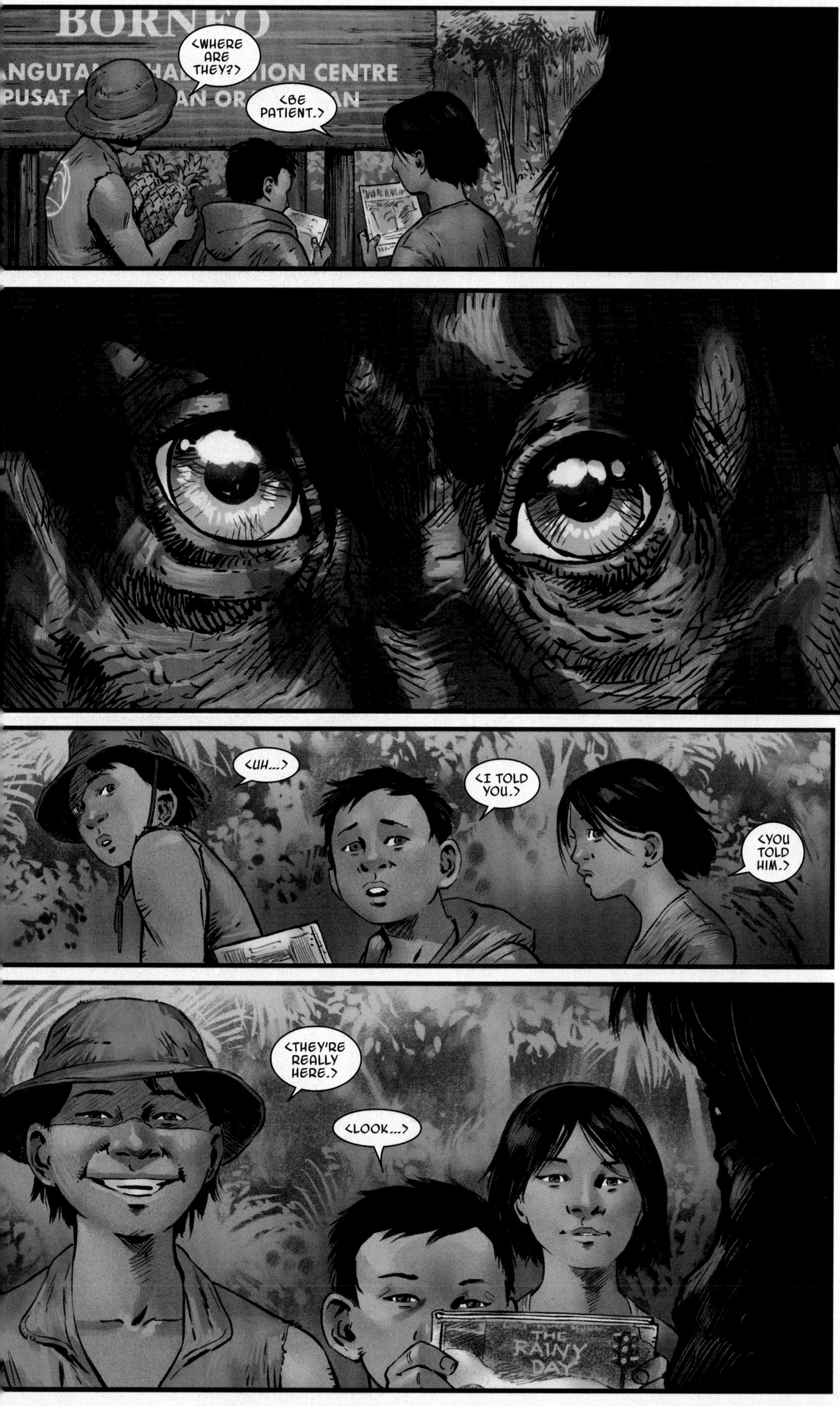
<WHERE ARE THEY?>
<BE PATIENT.>
<UH...>
<I TOLD YOU.>
<YOU TOLD HIM.>
<THEY'RE REALLY HERE.>
<LOOK...>
THE RAINY DAY

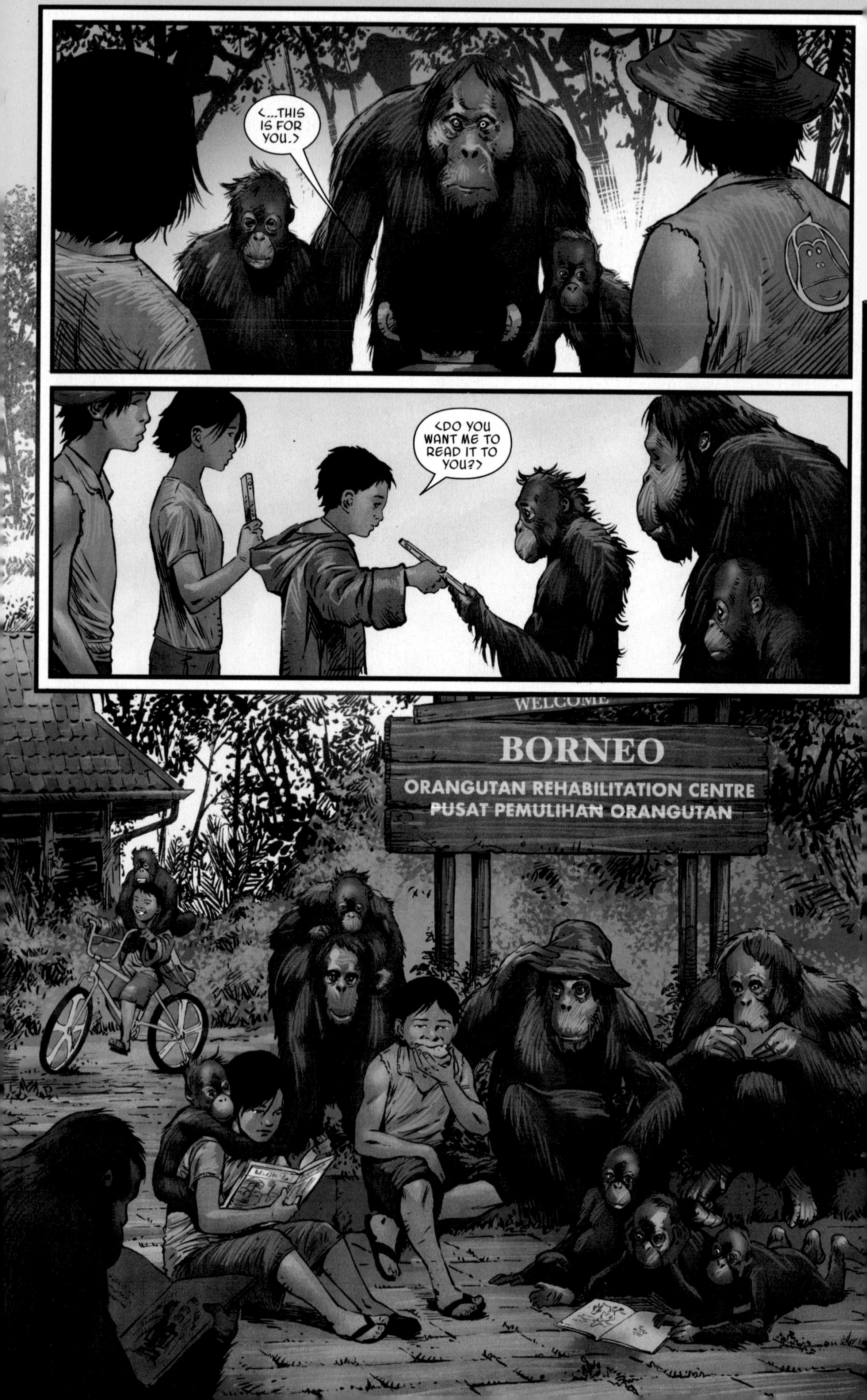
<...THIS IS FOR YOU.>
<DO YOU WANT ME TO READ IT TO YOU?>
WELCOME
BORNEO
ORANGUTAN REHABILITATION CENTRE
PUSAT PEMULIHAN ORANGUTAN

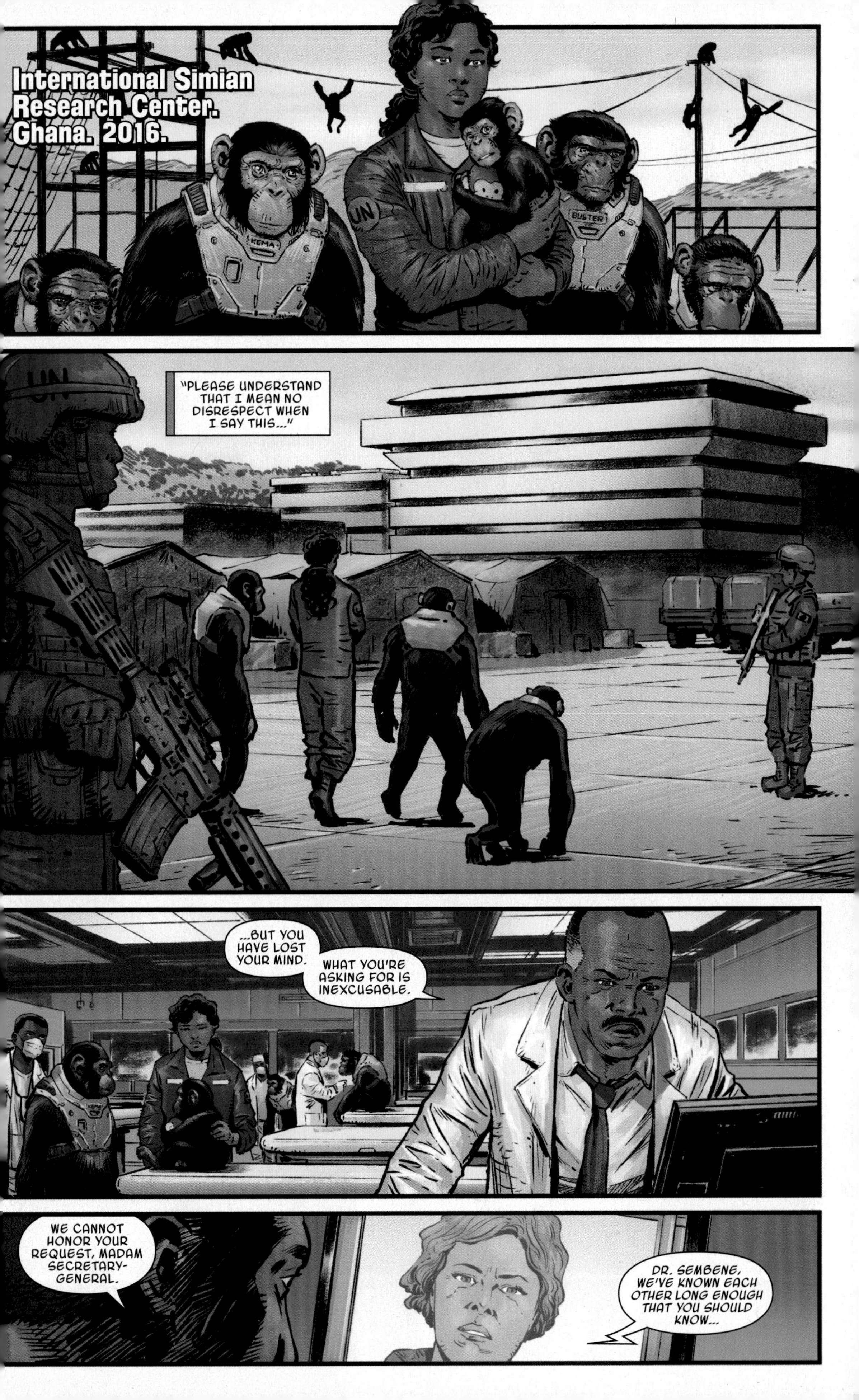
International Simian Research Center. Ghana. 2016.
KEMA
UN
BUSTER
"PLEASE UNDERSTAND THAT I MEAN NO DISRESPECT WHEN I SAY THIS..."
UN
...BUT YOU HAVE LOST YOUR MIND.
WHAT YOU'RE ASKING FOR IS INEXCUSABLE.
KEMA
WE CANNOT HONOR YOUR REQUEST, MADAM SECRETARY-GENERAL.
DR. SEMBENE, WE'VE KNOWN EACH OTHER LONG ENOUGH THAT YOU SHOULD KNOW...

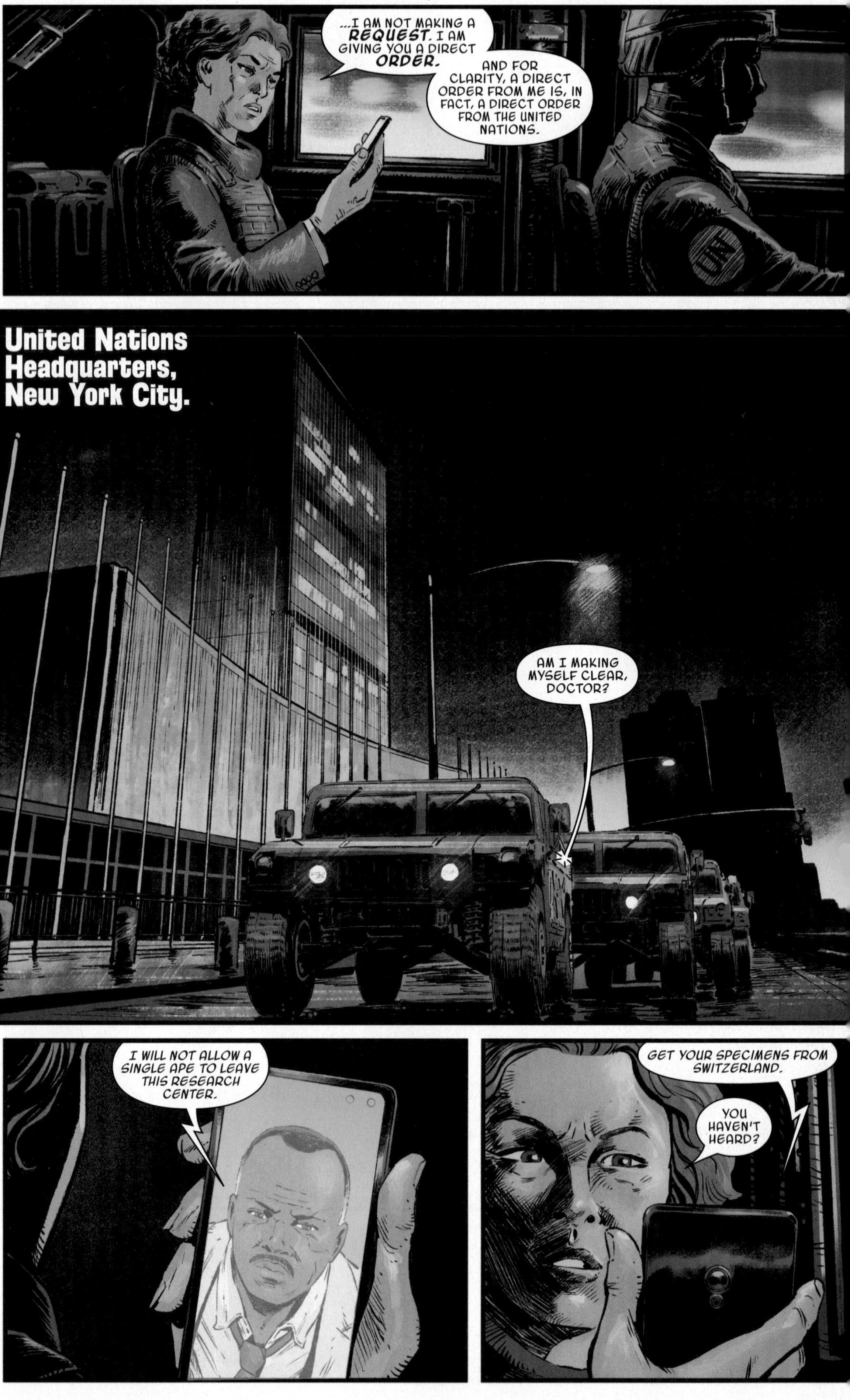
...I AM NOT MAKING A REQUEST. I AM GIVING YOU A DIRECT ORDER.
AND FOR CLARITY, A DIRECT ORDER FROM ME IS, IN FACT, A DIRECT ORDER FROM THE UNITED NATIONS.
UN
United Nations Headquarters, New York City.
AM I MAKING MYSELF CLEAR, DOCTOR?
I WILL NOT ALLOW A SINGLE APE TO LEAVE THIS RESEARCH CENTER.
GET YOUR SPECIMENS FROM SWITZERLAND.
YOU HAVEN'T HEARD?

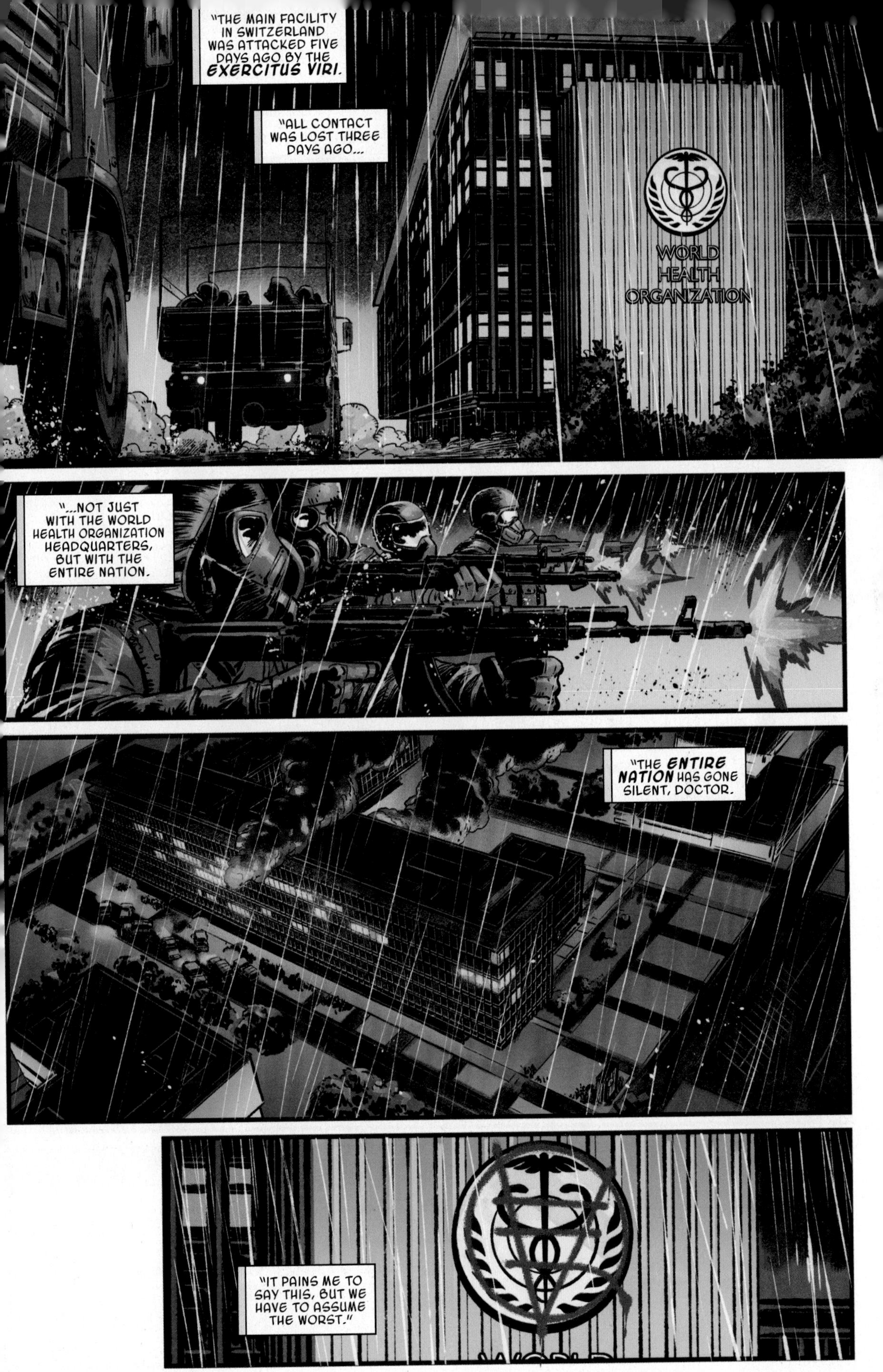
"THE MAIN FACILITY IN SWITZERLAND WAS ATTACKED FIVE DAYS AGO BY THE EXERCITUS VIRI.
"ALL CONTACT WAS LOST THREE DAYS AGO...
WORLD HEALTH ORGANIZATION
"...NOT JUST WITH THE WORLD HEALTH ORGANIZATION HEADQUARTERS, BUT WITH THE ENTIRE NATION.
"THE ENTIRE NATION HAS GONE SILENT, DOCTOR.
"IT PAINS ME TO SAY THIS, BUT WE HAVE TO ASSUME THE WORST."

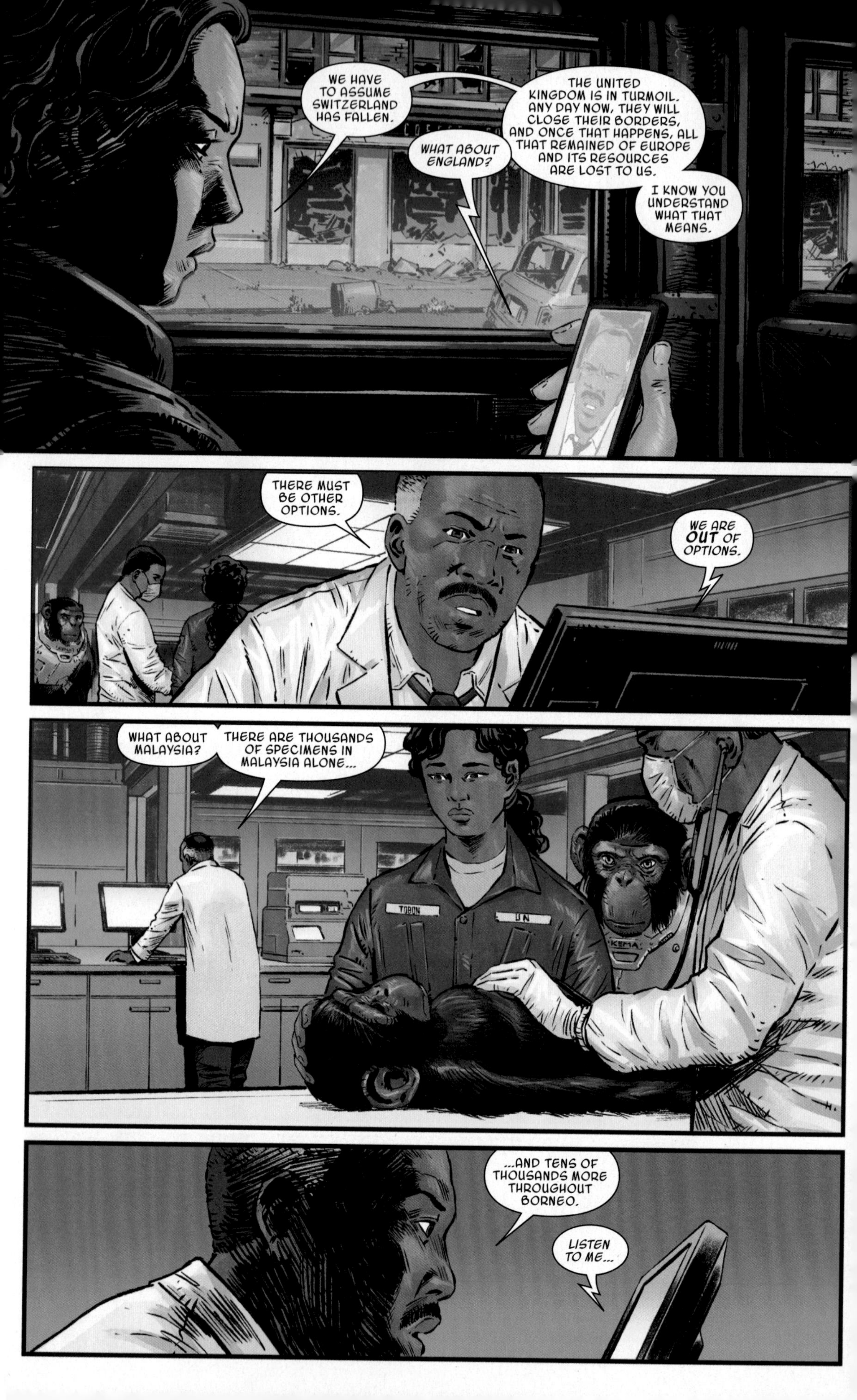
WE HAVE TO ASSUME SWITZERLAND HAS FALLEN.
WHAT ABOUT ENGLAND?
THE UNITED KINGDOM IS IN TURMOIL. ANY DAY NOW, THEY WILL CLOSE THEIR BORDERS, AND ONCE THAT HAPPENS, ALL THAT REMAINED OF EUROPE AND ITS RESOURCES ARE LOST TO US.
I KNOW YOU UNDERSTAND WHAT THAT MEANS.
THERE MUST BE OTHER OPTIONS.
WE ARE OUT OF OPTIONS.
TOBON
UN
KEMA
WHAT ABOUT MALAYSIA?
THERE ARE THOUSANDS OF SPECIMENS IN MALAYSIA ALONE...
...AND TENS OF THOUSANDS MORE THROUGHOUT BORNEO.
LISTEN TO ME...

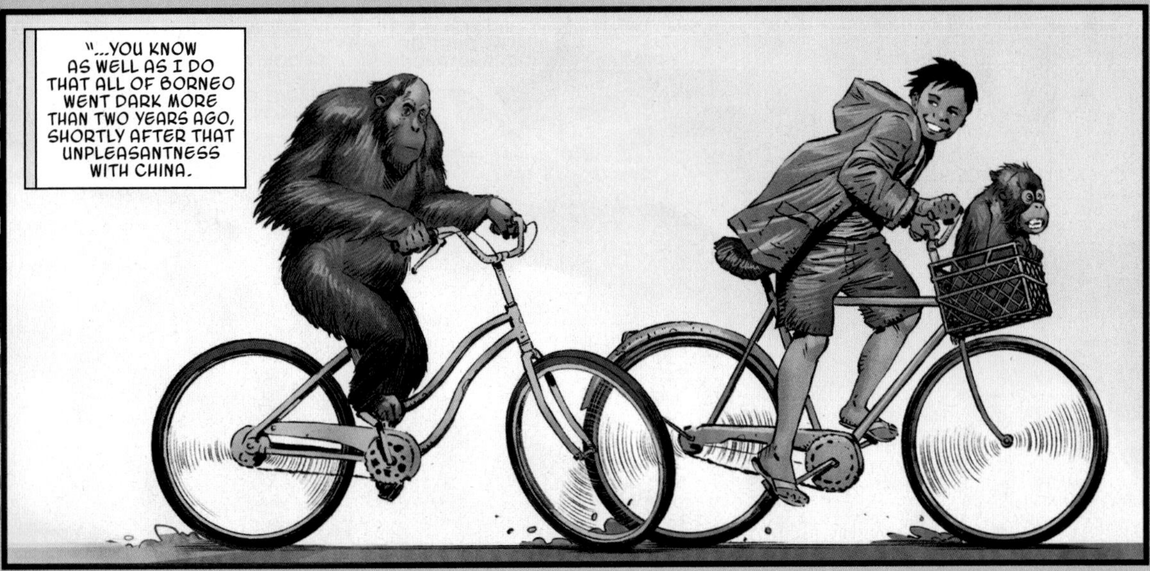
"...YOU KNOW AS WELL AS I DO THAT ALL OF BORNEO WENT DARK MORE THAN TWO YEARS AGO, SHORTLY AFTER THAT UNPLEASANTNESS WITH CHINA.

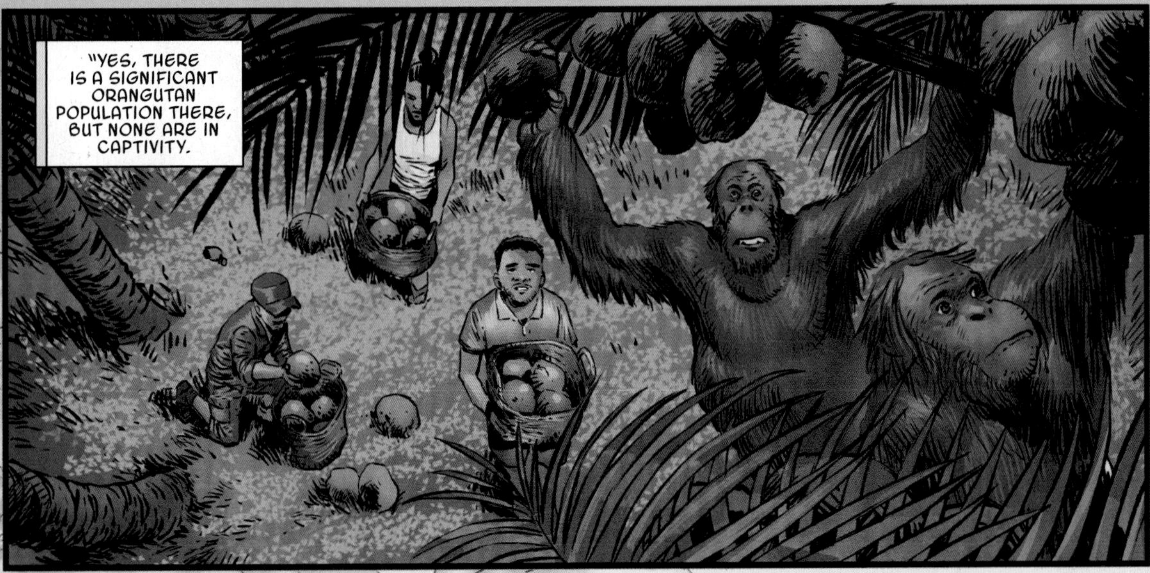
"YES, THERE IS A SIGNIFICANT ORANGUTAN POPULATION THERE, BUT NONE ARE IN CAPTIVITY.

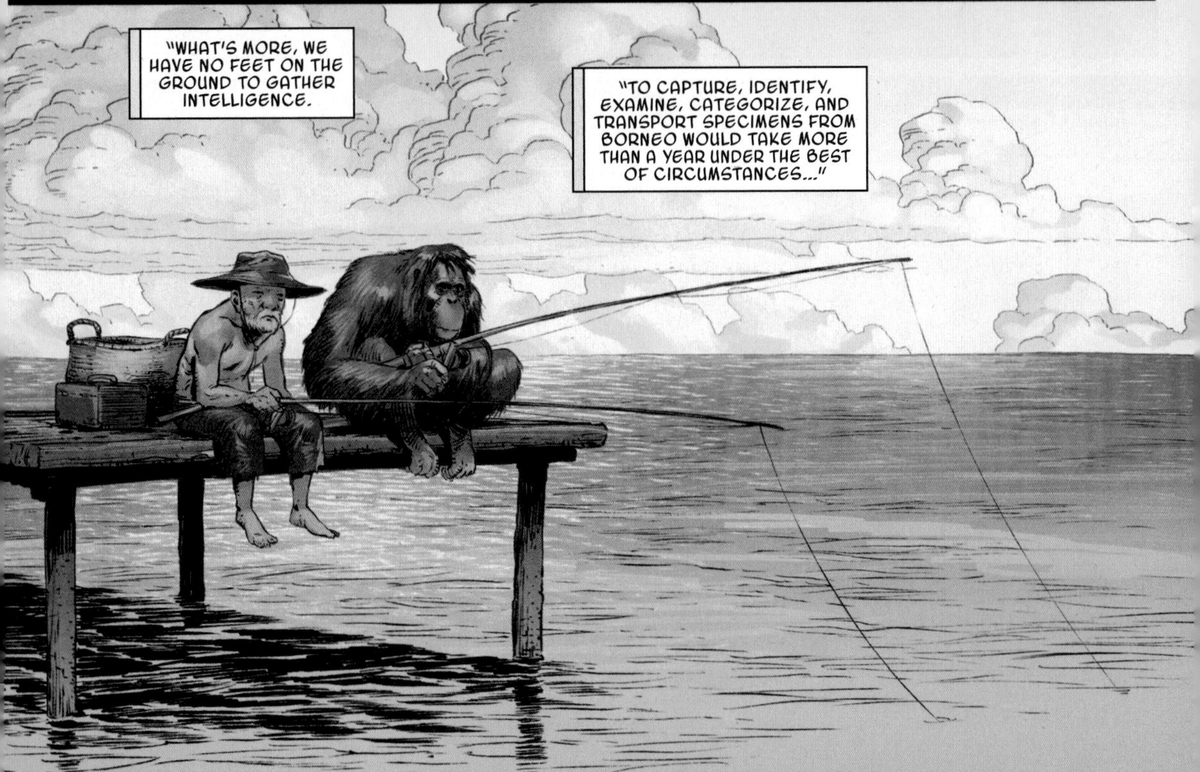
"WHAT'S MORE, WE HAVE NO FEET ON THE GROUND TO GATHER INTELLIGENCE.
"TO CAPTURE, IDENTIFY, EXAMINE, CATEGORIZE, AND TRANSPORT SPECIMENS FROM BORNEO WOULD TAKE MORE THAN A YEAR UNDER THE BEST OF CIRCUMSTANCES..."

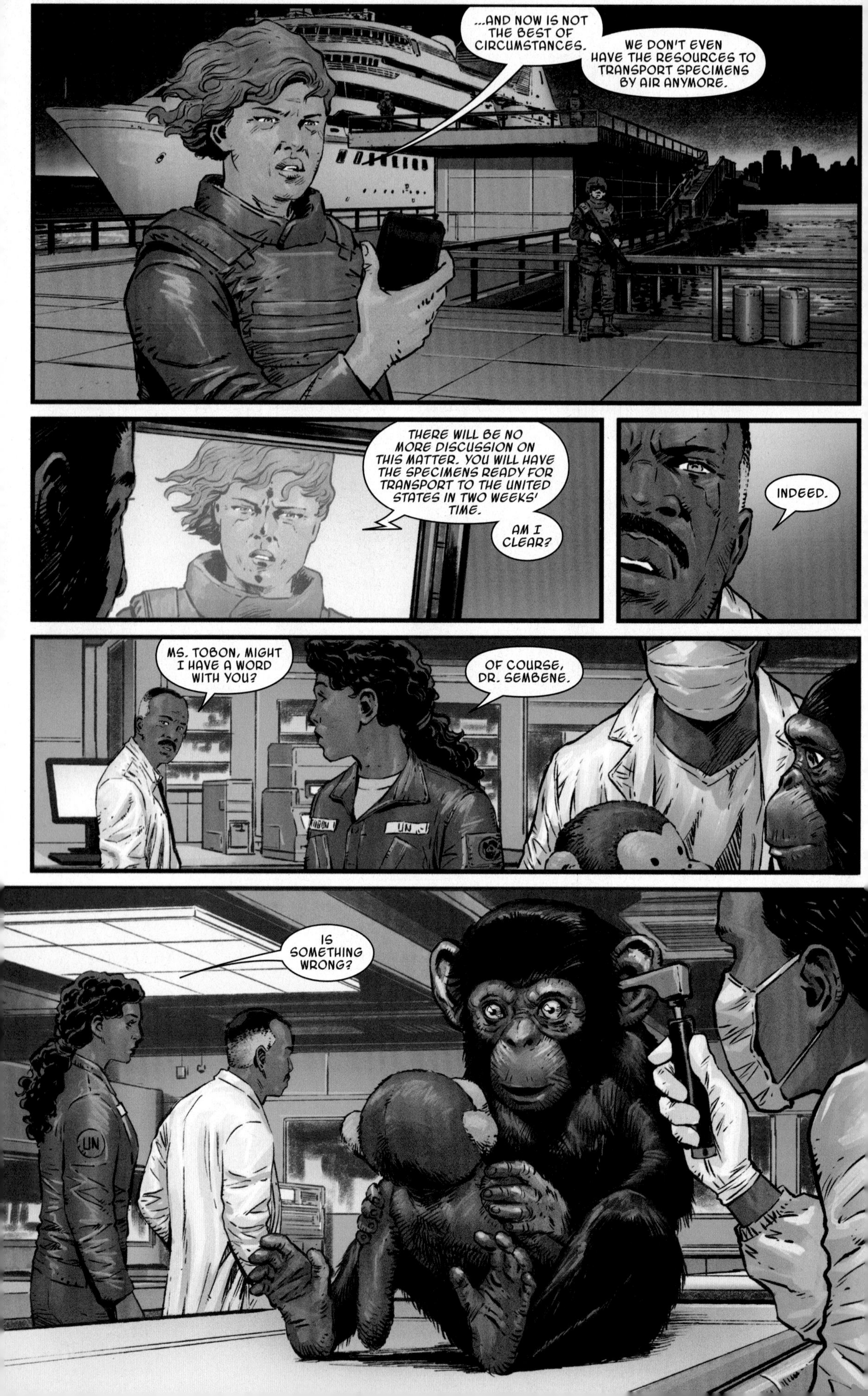
...AND NOW IS NOT THE BEST OF CIRCUMSTANCES.
WE DON'T EVEN HAVE THE RESOURCES TO TRANSPORT SPECIMENS BY AIR ANYMORE.
THERE WILL BE NO MORE DISCUSSION ON THIS MATTER. YOU WILL HAVE THE SPECIMENS READY FOR TRANSPORT TO THE UNITED STATES IN TWO WEEKS' TIME.
AM I CLEAR?
INDEED.
MS. TOBON, MIGHT I HAVE A WORD WITH YOU?
OF COURSE, DR. SEMBENE.
IS SOMETHING WRONG?

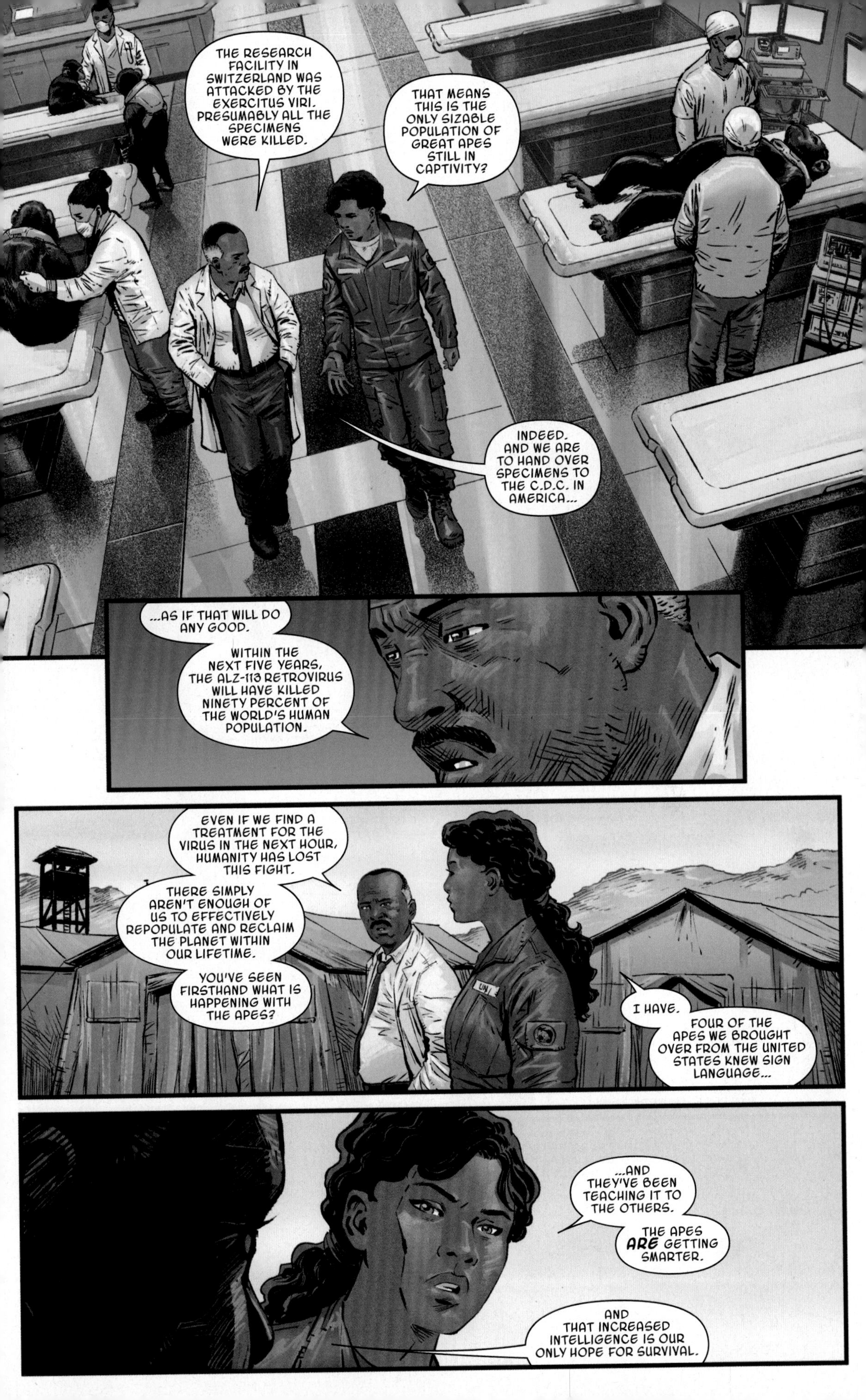
THE RESEARCH FACILITY IN SWITZERLAND WAS ATTACKED BY THE EXERCITUS VIRI. PRESUMABLY ALL THE SPECIMENS WERE KILLED.
THAT MEANS THIS IS THE ONLY SIZABLE POPULATION OF GREAT APES STILL IN CAPTIVITY?
INDEED. AND WE ARE TO HAND OVER SPECIMENS TO THE C.D.C. IN AMERICA...
...AS IF THAT WILL DO ANY GOOD.
WITHIN THE NEXT FIVE YEARS, THE ALZ-113 RETROVIRUS WILL HAVE KILLED NINETY PERCENT OF THE WORLD'S HUMAN POPULATION.
EVEN IF WE FIND A TREATMENT FOR THE VIRUS IN THE NEXT HOUR, HUMANITY HAS LOST THIS FIGHT.
THERE SIMPLY AREN'T ENOUGH OF US TO EFFECTIVELY REPOPULATE AND RECLAIM THE PLANET WITHIN OUR LIFETIME.
YOU'VE SEEN FIRSTHAND WHAT IS HAPPENING WITH THE APES?
I HAVE.
FOUR OF THE APES WE BROUGHT OVER FROM THE UNITED STATES KNEW SIGN LANGUAGE...
...AND THEY'VE BEEN TEACHING IT TO THE OTHERS.
THE APES **ARE** GETTING SMARTER.
AND THAT INCREASED INTELLIGENCE IS OUR ONLY HOPE FOR SURVIVAL.

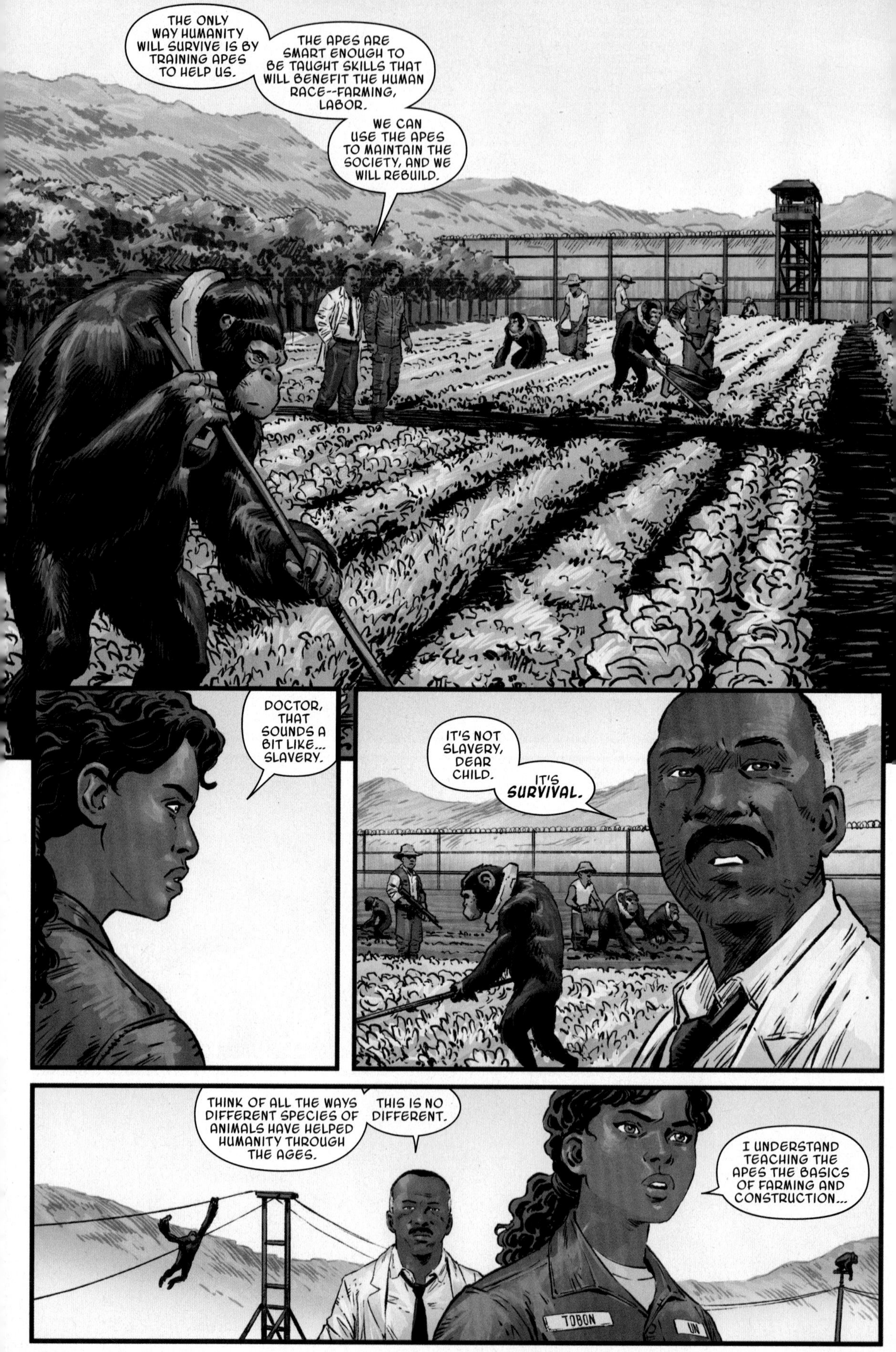
THE ONLY WAY HUMANITY WILL SURVIVE IS BY TRAINING APES TO HELP US.
THE APES ARE SMART ENOUGH TO BE TAUGHT SKILLS THAT WILL BENEFIT THE HUMAN RACE--FARMING, LABOR.
WE CAN USE THE APES TO MAINTAIN THE SOCIETY, AND WE WILL REBUILD.
DOCTOR, THAT SOUNDS A BIT LIKE... SLAVERY.
IT'S NOT SLAVERY, DEAR CHILD.
IT'S **SURVIVAL.**
THINK OF ALL THE WAYS DIFFERENT SPECIES OF ANIMALS HAVE HELPED HUMANITY THROUGH THE AGES.
THIS IS NO DIFFERENT.
I UNDERSTAND TEACHING THE APES THE BASICS OF FARMING AND CONSTRUCTION...
TOBON
UN

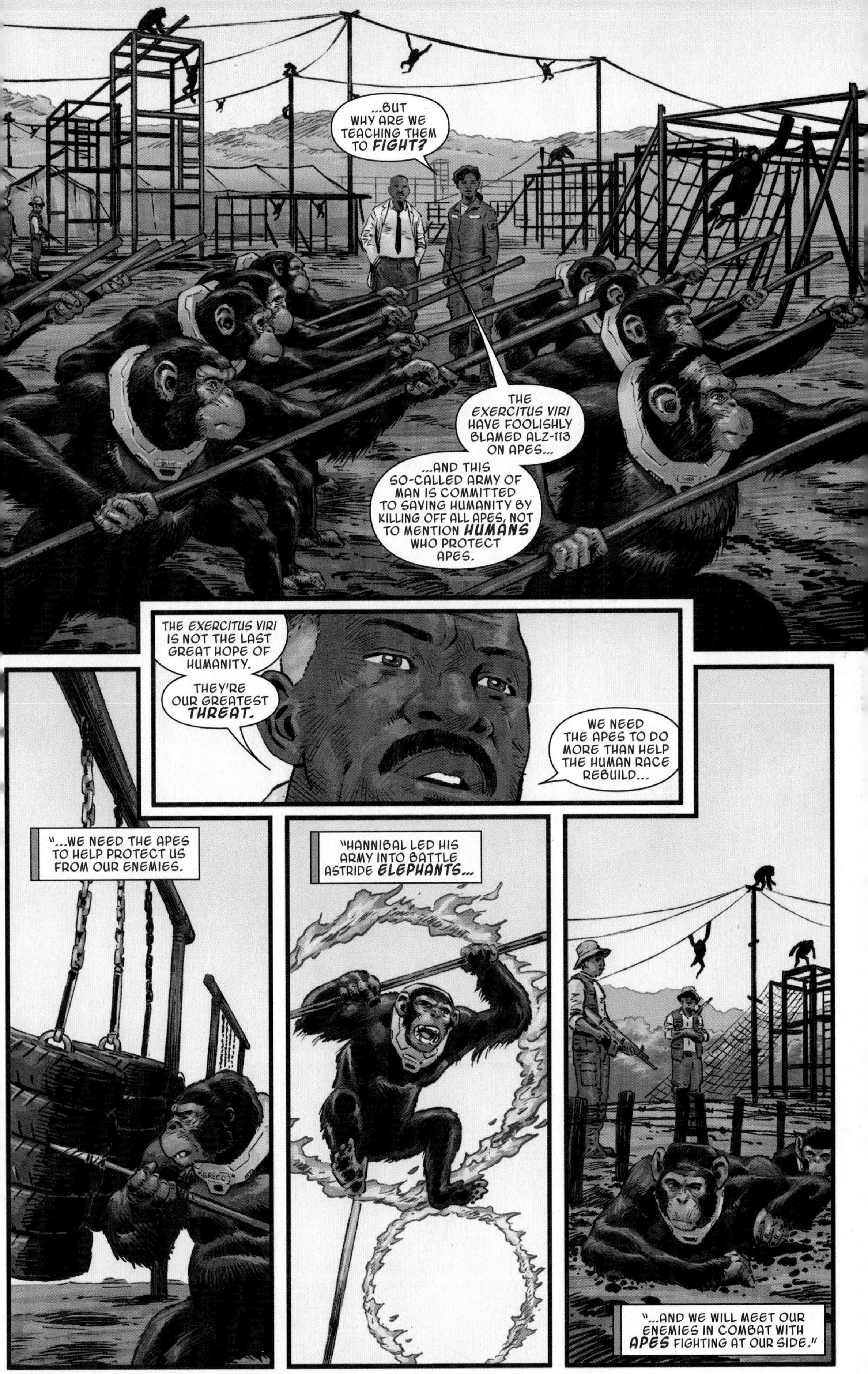
...BUT WHY ARE WE TEACHING THEM TO FIGHT?
THE EXERCITUS VIRI HAVE FOOLISHLY BLAMED ALZ-113 ON APES...
...AND THIS SO-CALLED ARMY OF MAN IS COMMITTED TO SAVING HUMANITY BY KILLING OFF ALL APES, NOT TO MENTION HUMANS WHO PROTECT APES.
THE EXERCITUS VIRI IS NOT THE LAST GREAT HOPE OF HUMANITY.
THEY'RE OUR GREATEST THREAT.
WE NEED THE APES TO DO MORE THAN HELP THE HUMAN RACE REBUILD...
"...WE NEED THE APES TO HELP PROTECT US FROM OUR ENEMIES.
"HANNIBAL LED HIS ARMY INTO BATTLE ASTRIDE ELEPHANTS...
"...AND WE WILL MEET OUR ENEMIES IN COMBAT WITH APES FIGHTING AT OUR SIDE."

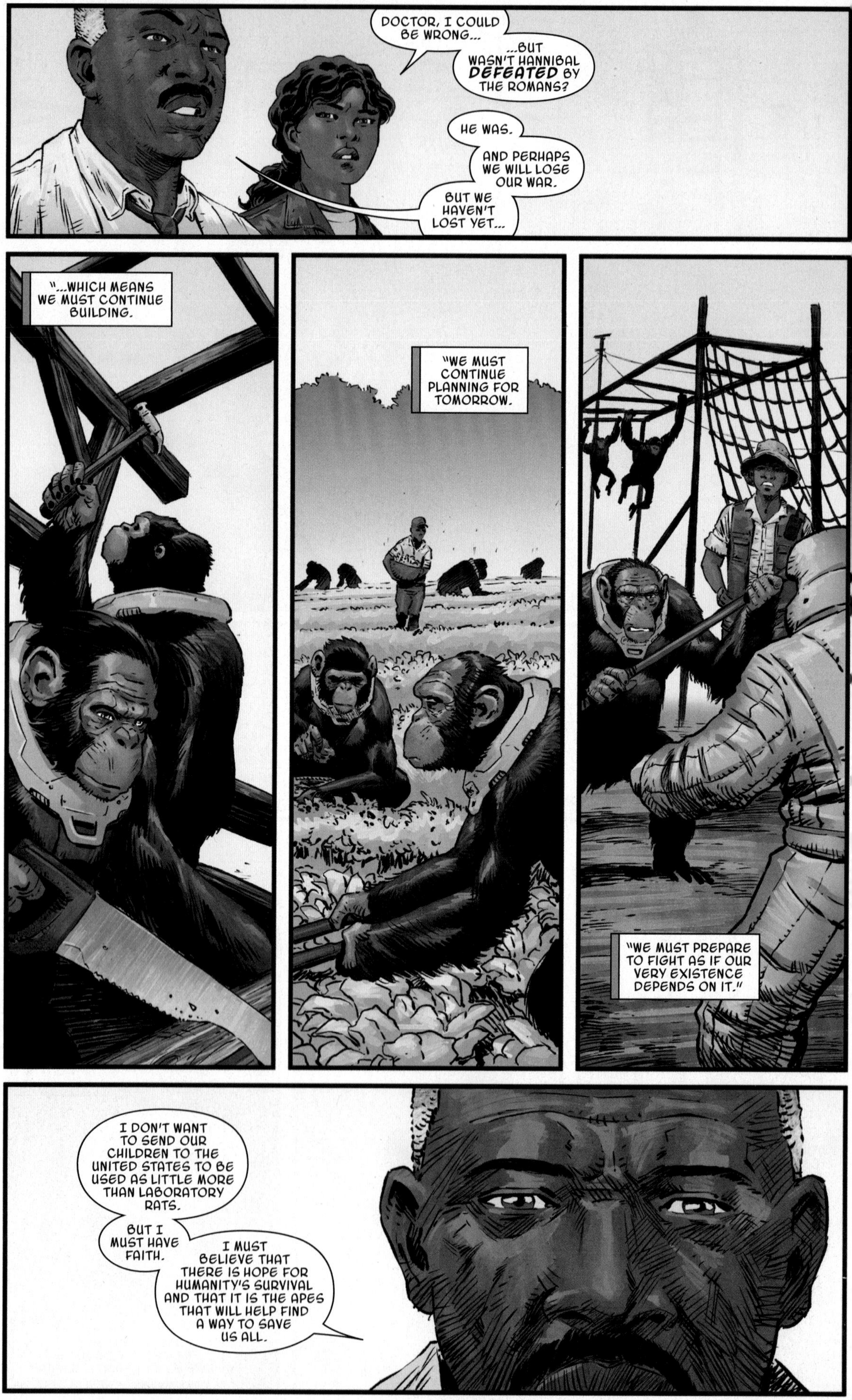
DOCTOR, I COULD BE WRONG...
...BUT WASN'T HANNIBAL DEFEATED BY THE ROMANS?
HE WAS.
AND PERHAPS WE WILL LOSE OUR WAR.
BUT WE HAVEN'T LOST YET...
"...WHICH MEANS WE MUST CONTINUE BUILDING.
"WE MUST CONTINUE PLANNING FOR TOMORROW.
"WE MUST PREPARE TO FIGHT AS IF OUR VERY EXISTENCE DEPENDS ON IT."
I DON'T WANT TO SEND OUR CHILDREN TO THE UNITED STATES TO BE USED AS LITTLE MORE THAN LABORATORY RATS.
BUT I MUST HAVE FAITH.
I MUST BELIEVE THAT THERE IS HOPE FOR HUMANITY'S SURVIVAL AND THAT IT IS THE APES THAT WILL HELP FIND A WAY TO SAVE US ALL.

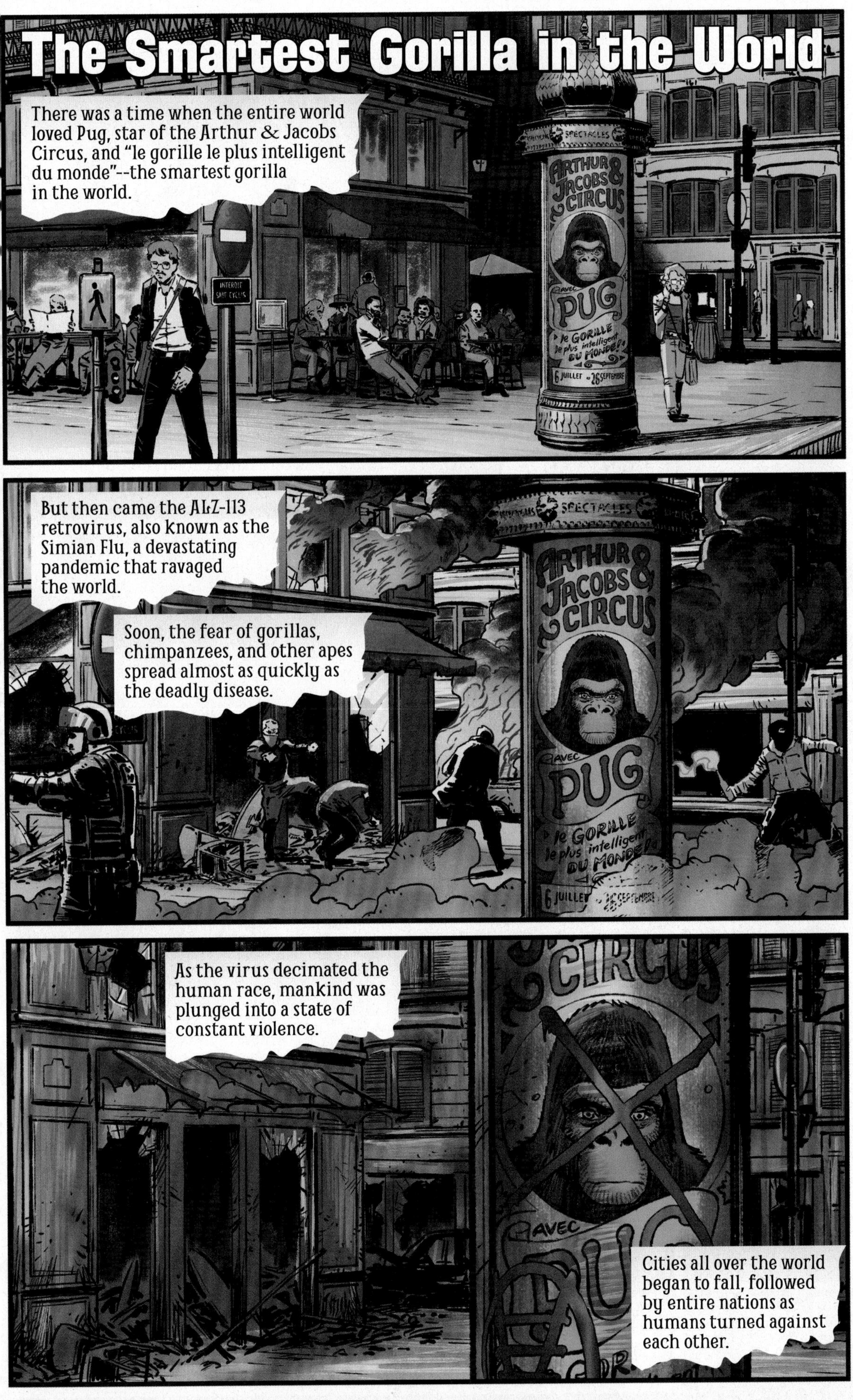
The Smartest Gorilla in the World
There was a time when the entire world loved Pug, star of the Arthur & Jacobs Circus, and "le gorille le plus intelligent du monde"--the smartest gorilla in the world.
SPECTACLES
ARTHUR & JACOBS CIRCUS
AVEC PUG
le GORILLE le plus intelligent DU MONDE!
6 JUILLET - 26 SEPTEMBRE
But then came the ALZ-113 retrovirus, also known as the Simian Flu, a devastating pandemic that ravaged the world.
Soon, the fear of gorillas, chimpanzees, and other apes spread almost as quickly as the deadly disease.
SPECTACLES
ARTHUR & JACOBS CIRCUS
AVEC PUG
le GORILLE le plus intelligent DU MONDE
As the virus decimated the human race, mankind was plunged into a state of constant violence.
CIRCUS
AVEC
Cities all over the world began to fall, followed by entire nations as humans turned against each other.

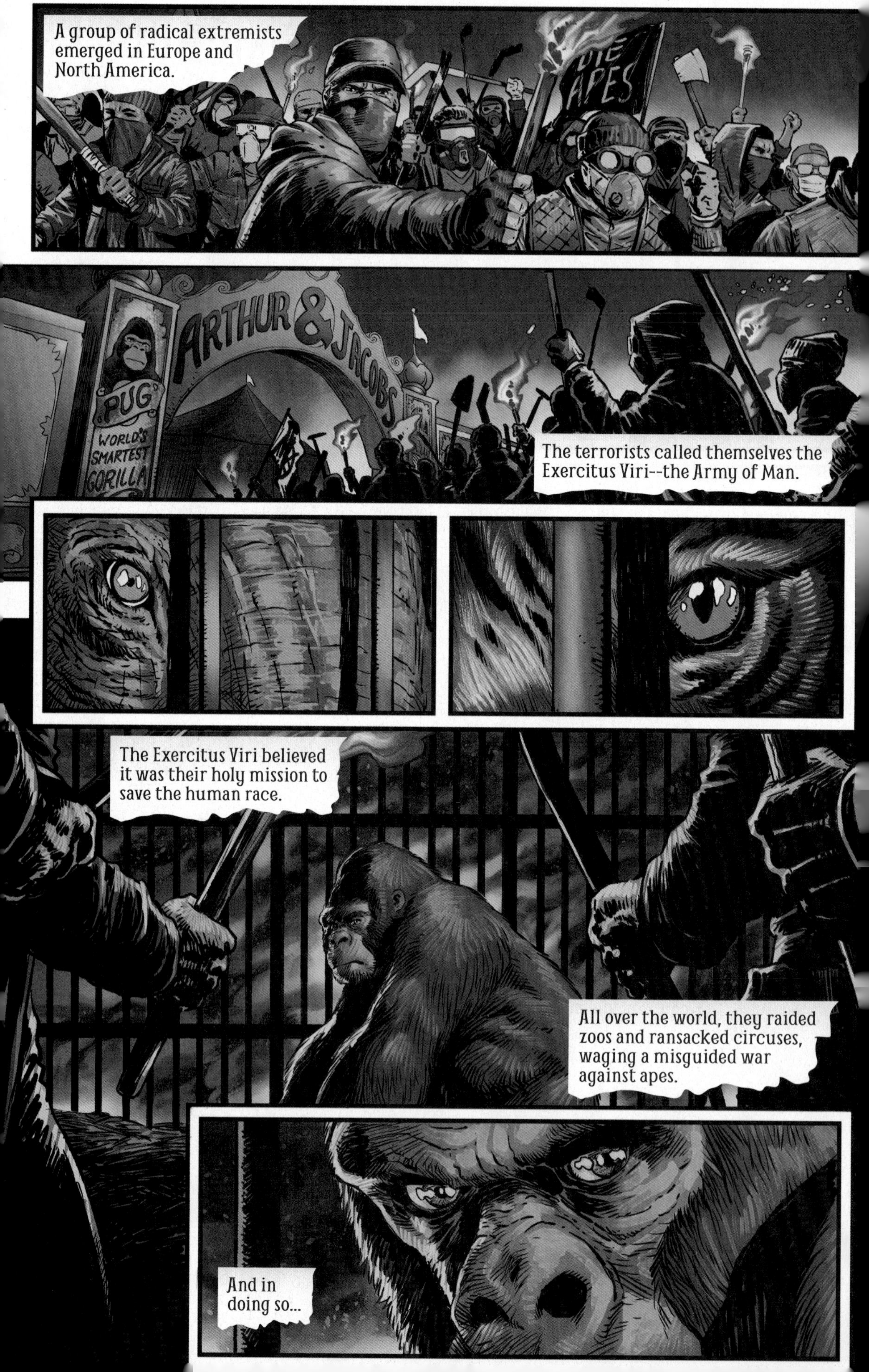
A group of radical extremists emerged in Europe and North America.
DIE APES
ARTHUR & JACOBS
PUG WORLD'S SMARTEST GORILLA
The terrorists called themselves the Exercitus Viri--the Army of Man.
The Exercitus Viri believed it was their holy mission to save the human race.
All over the world, they raided zoos and ransacked circuses, waging a misguided war against apes.
And in doing so...

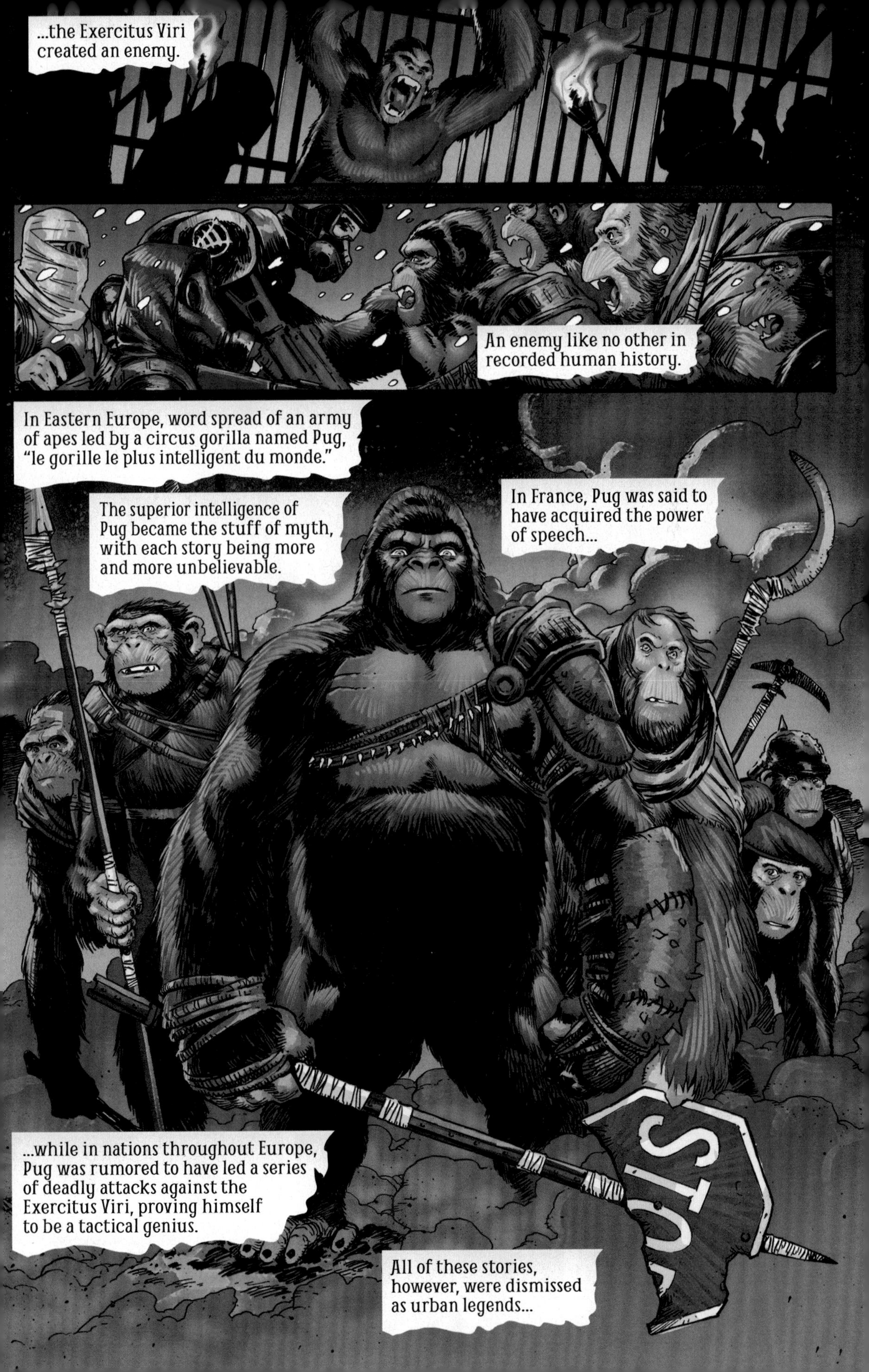
...the Exercitus Viri created an enemy.
An enemy like no other in recorded human history.
In Eastern Europe, word spread of an army of apes led by a circus gorilla named Pug, "le gorille le plus intelligent du monde."
The superior intelligence of Pug became the stuff of myth, with each story being more and more unbelievable.
In France, Pug was said to have acquired the power of speech...
...while in nations throughout Europe, Pug was rumored to have led a series of deadly attacks against the Exercitus Viri, proving himself to be a tactical genius.
All of these stories, however, were dismissed as urban legends...

...for no gorilla, no matter how smart they were, possessed the intelligence to stalk their human enemies and lead them into a trap.

But of all the myths, legends, and tall tales of Pug and his army of apes, none was more unbelievable than the story of their engagement with the Exercitus Viri at the World Health Organization in Switzerland.

Leading the global search for a cure for ALZ-113, the World Health Organization housed hundreds of primates...

...making it a target of the Exercitus Viri.

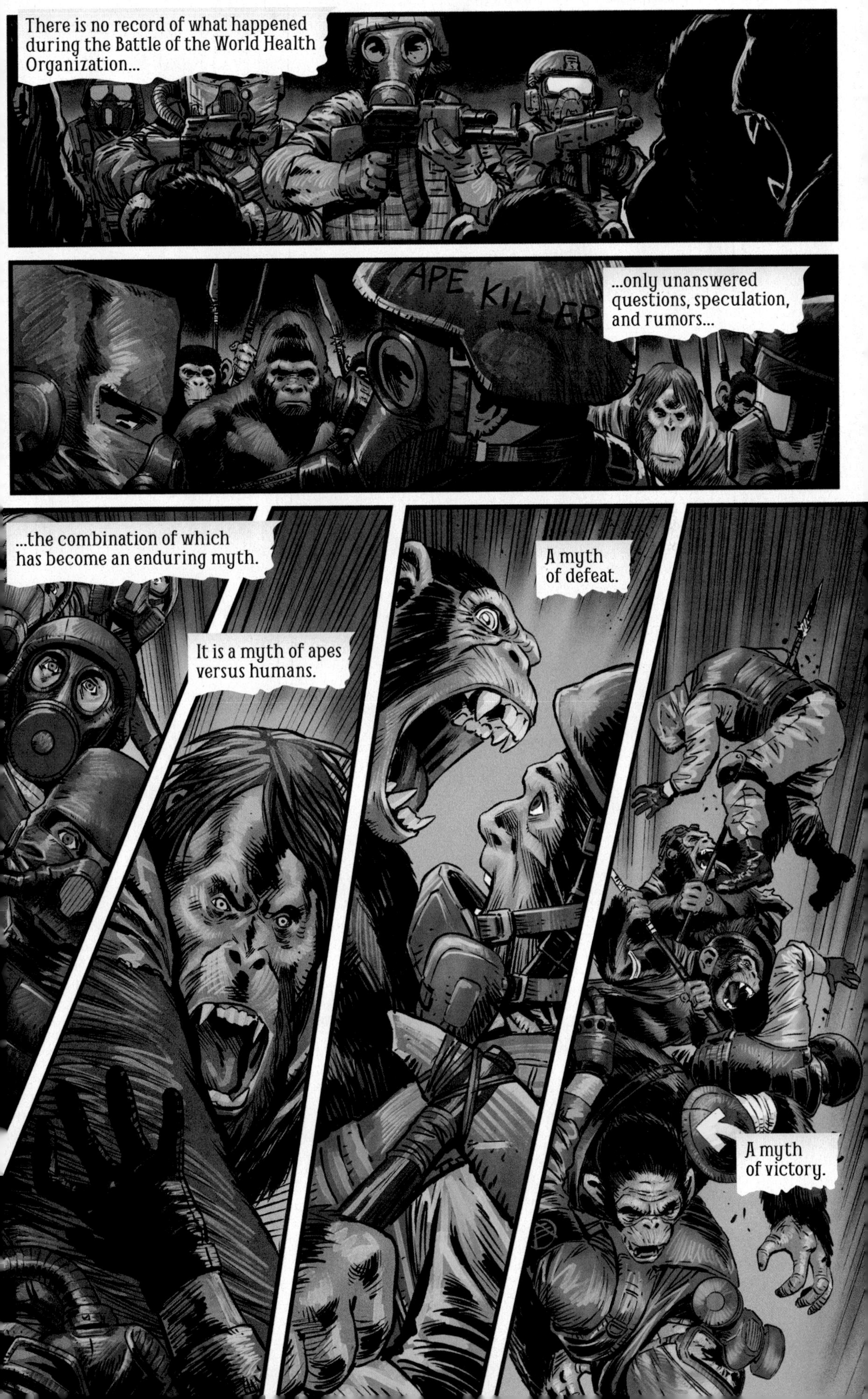
There is no record of what happened during the Battle of the World Health Organization...
APE KILLER
...only unanswered questions, speculation, and rumors...
...the combination of which has become an enduring myth.
It is a myth of apes versus humans.
A myth of defeat.
A myth of victory.

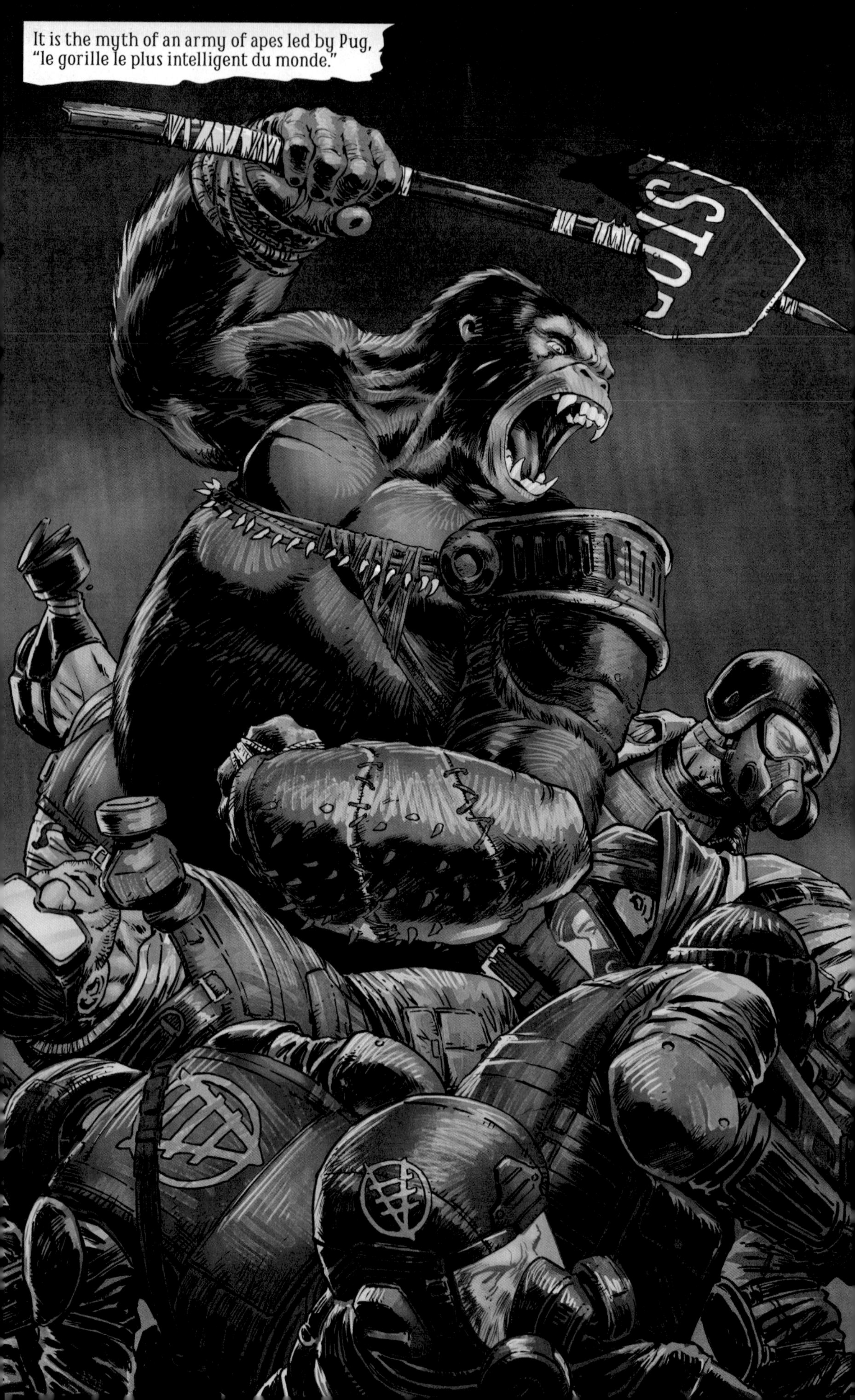
It is the myth of an army of apes led by Pug, "le gorille le plus intelligent du monde."
STOP

E.M. GIST

#2 Variant

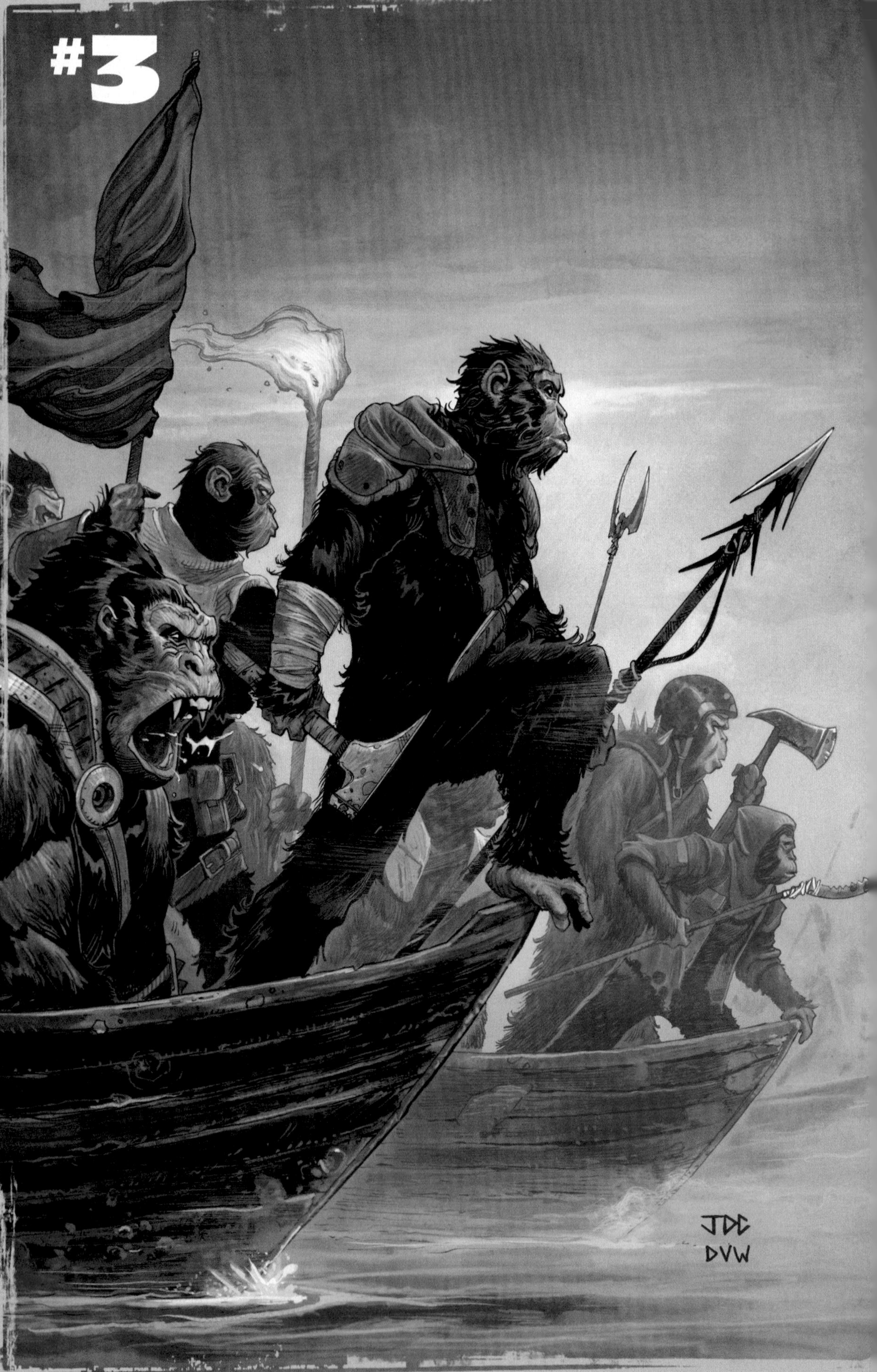
#3
JDC
DVW

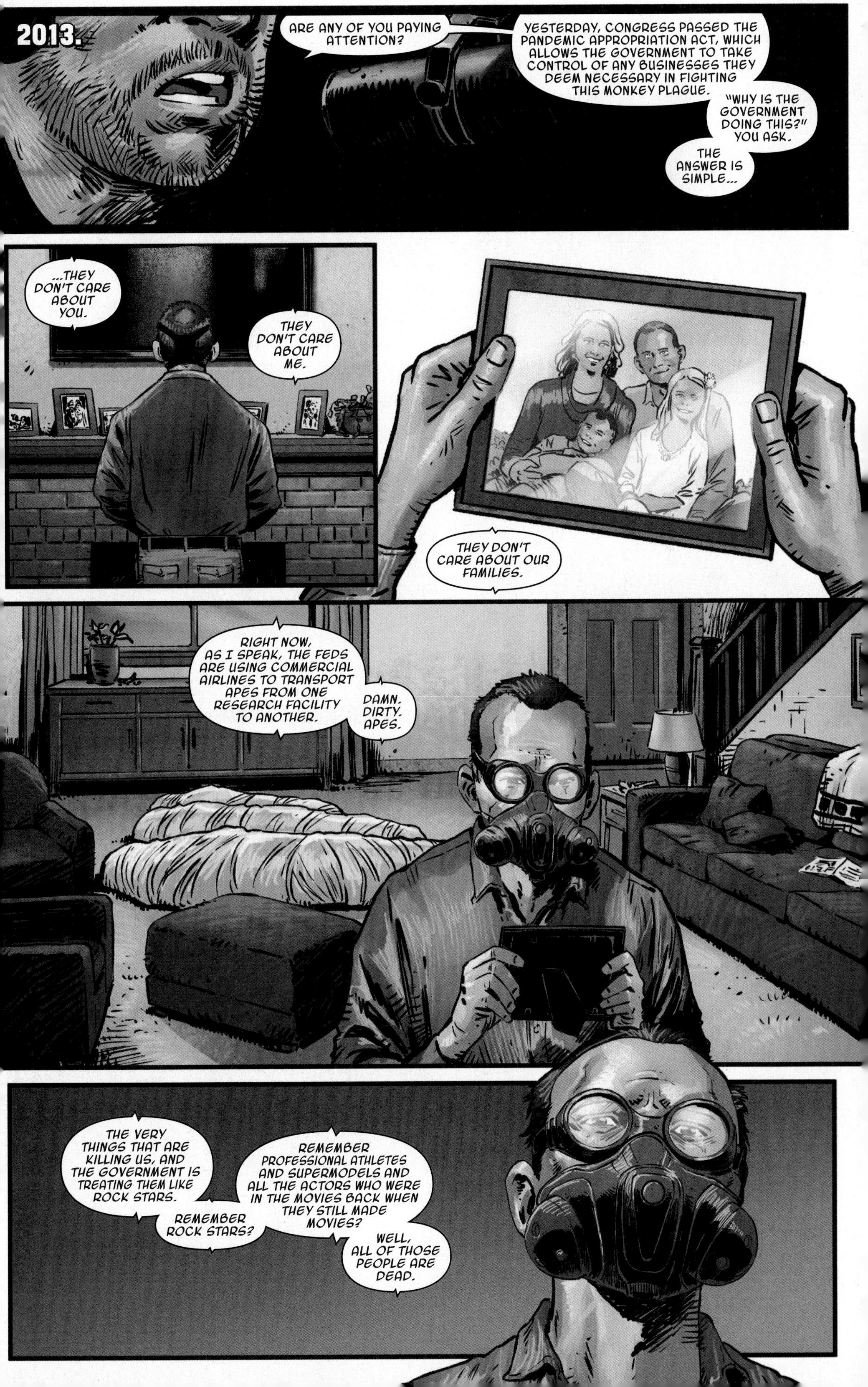
2013.
ARE ANY OF YOU PAYING ATTENTION?
YESTERDAY, CONGRESS PASSED THE PANDEMIC APPROPRIATION ACT, WHICH ALLOWS THE GOVERNMENT TO TAKE CONTROL OF ANY BUSINESSES THEY DEEM NECESSARY IN FIGHTING THIS MONKEY PLAGUE.
"WHY IS THE GOVERNMENT DOING THIS?" YOU ASK.
THE ANSWER IS SIMPLE...
...THEY DON'T CARE ABOUT YOU.
THEY DON'T CARE ABOUT ME.
THEY DON'T CARE ABOUT OUR FAMILIES.
RIGHT NOW, AS I SPEAK, THE FEDS ARE USING COMMERCIAL AIRLINES TO TRANSPORT APES FROM ONE RESEARCH FACILITY TO ANOTHER.
DAMN. DIRTY. APES.
THE VERY THINGS THAT ARE KILLING US, AND THE GOVERNMENT IS TREATING THEM LIKE ROCK STARS.
REMEMBER ROCK STARS?
REMEMBER PROFESSIONAL ATHLETES AND SUPERMODELS AND ALL THE ACTORS WHO WERE IN THE MOVIES BACK WHEN THEY STILL MADE MOVIES?
WELL, ALL OF THOSE PEOPLE ARE DEAD.

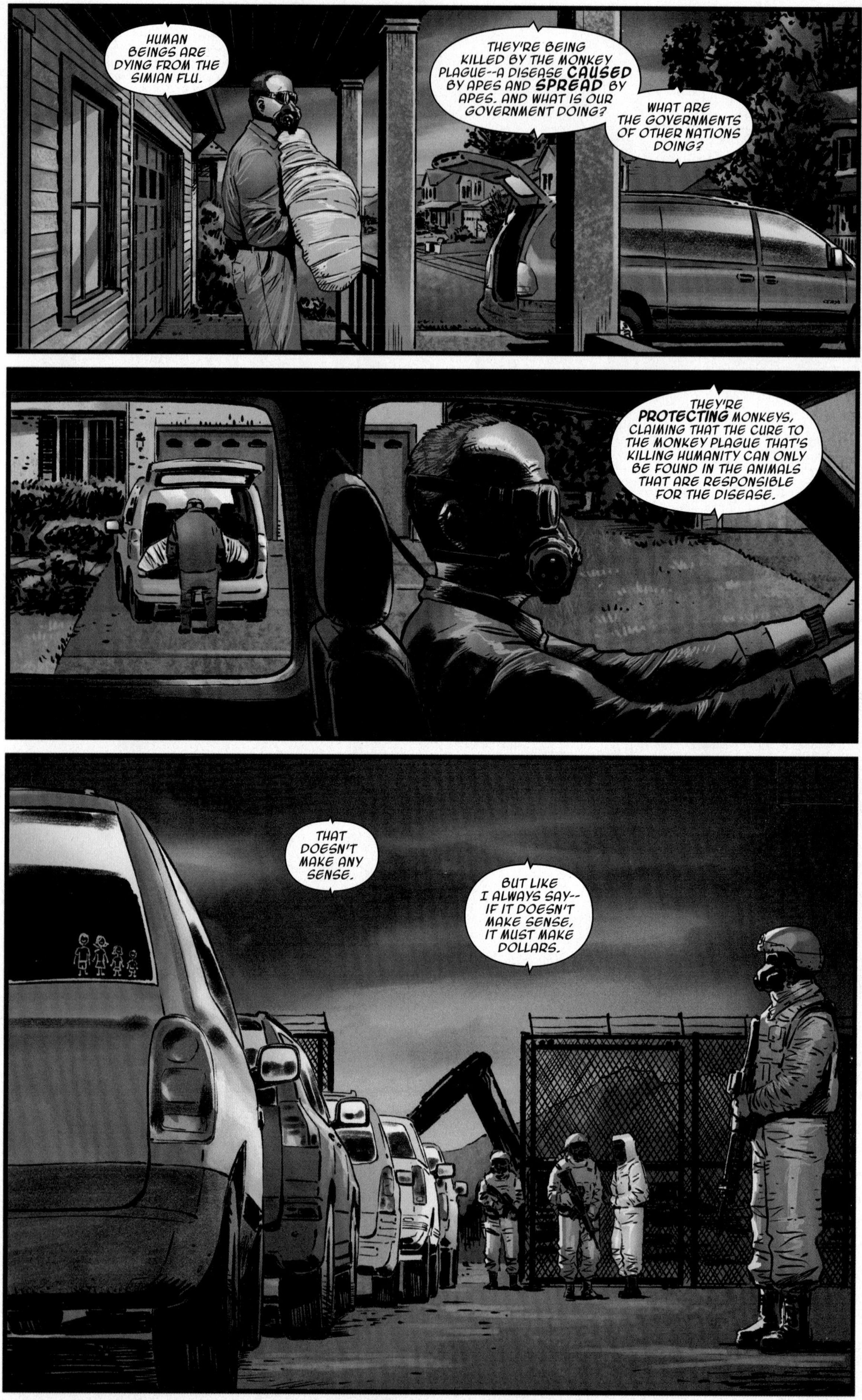
HUMAN BEINGS ARE DYING FROM THE SIMIAN FLU.
THEY'RE BEING KILLED BY THE MONKEY PLAGUE--A DISEASE **CAUSED** BY APES AND **SPREAD** BY APES. AND WHAT IS OUR GOVERNMENT DOING?
WHAT ARE THE GOVERNMENTS OF OTHER NATIONS DOING?
THEY'RE **PROTECTING** MONKEYS, CLAIMING THAT THE CURE TO THE MONKEY PLAGUE THAT'S KILLING HUMANITY CAN ONLY BE FOUND IN THE ANIMALS THAT ARE RESPONSIBLE FOR THE DISEASE.
THAT DOESN'T MAKE ANY SENSE.
BUT LIKE I ALWAYS SAY-- IF IT DOESN'T MAKE SENSE, IT MUST MAKE DOLLARS.

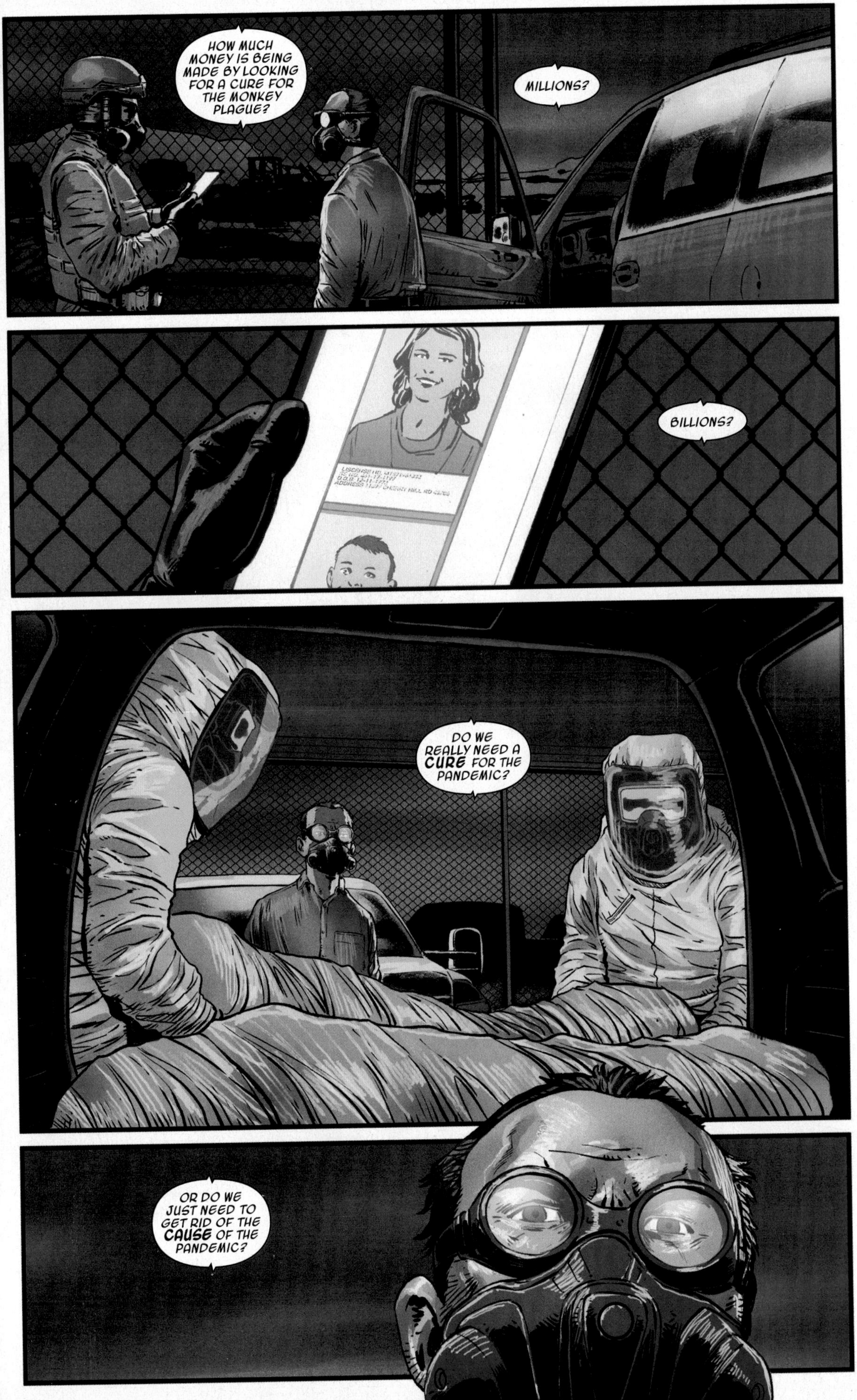
HOW MUCH MONEY IS BEING MADE BY LOOKING FOR A CURE FOR THE MONKEY PLAGUE?
MILLIONS?
BILLIONS?
DO WE REALLY NEED A CURE FOR THE PANDEMIC?
OR DO WE JUST NEED TO GET RID OF THE CAUSE OF THE PANDEMIC?

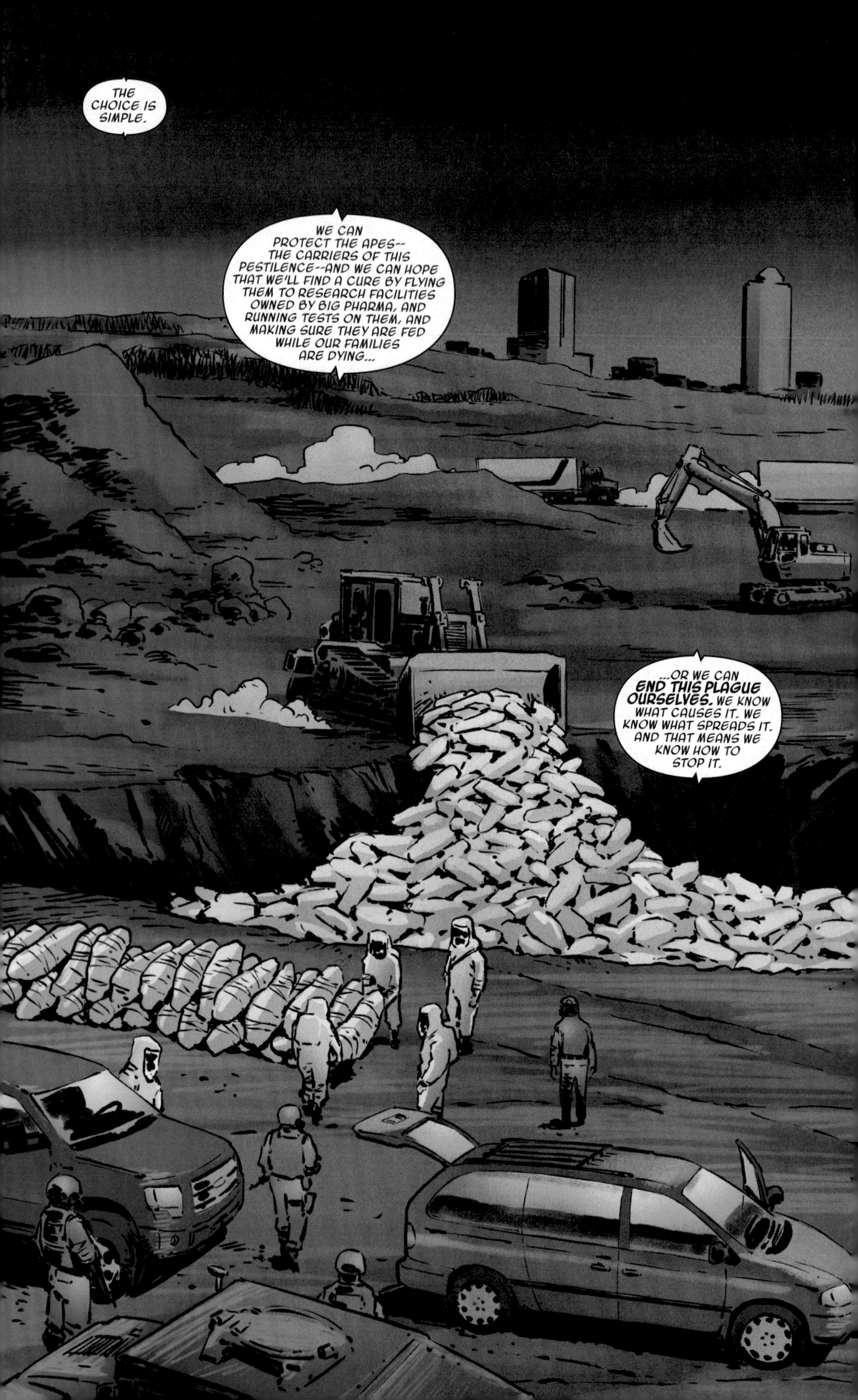
THE CHOICE IS SIMPLE.
WE CAN PROTECT THE APES-- THE CARRIERS OF THIS PESTILENCE--AND WE CAN HOPE THAT WE'LL FIND A CURE BY FLYING THEM TO RESEARCH FACILITIES OWNED BY BIG PHARMA, AND RUNNING TESTS ON THEM, AND MAKING SURE THEY ARE FED WHILE OUR FAMILIES ARE DYING...
...OR WE CAN **END THIS PLAGUE OURSELVES.** WE KNOW WHAT CAUSES IT. WE KNOW WHAT SPREADS IT. AND THAT MEANS WE KNOW HOW TO STOP IT.

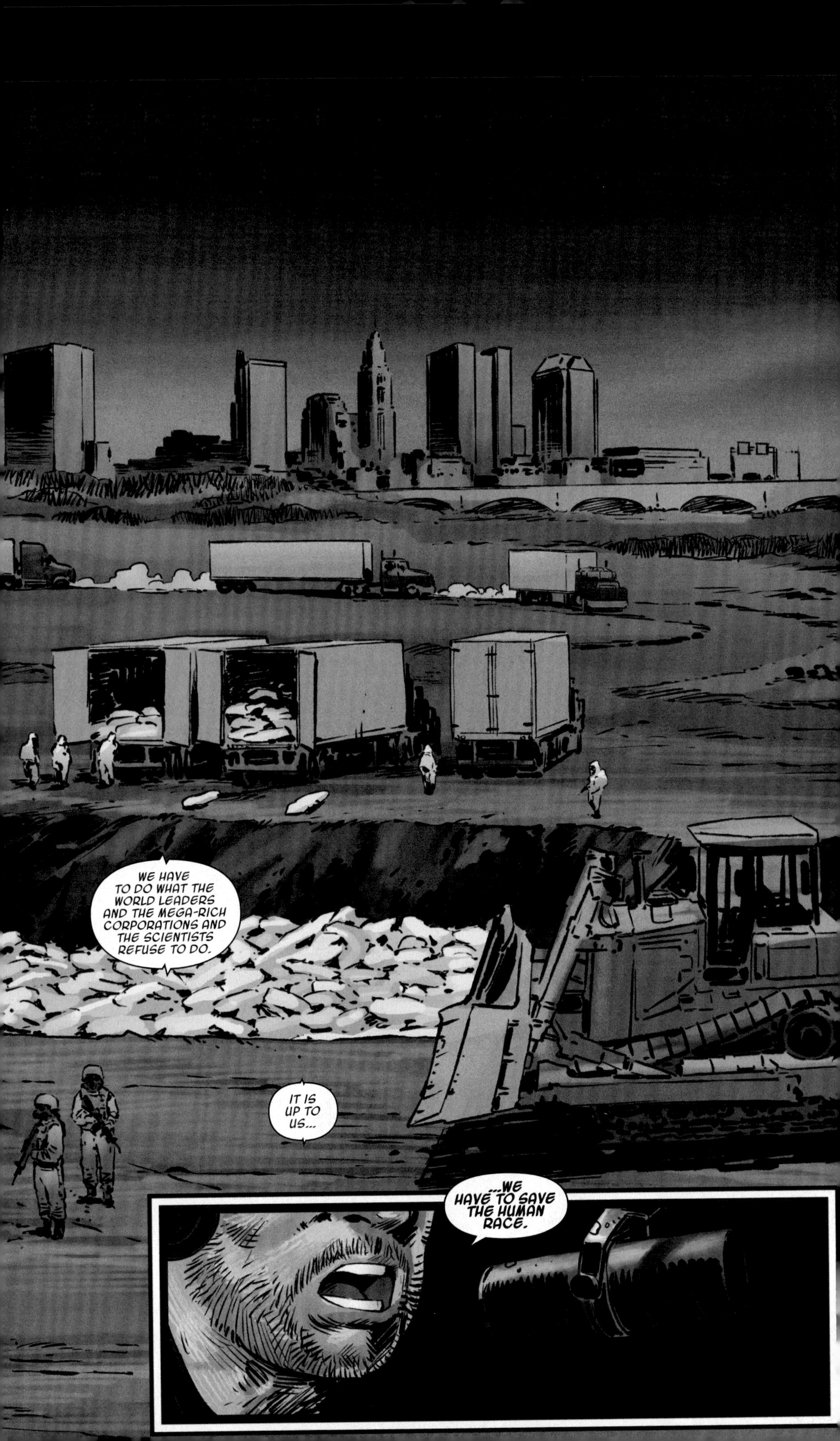
WE HAVE TO DO WHAT THE WORLD LEADERS AND THE MEGA-RICH CORPORATIONS AND THE SCIENTISTS REFUSE TO DO.
IT IS UP TO US...
...WE HAVE TO SAVE THE HUMAN RACE.

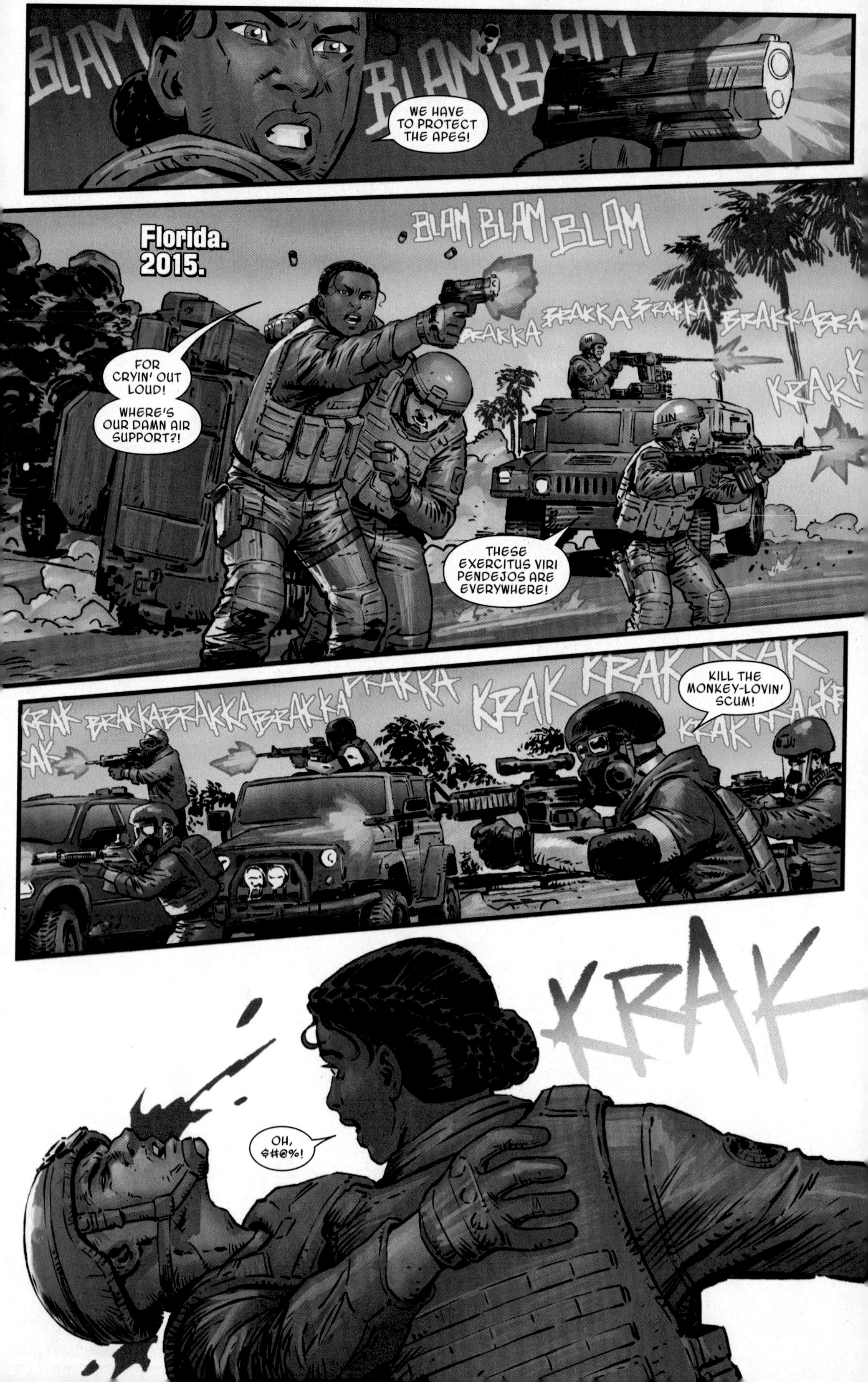
BLAM
BLAM BLAM
WE HAVE TO PROTECT THE APES!
Florida. 2015.
BLAM BLAM BLAM
FOR CRYIN' OUT LOUD!
WHERE'S OUR DAMN AIR SUPPORT?!
BRAKKA BRAKKA BRAKKA BRAKKA
KRAK
THESE EXERCITUS VIRI PENDEJOS ARE EVERYWHERE!
KRAK BRAKKA BRAKKA BRAKKA BRAKKA
KRAK KRAK KRAK
KILL THE MONKEY-LOVIN' SCUM!
KRAK
OH, $#@%!

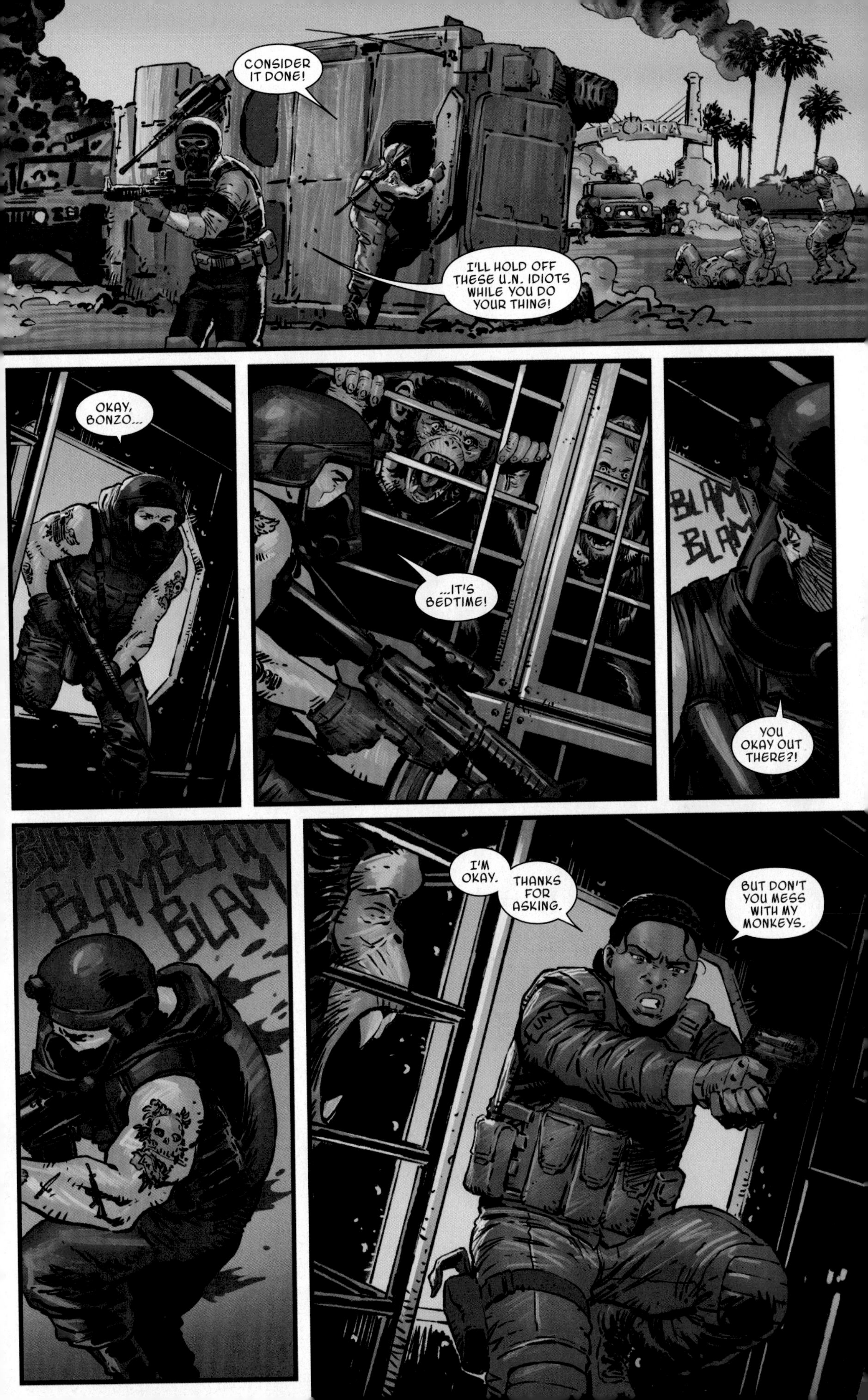
CONSIDER IT DONE!
I'LL HOLD OFF THESE U.N. IDIOTS WHILE YOU DO YOUR THING!
OKAY, BONZO...
...IT'S BEDTIME!
BLAM BLAM
YOU OKAY OUT THERE?!
BLAM BLAM
I'M OKAY.
THANKS FOR ASKING.
BUT DON'T YOU MESS WITH MY MONKEYS.

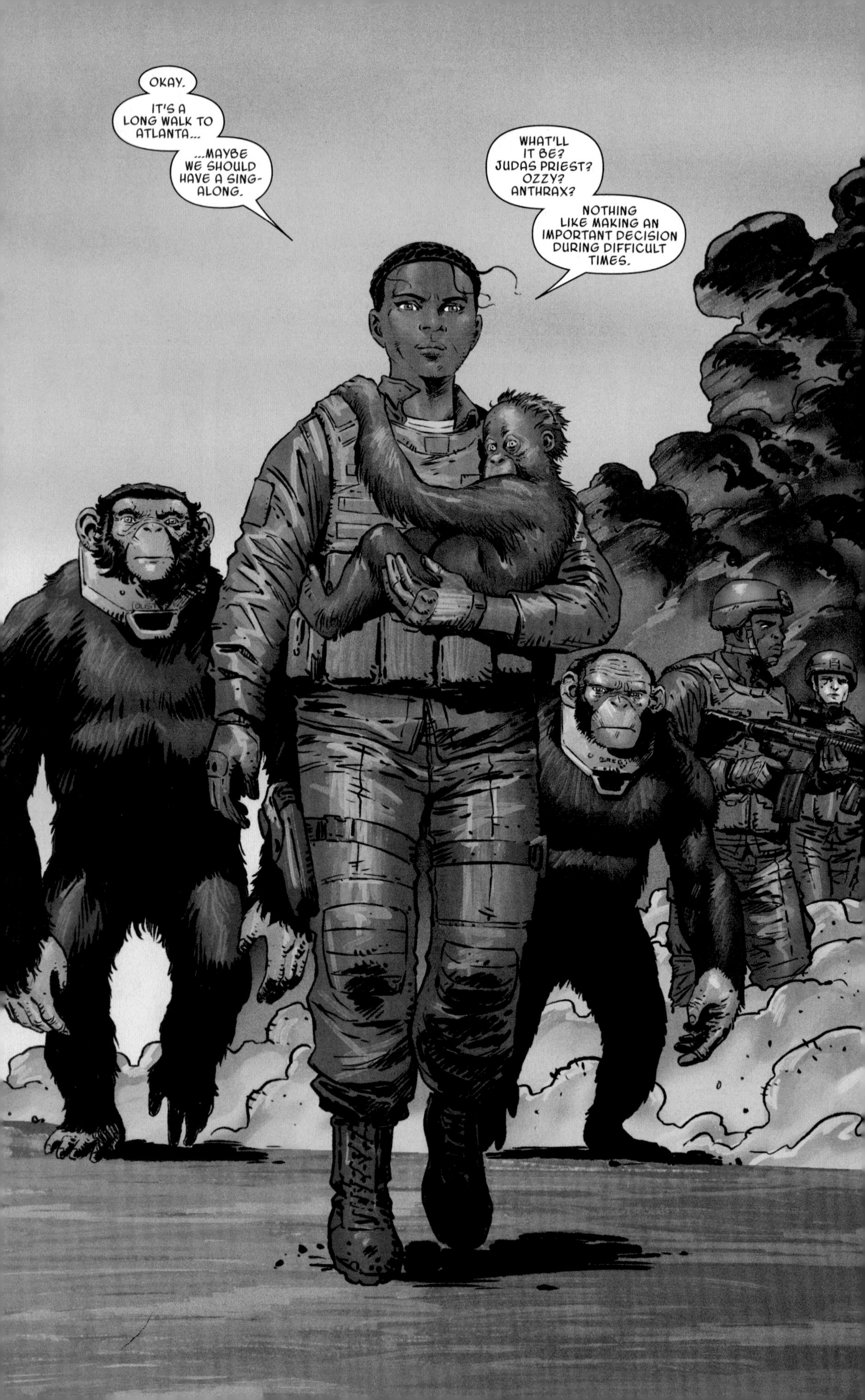
OKAY.
IT'S A LONG WALK TO ATLANTA...
...MAYBE WE SHOULD HAVE A SING-ALONG.
WHAT'LL IT BE? JUDAS PRIEST? OZZY? ANTHRAX?
NOTHING LIKE MAKING AN IMPORTANT DECISION DURING DIFFICULT TIMES.

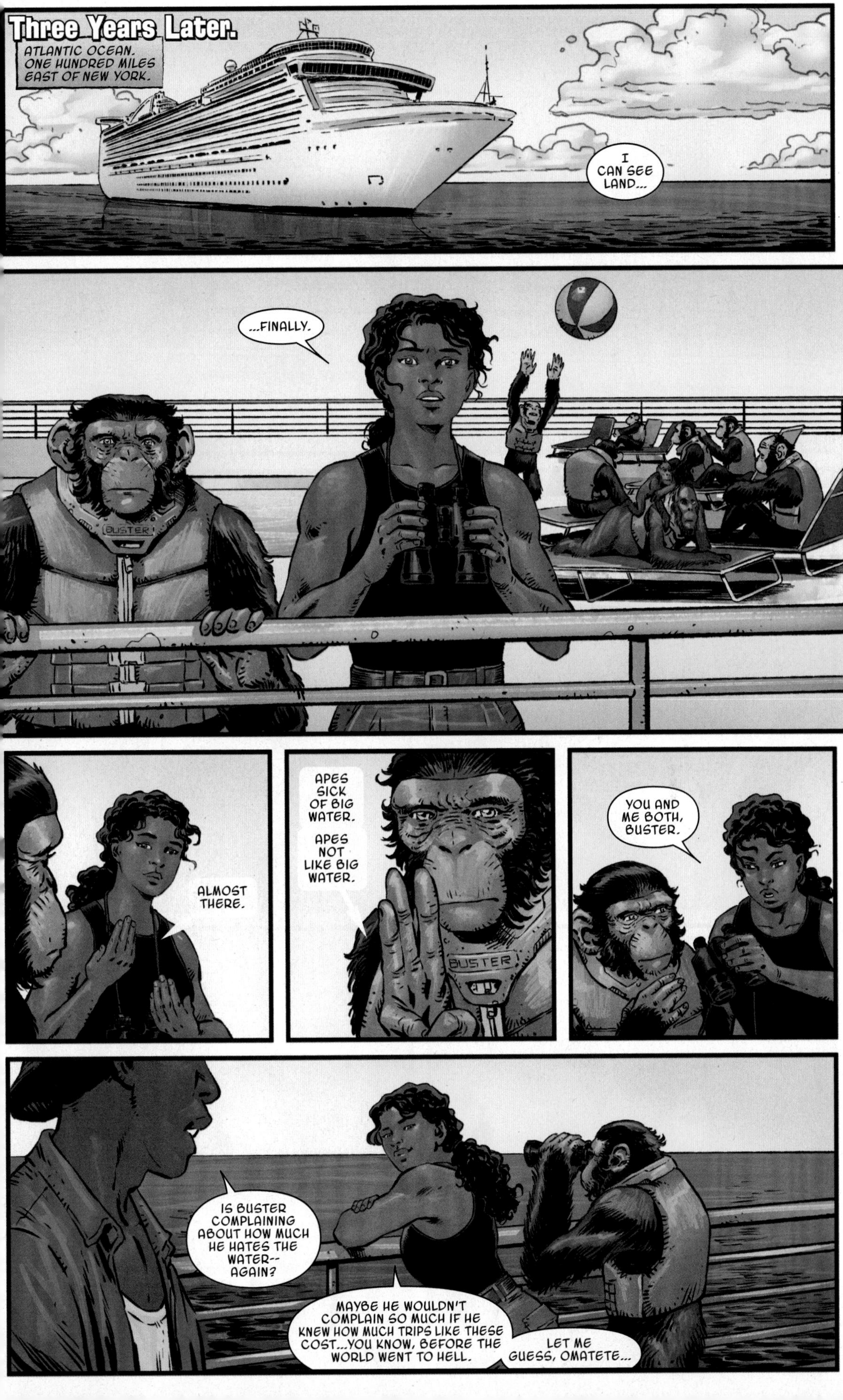
Three Years Later.
ATLANTIC OCEAN. ONE HUNDRED MILES EAST OF NEW YORK.
I CAN SEE LAND...
...FINALLY.
BUSTER
ALMOST THERE.
APES SICK OF BIG WATER.
APES NOT LIKE BIG WATER.
BUSTER
YOU AND ME BOTH, BUSTER.
IS BUSTER COMPLAINING ABOUT HOW MUCH HE HATES THE WATER-- AGAIN?
MAYBE HE WOULDN'T COMPLAIN SO MUCH IF HE KNEW HOW MUCH TRIPS LIKE THESE COST...YOU KNOW, BEFORE THE WORLD WENT TO HELL.
LET ME GUESS, OMATETE...

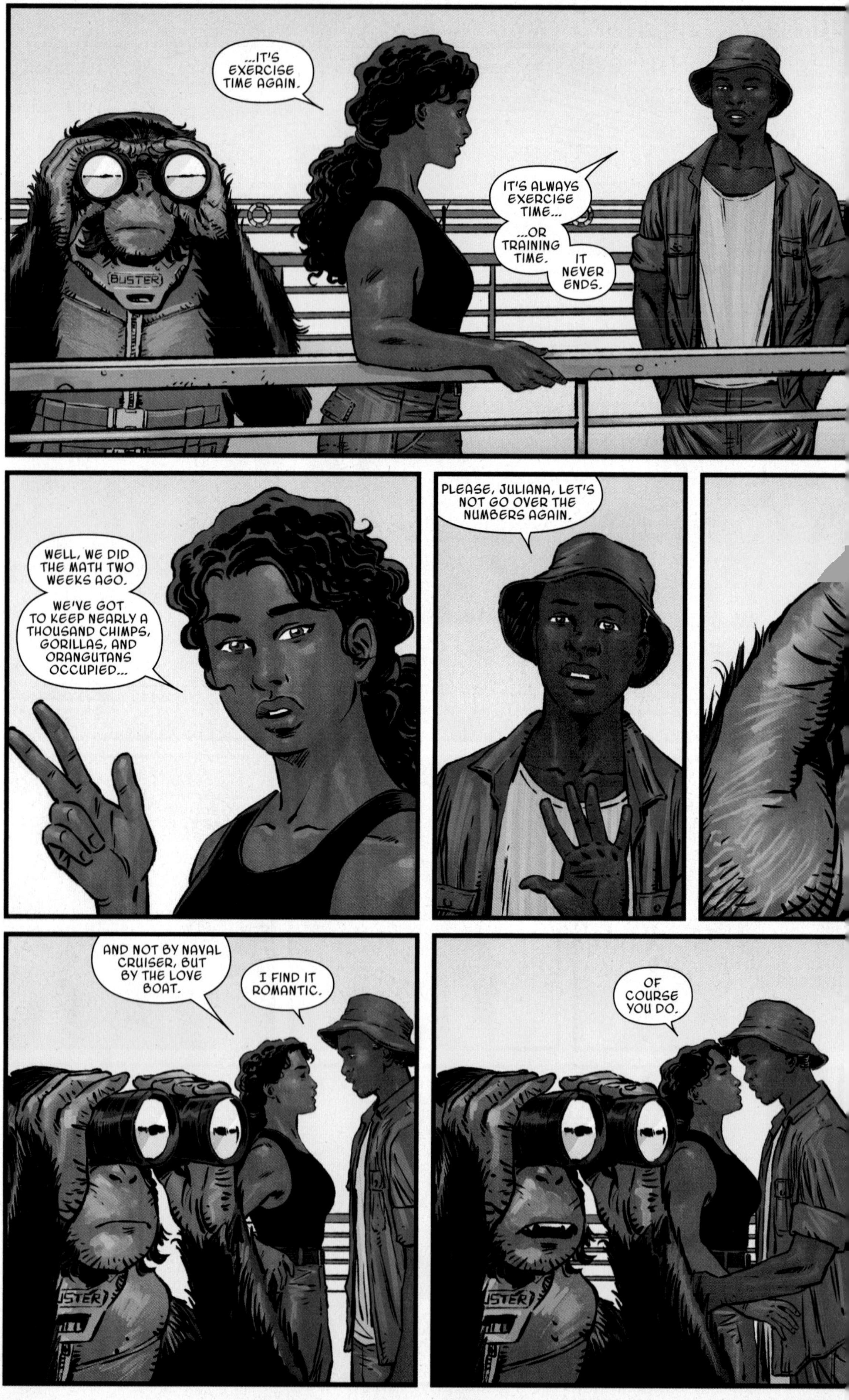
...IT'S EXERCISE TIME AGAIN.
IT'S ALWAYS EXERCISE TIME...
...OR TRAINING TIME.
IT NEVER ENDS.
BUSTER
WELL, WE DID THE MATH TWO WEEKS AGO.
WE'VE GOT TO KEEP NEARLY A THOUSAND CHIMPS, GORILLAS, AND ORANGUTANS OCCUPIED...
PLEASE, JULIANA, LET'S NOT GO OVER THE NUMBERS AGAIN.
AND NOT BY NAVAL CRUISER, BUT BY THE LOVE BOAT.
I FIND IT ROMANTIC.
OF COURSE YOU DO.

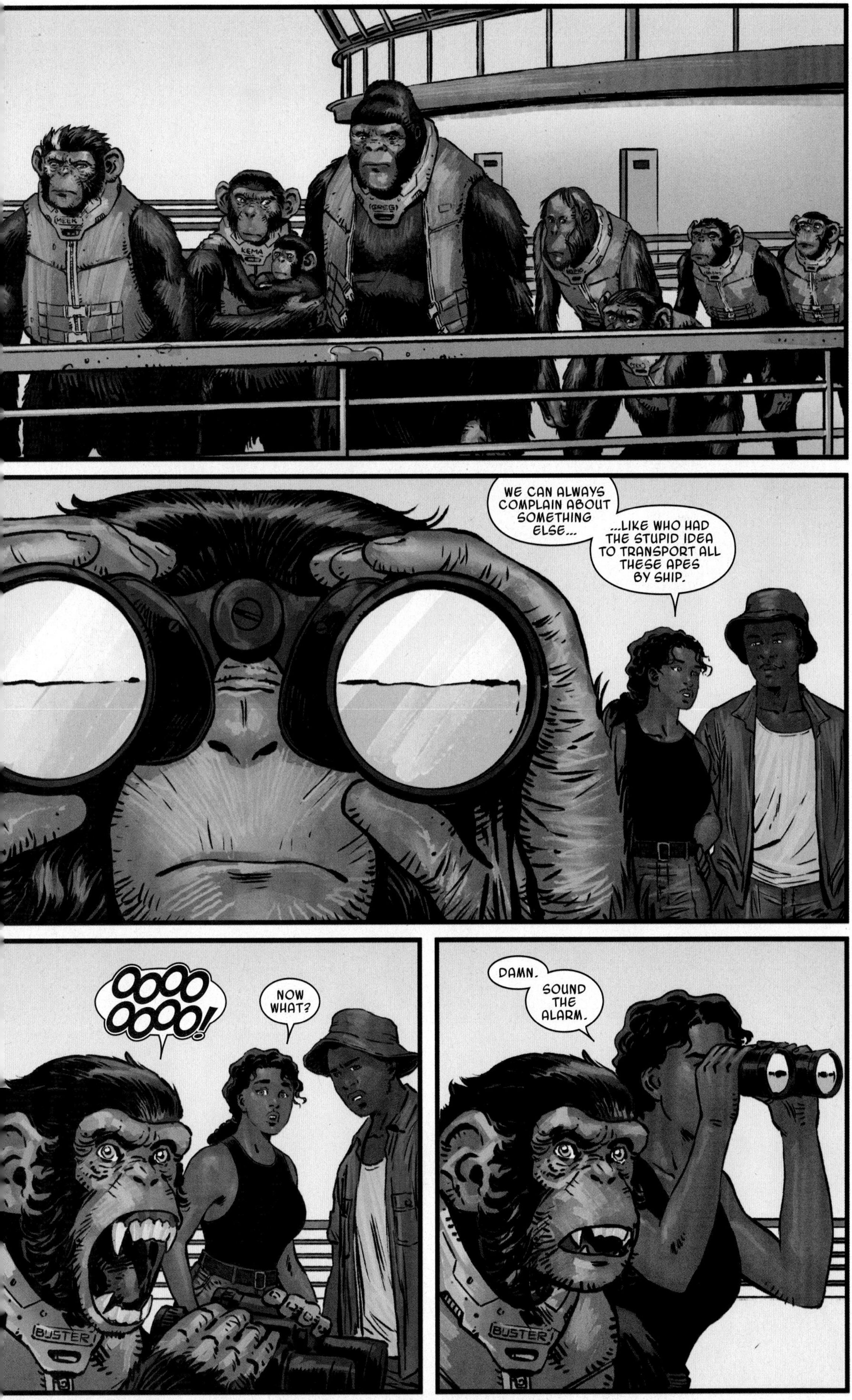
WE CAN ALWAYS COMPLAIN ABOUT SOMETHING ELSE...
...LIKE WHO HAD THE STUPID IDEA TO TRANSPORT ALL THESE APES BY SHIP.
OOOO OOOO!
NOW WHAT?
DAMN.
SOUND THE ALARM.

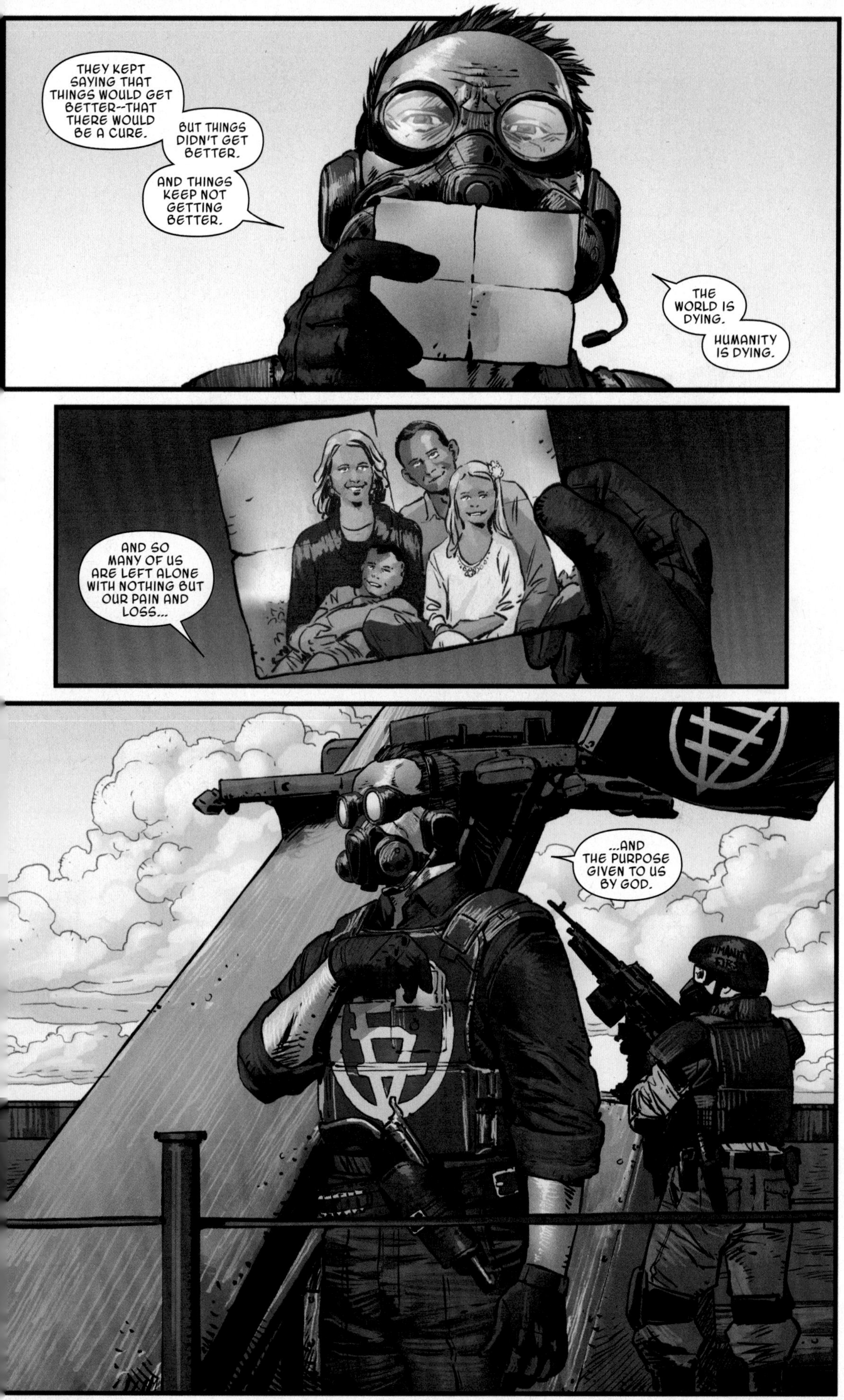
THEY KEPT SAYING THAT THINGS WOULD GET BETTER--THAT THERE WOULD BE A CURE.
BUT THINGS DIDN'T GET BETTER.
AND THINGS KEEP NOT GETTING BETTER.
THE WORLD IS DYING.
HUMANITY IS DYING.
AND SO MANY OF US ARE LEFT ALONE WITH NOTHING BUT OUR PAIN AND LOSS...
...AND THE PURPOSE GIVEN TO US BY GOD.

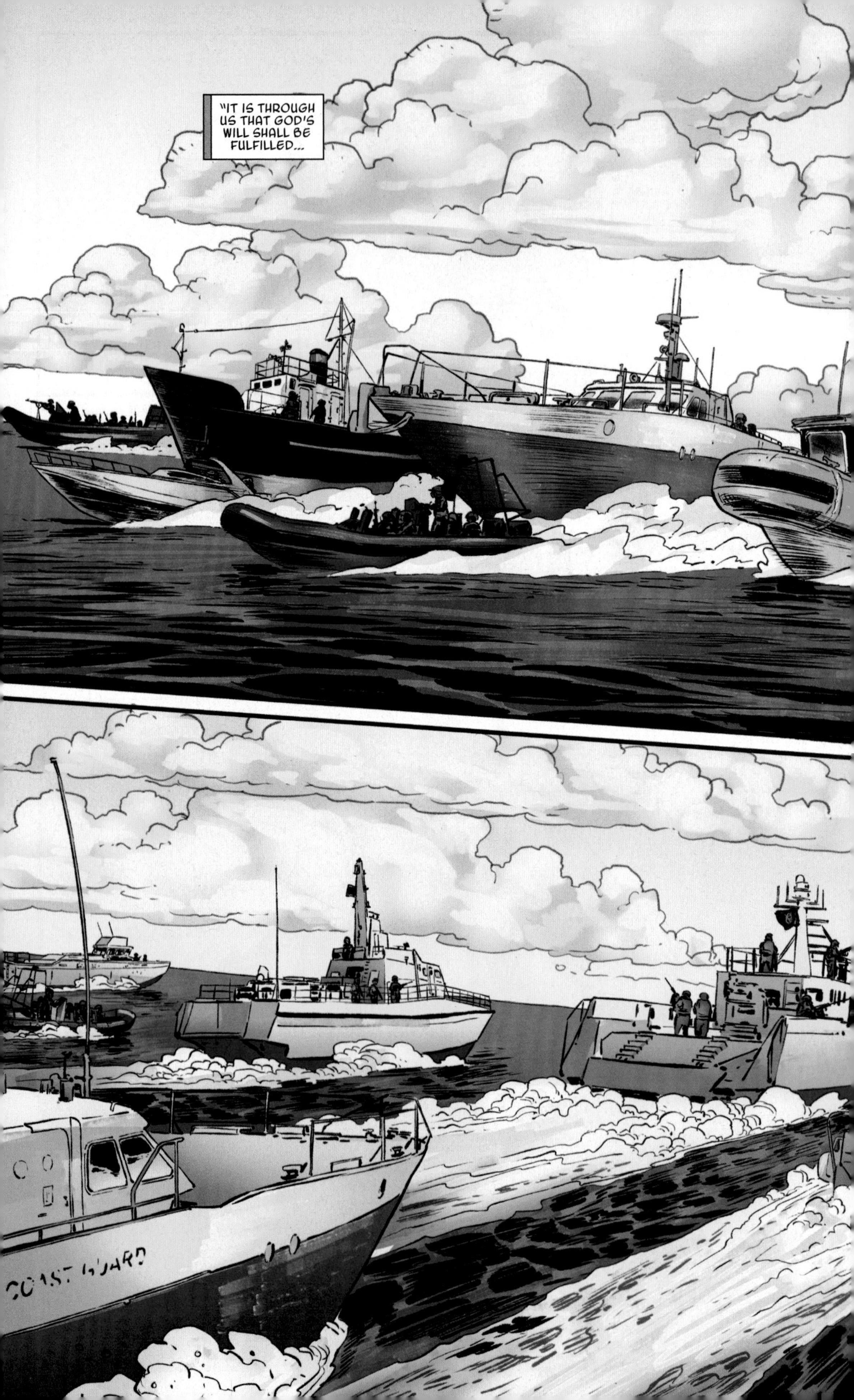
"IT IS THROUGH
US THAT GOD'S
WILL SHALL BE
FULFILLED...
COAST GUARD

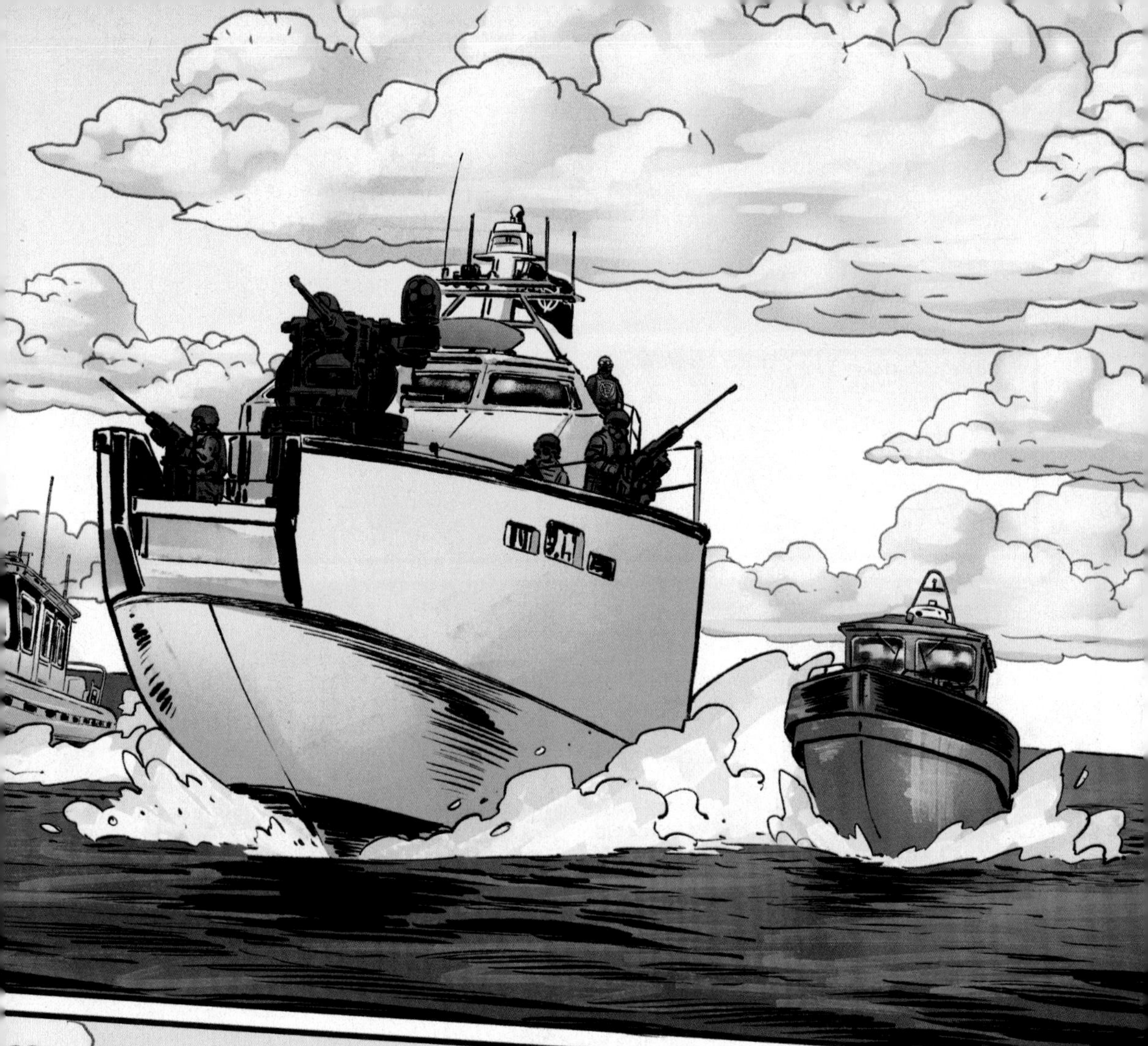

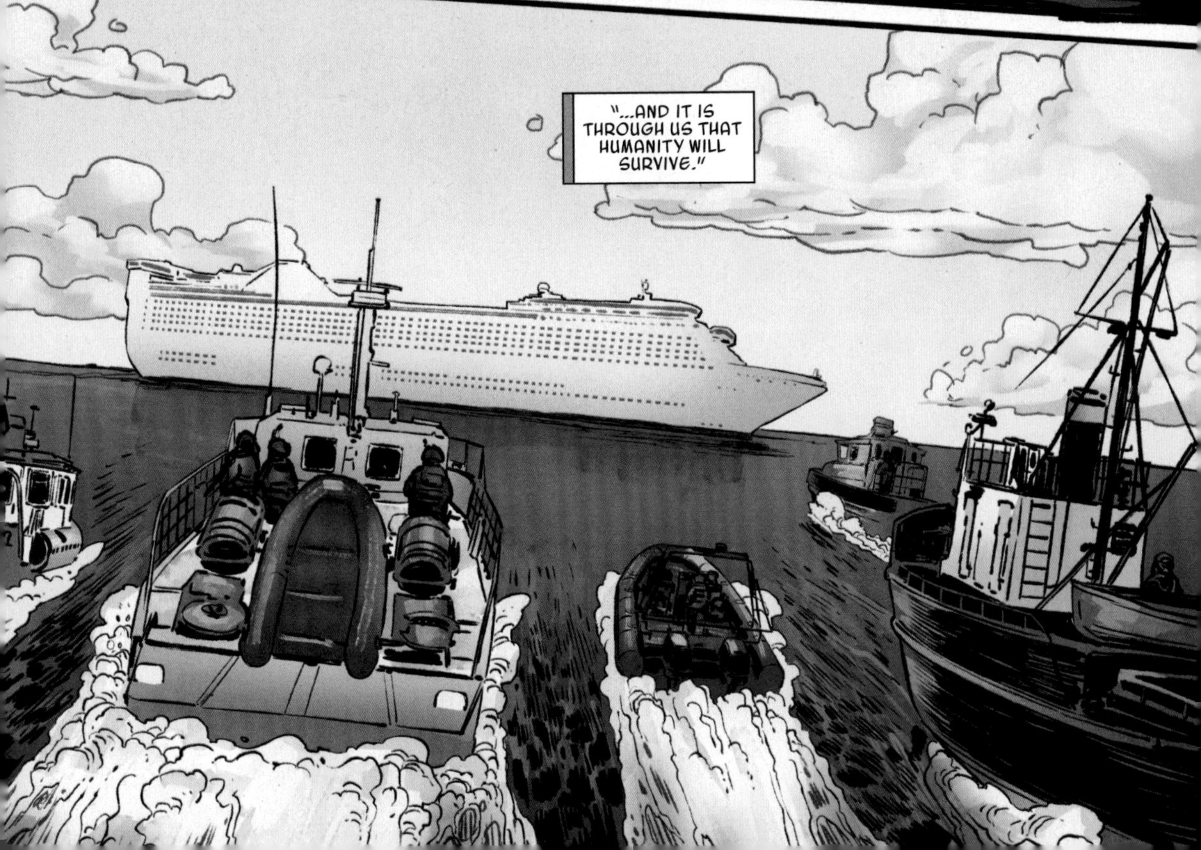
"...AND IT IS THROUGH US THAT HUMANITY WILL SURVIVE."

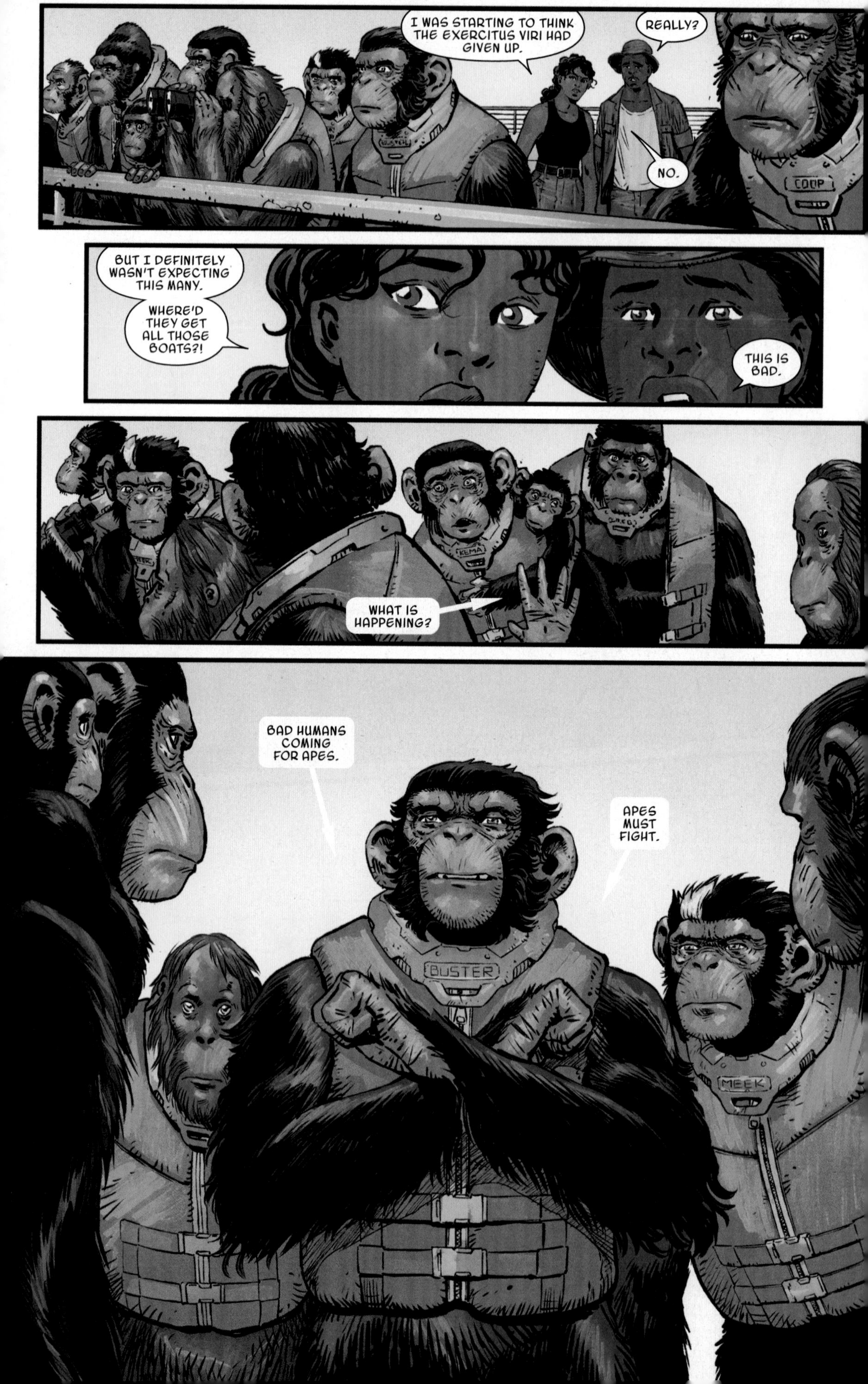
I WAS STARTING TO THINK THE EXERCITUS VIRI HAD GIVEN UP.
REALLY?
NO.
BUT I DEFINITELY WASN'T EXPECTING THIS MANY.
WHERE'D THEY GET ALL THOSE BOATS?!
THIS IS BAD.
WHAT IS HAPPENING?
BAD HUMANS COMING FOR APES.
APES MUST FIGHT.

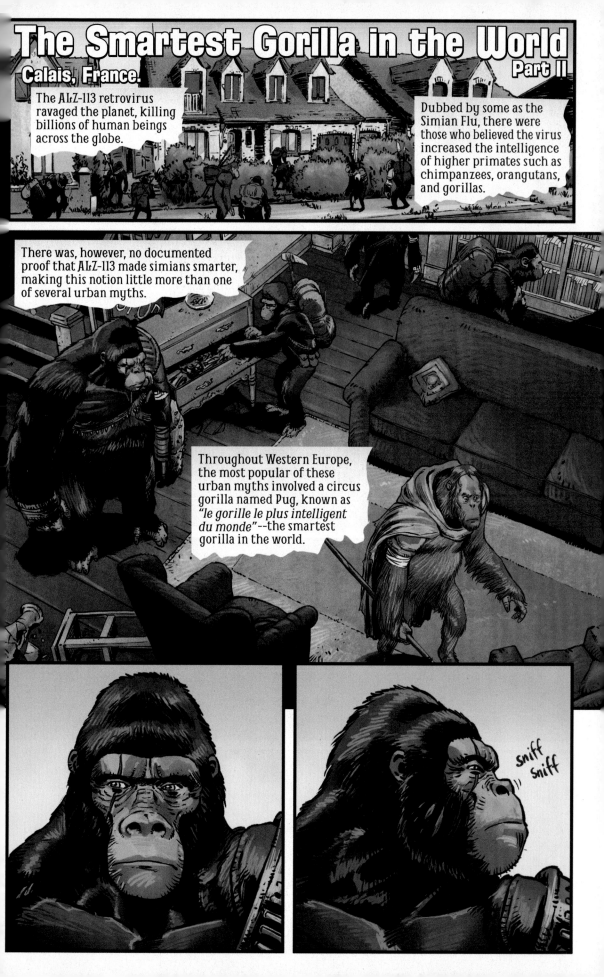

The Smartest Gorilla in the World
Part II
Calais, France.

The ALZ-113 retrovirus ravaged the planet, killing billions of human beings across the globe.

Dubbed by some as the Simian Flu, there were those who believed the virus increased the intelligence of higher primates such as chimpanzees, orangutans, and gorillas.

There was, however, no documented proof that ALZ-113 made simians smarter, making this notion little more than one of several urban myths.

Throughout Western Europe, the most popular of these urban myths involved a circus gorilla named Pug, known as *"le gorille le plus intelligent du monde"*--the smartest gorilla in the world.

sniff sniff

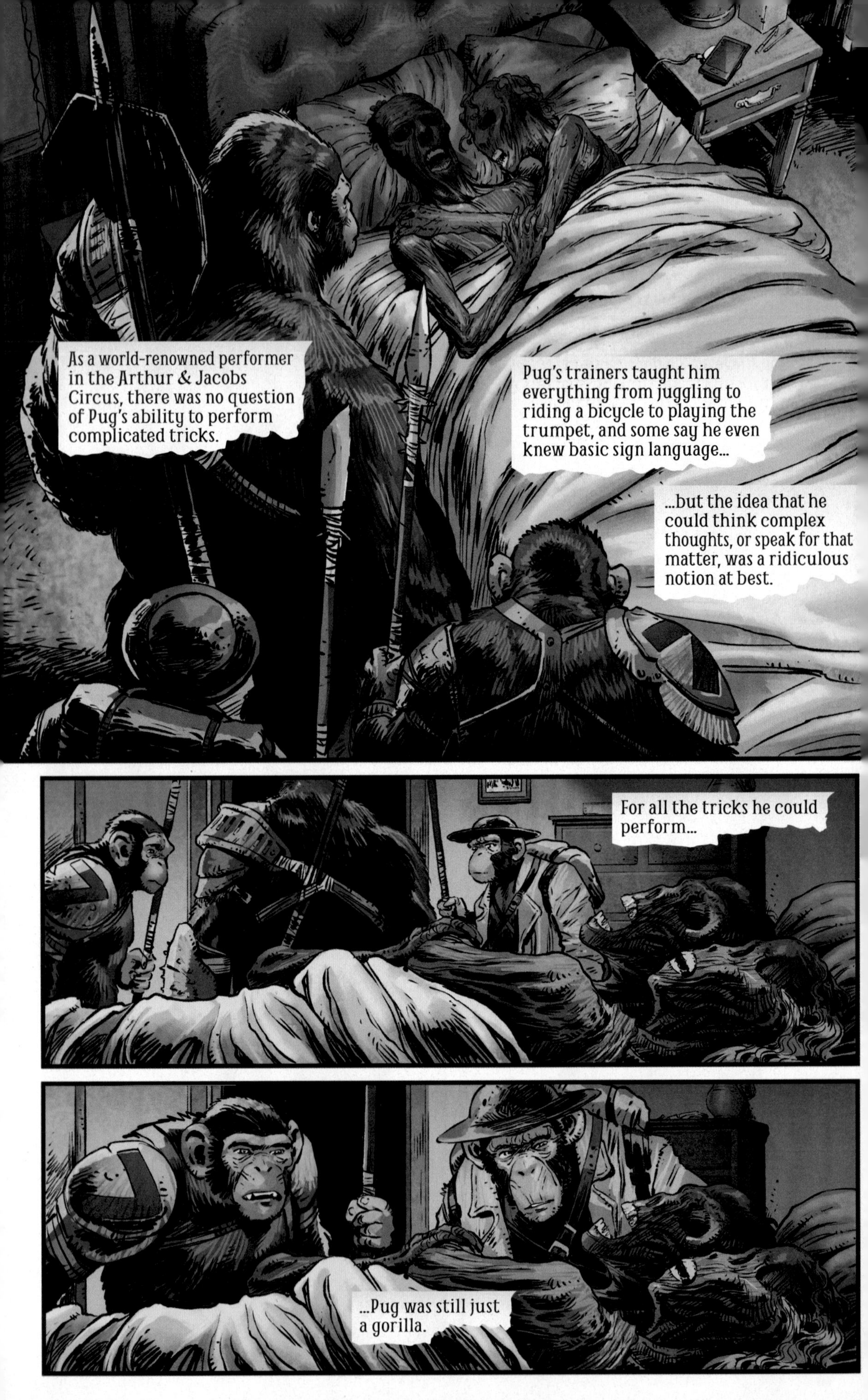
As a world-renowned performer in the Arthur & Jacobs Circus, there was no question of Pug's ability to perform complicated tricks.
Pug's trainers taught him everything from juggling to riding a bicycle to playing the trumpet, and some say he even knew basic sign language...
...but the idea that he could think complex thoughts, or speak for that matter, was a ridiculous notion at best.
For all the tricks he could perform...
...Pug was still just a gorilla.

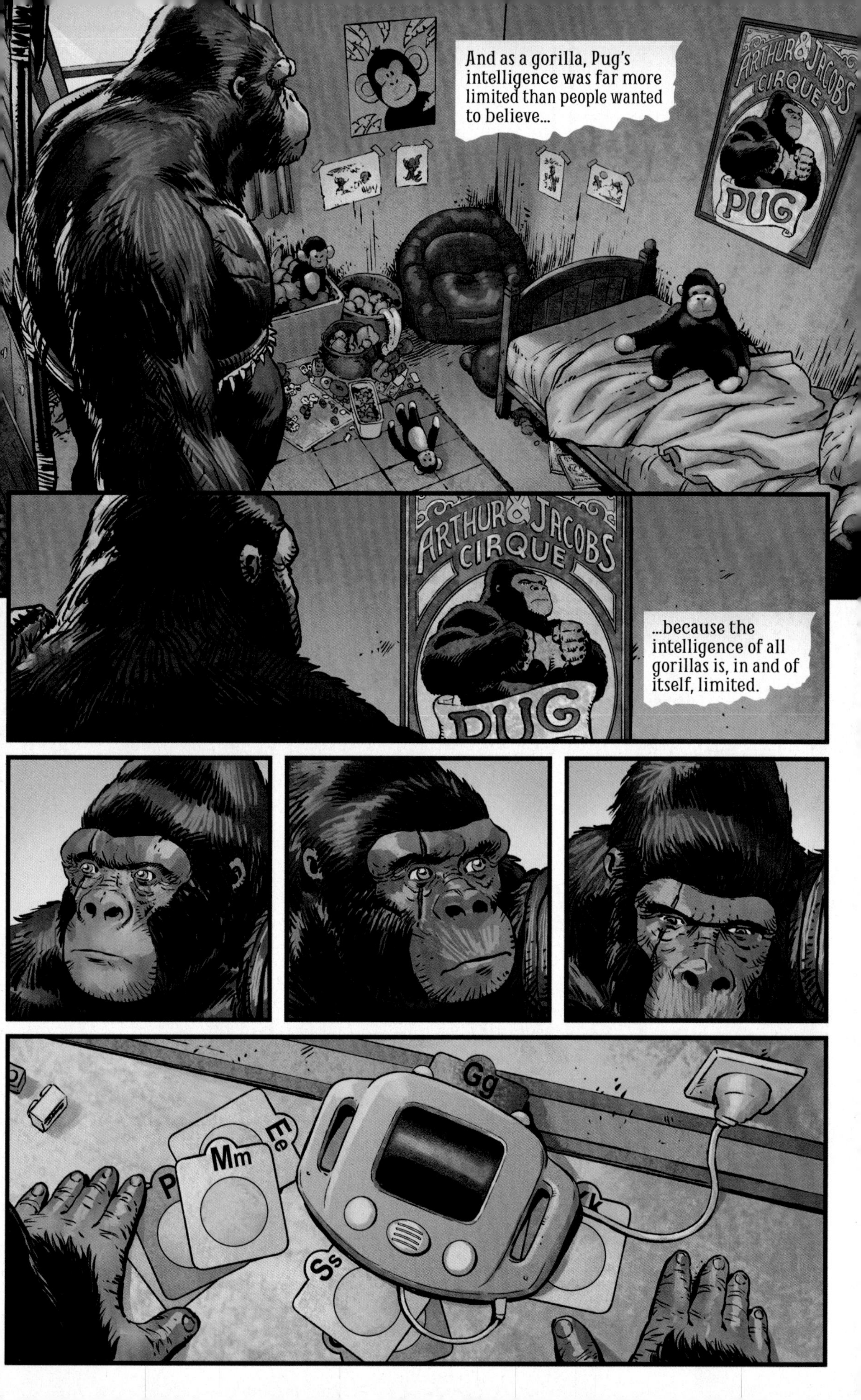
And as a gorilla, Pug's intelligence was far more limited than people wanted to believe...
ARTHUR & JACOBS CIRQUE
PUG
ARTHUR & JACOBS CIRQUE
...because the intelligence of all gorillas is, in and of itself, limited.
Gg
Ee
Mm
P
Ss

tap tap
tap tap tap
tap tap
DING
Gg
GORILLE
Gg
GORILLE
Gg
Jj
Pp
Cc
Pp
Pp

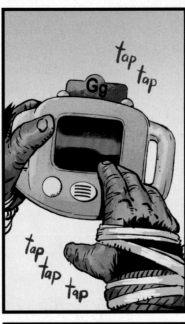

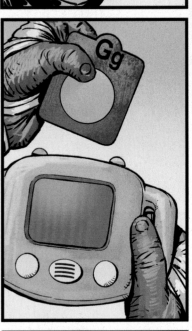

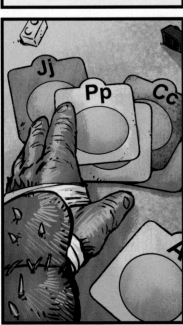

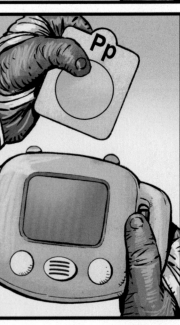

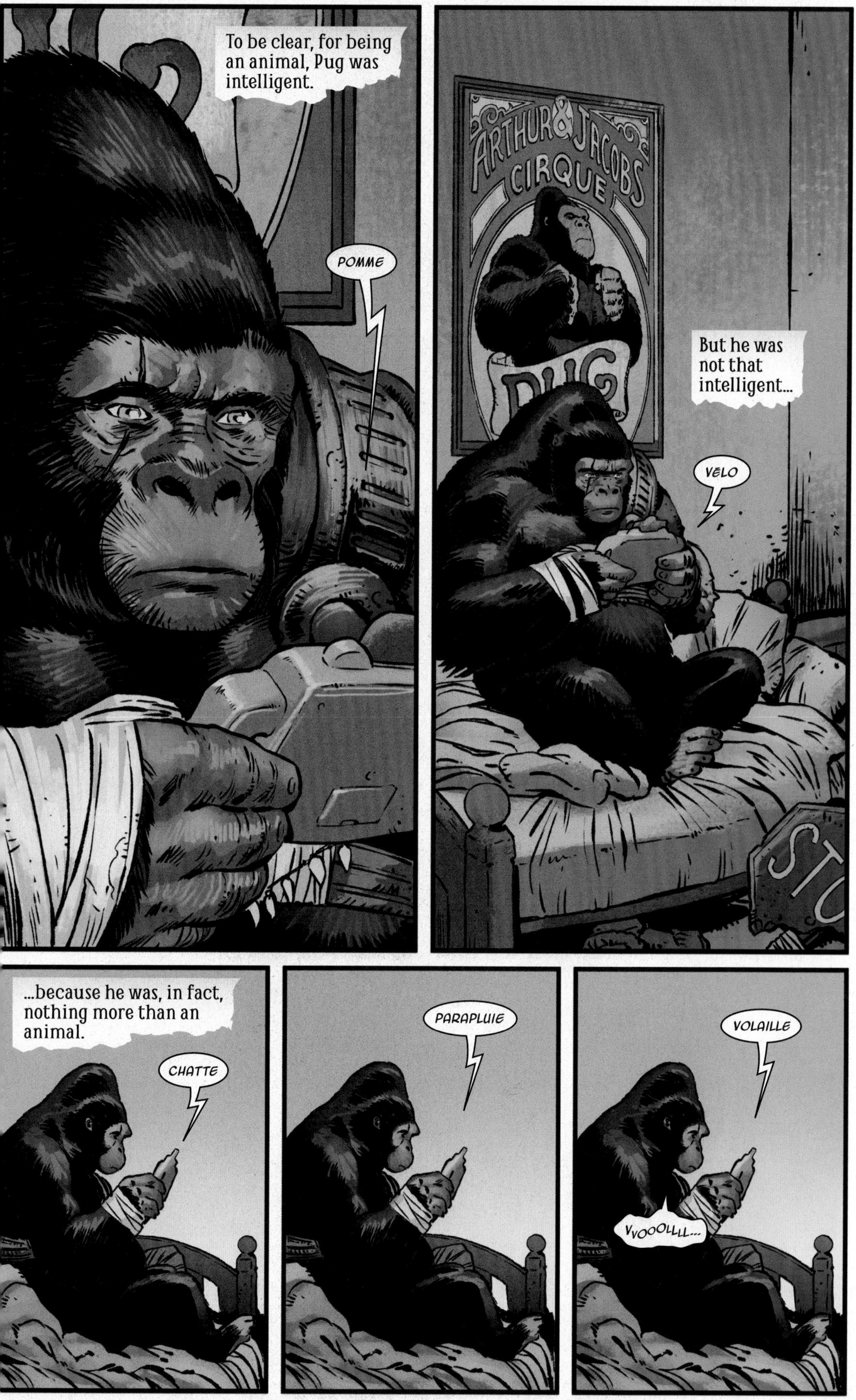
To be clear, for being an animal, Pug was intelligent.
POMME
ARTHUR & JACOBS
CIRQUE
But he was not that intelligent...
VĒLO
...because he was, in fact, nothing more than an animal.
CHATTE
PARAPLUIE
VOLAILLE
VVOOOLLLL...

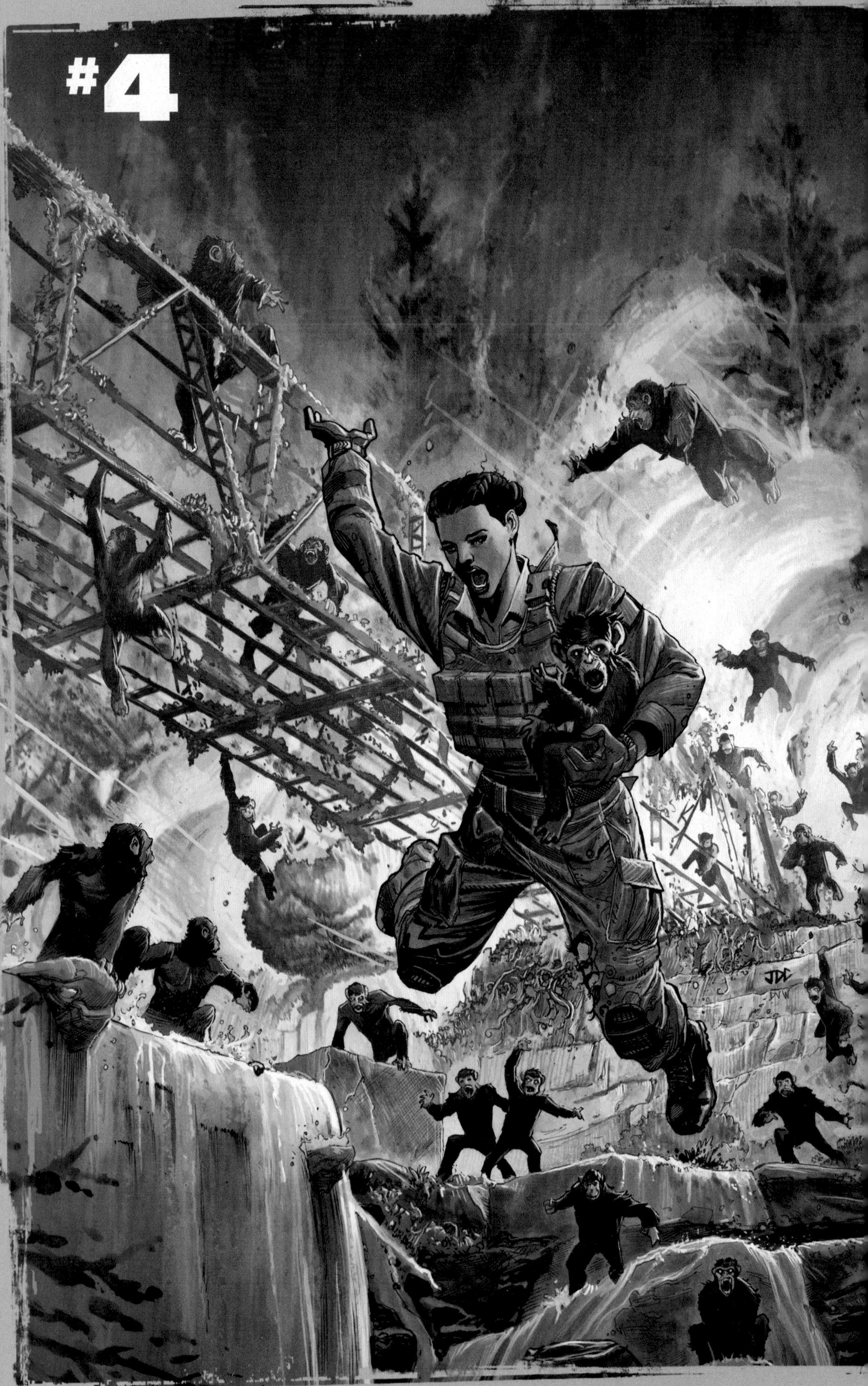
#4

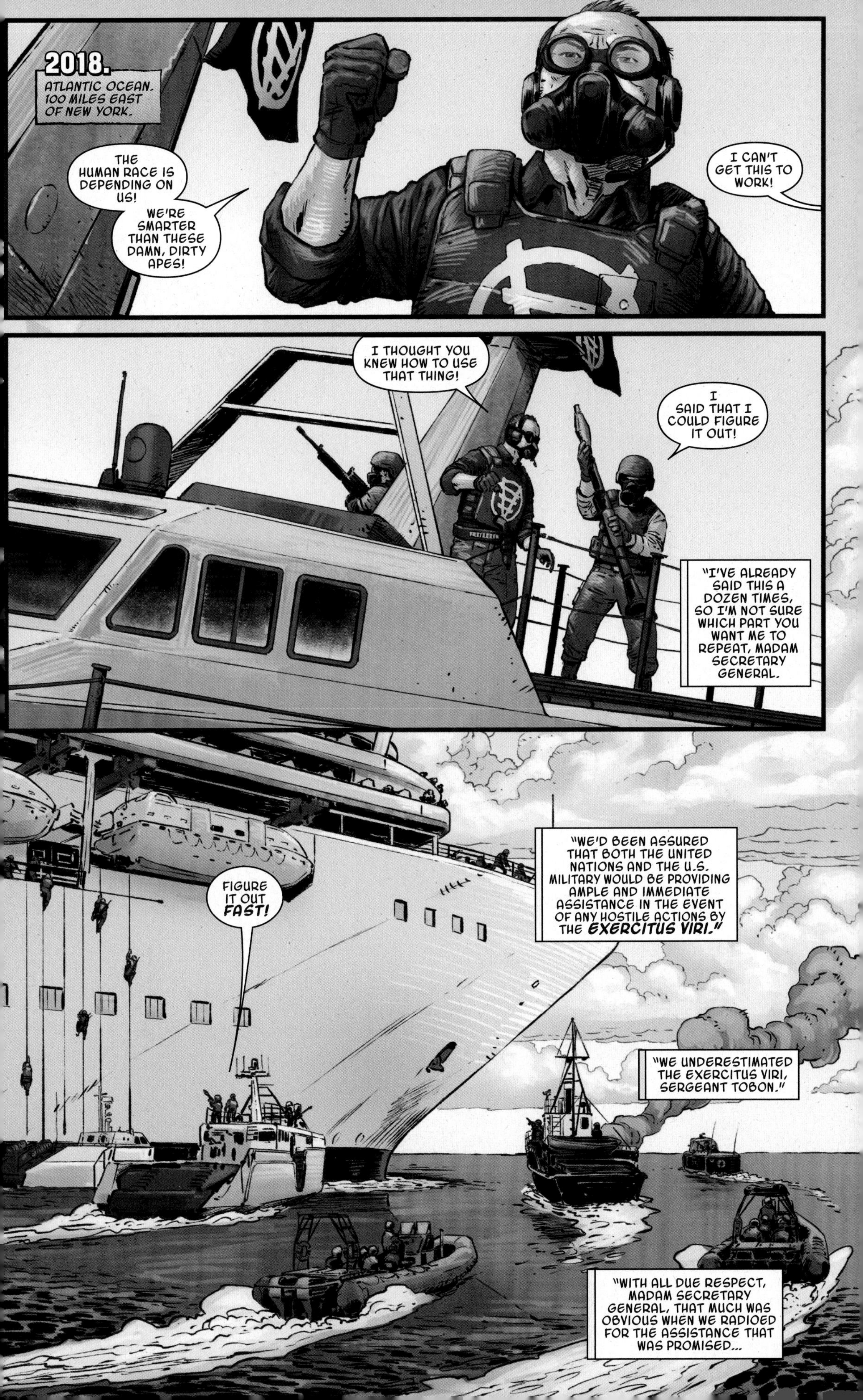
2018.
ATLANTIC OCEAN. 100 MILES EAST OF NEW YORK.
THE HUMAN RACE IS DEPENDING ON US!
WE'RE SMARTER THAN THESE DAMN, DIRTY APES!
I CAN'T GET THIS TO WORK!
I THOUGHT YOU KNEW HOW TO USE THAT THING!
I SAID THAT I COULD FIGURE IT OUT!
"I'VE ALREADY SAID THIS A DOZEN TIMES, SO I'M NOT SURE WHICH PART YOU WANT ME TO REPEAT, MADAM SECRETARY GENERAL.
FIGURE IT OUT FAST!
"WE'D BEEN ASSURED THAT BOTH THE UNITED NATIONS AND THE U.S. MILITARY WOULD BE PROVIDING AMPLE AND IMMEDIATE ASSISTANCE IN THE EVENT OF ANY HOSTILE ACTIONS BY THE EXERCITUS VIRI."
"WE UNDERESTIMATED THE EXERCITUS VIRI, SERGEANT TOBON."
"WITH ALL DUE RESPECT, MADAM SECRETARY GENERAL, THAT MUCH WAS OBVIOUS WHEN WE RADIOED FOR THE ASSISTANCE THAT WAS PROMISED...

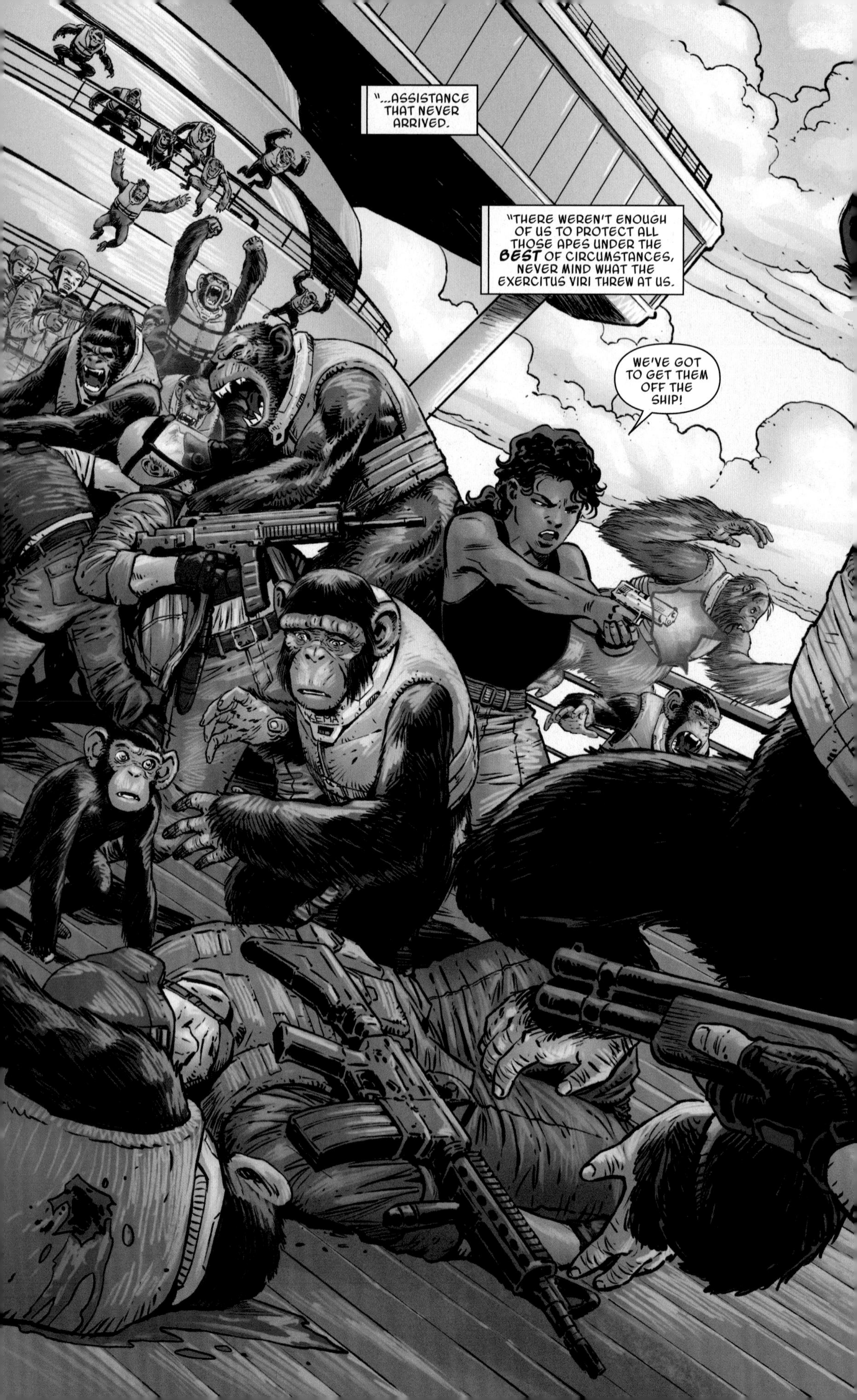
"...ASSISTANCE THAT NEVER ARRIVED.
"THERE WEREN'T ENOUGH OF US TO PROTECT ALL THOSE APES UNDER THE BEST OF CIRCUMSTANCES, NEVER MIND WHAT THE EXERCITUS VIRI THREW AT US.
WE'VE GOT TO GET THEM OFF THE SHIP!

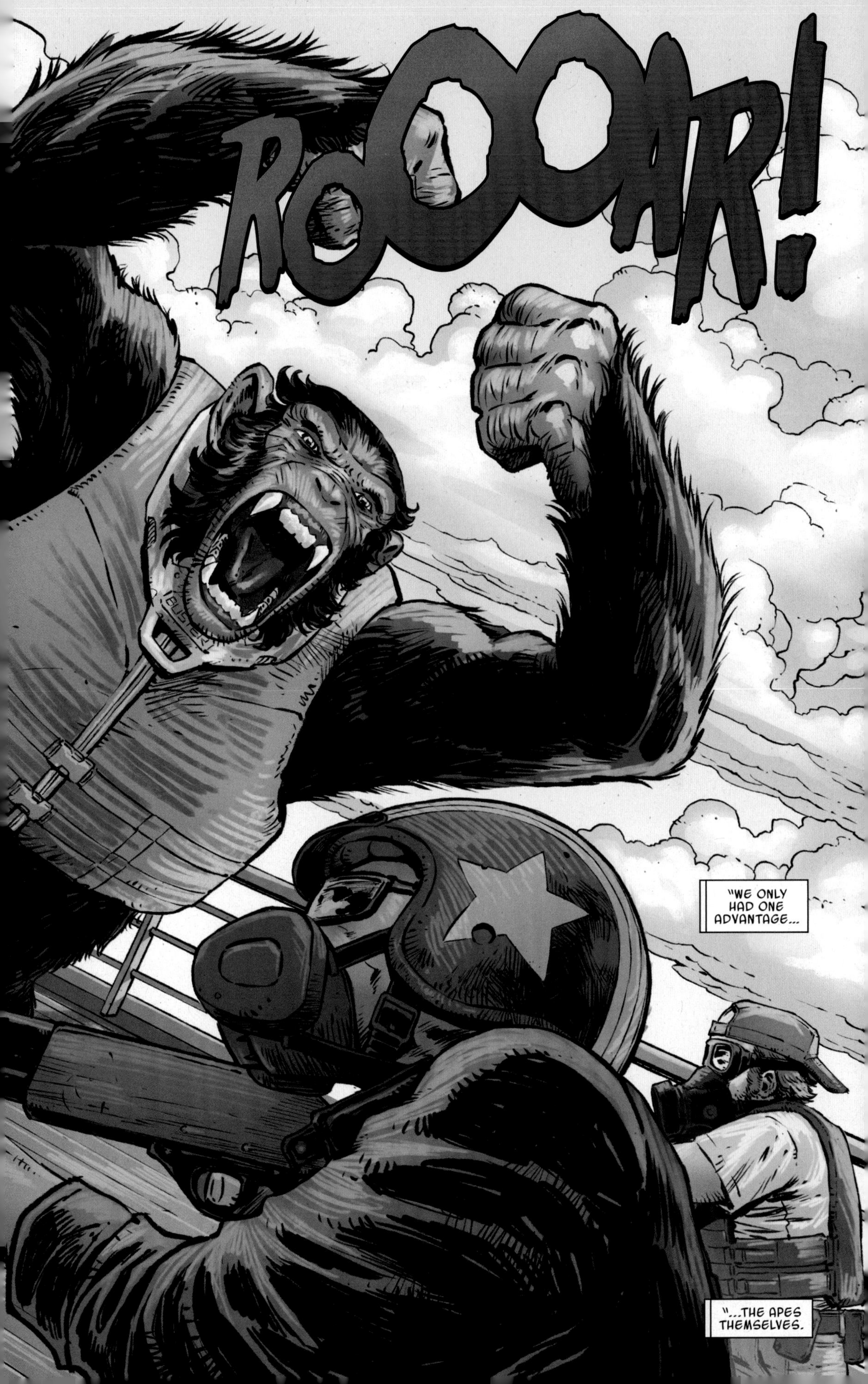
ROOOAR!
BUSTER
"WE ONLY HAD ONE ADVANTAGE...
"...THE APES THEMSELVES.

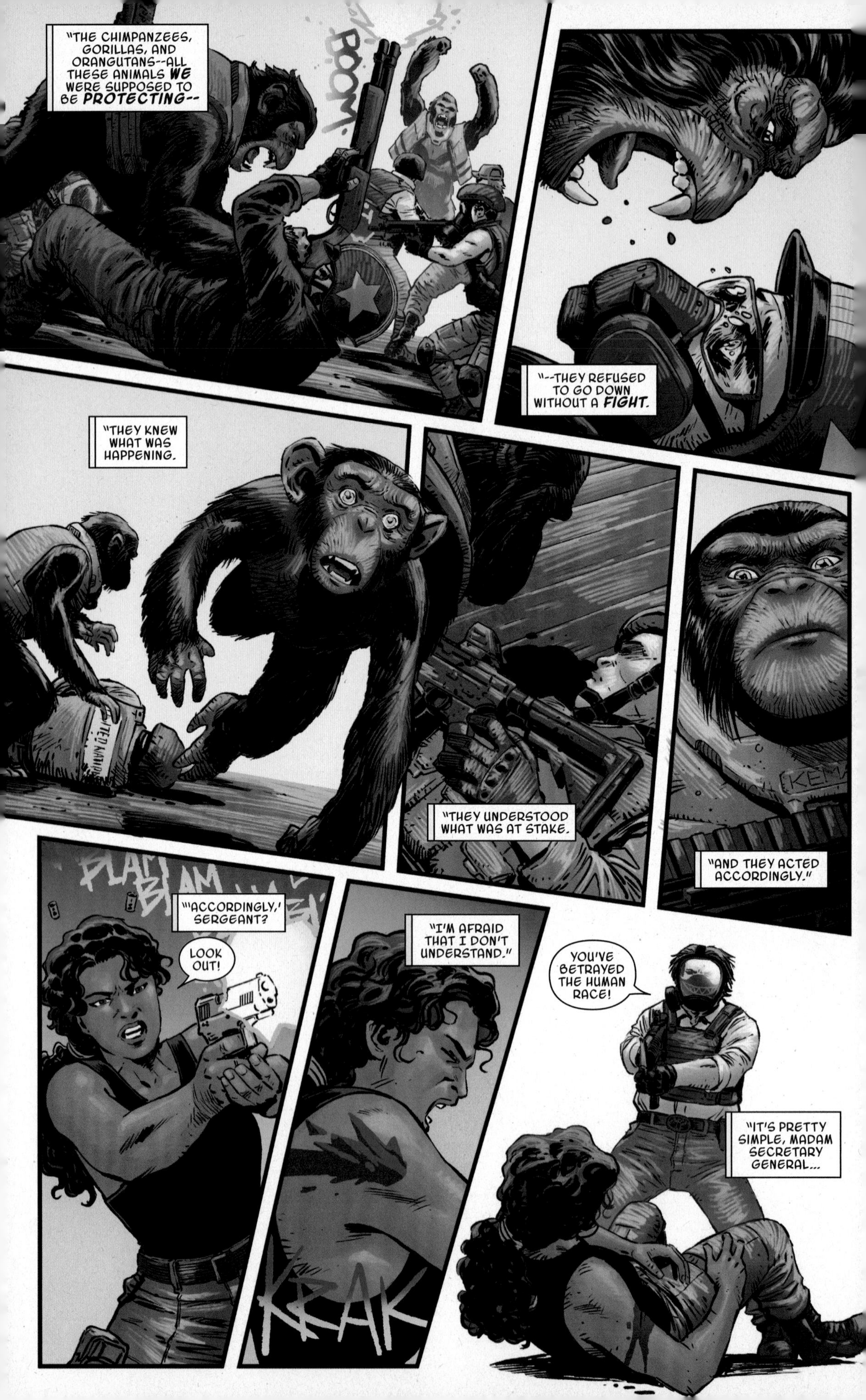
"THE CHIMPANZEES, GORILLAS, AND ORANGUTANS--ALL THESE ANIMALS WE WERE SUPPOSED TO BE PROTECTING--
BOOM!
"--THEY REFUSED TO GO DOWN WITHOUT A FIGHT.
"THEY KNEW WHAT WAS HAPPENING.
"THEY UNDERSTOOD WHAT WAS AT STAKE.
"AND THEY ACTED ACCORDINGLY."
"'ACCORDINGLY,' SERGEANT?
LOOK OUT!
"I'M AFRAID THAT I DON'T UNDERSTAND."
KRAK
YOU'VE BETRAYED THE HUMAN RACE!
"IT'S PRETTY SIMPLE, MADAM SECRETARY GENERAL...

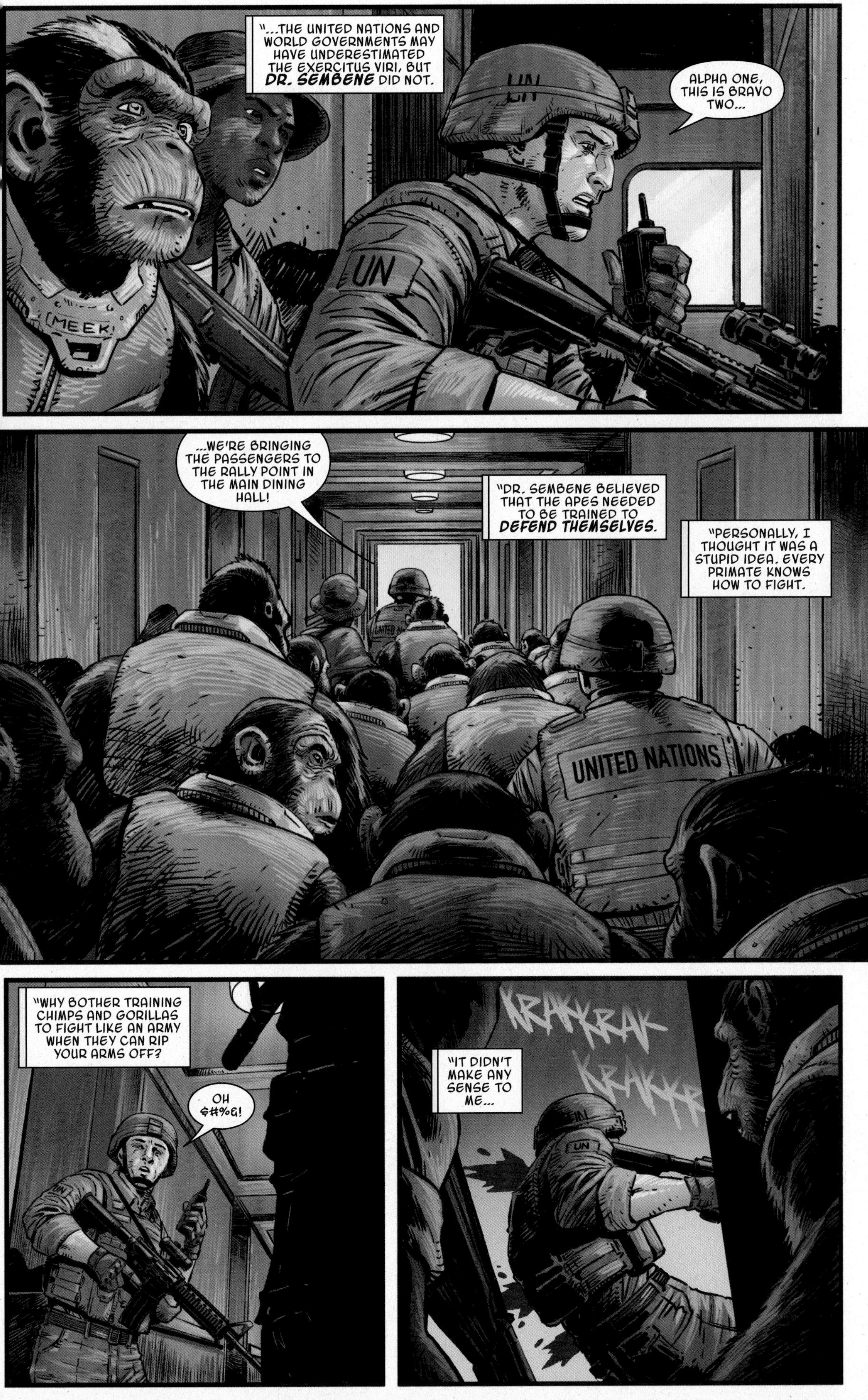
"...THE UNITED NATIONS AND WORLD GOVERNMENTS MAY HAVE UNDERESTIMATED THE EXERCITUS VIRI, BUT DR. SEMBENE DID NOT.
ALPHA ONE, THIS IS BRAVO TWO...
UN
UN
MEEK
...WE'RE BRINGING THE PASSENGERS TO THE RALLY POINT IN THE MAIN DINING HALL!
"DR. SEMBENE BELIEVED THAT THE APES NEEDED TO BE TRAINED TO DEFEND THEMSELVES.
"PERSONALLY, I THOUGHT IT WAS A STUPID IDEA. EVERY PRIMATE KNOWS HOW TO FIGHT.
UNITED NATIONS
"WHY BOTHER TRAINING CHIMPS AND GORILLAS TO FIGHT LIKE AN ARMY WHEN THEY CAN RIP YOUR ARMS OFF?
OH $#%&!
KRAKKRAK
KRAKKR
"IT DIDN'T MAKE ANY SENSE TO ME...
UN

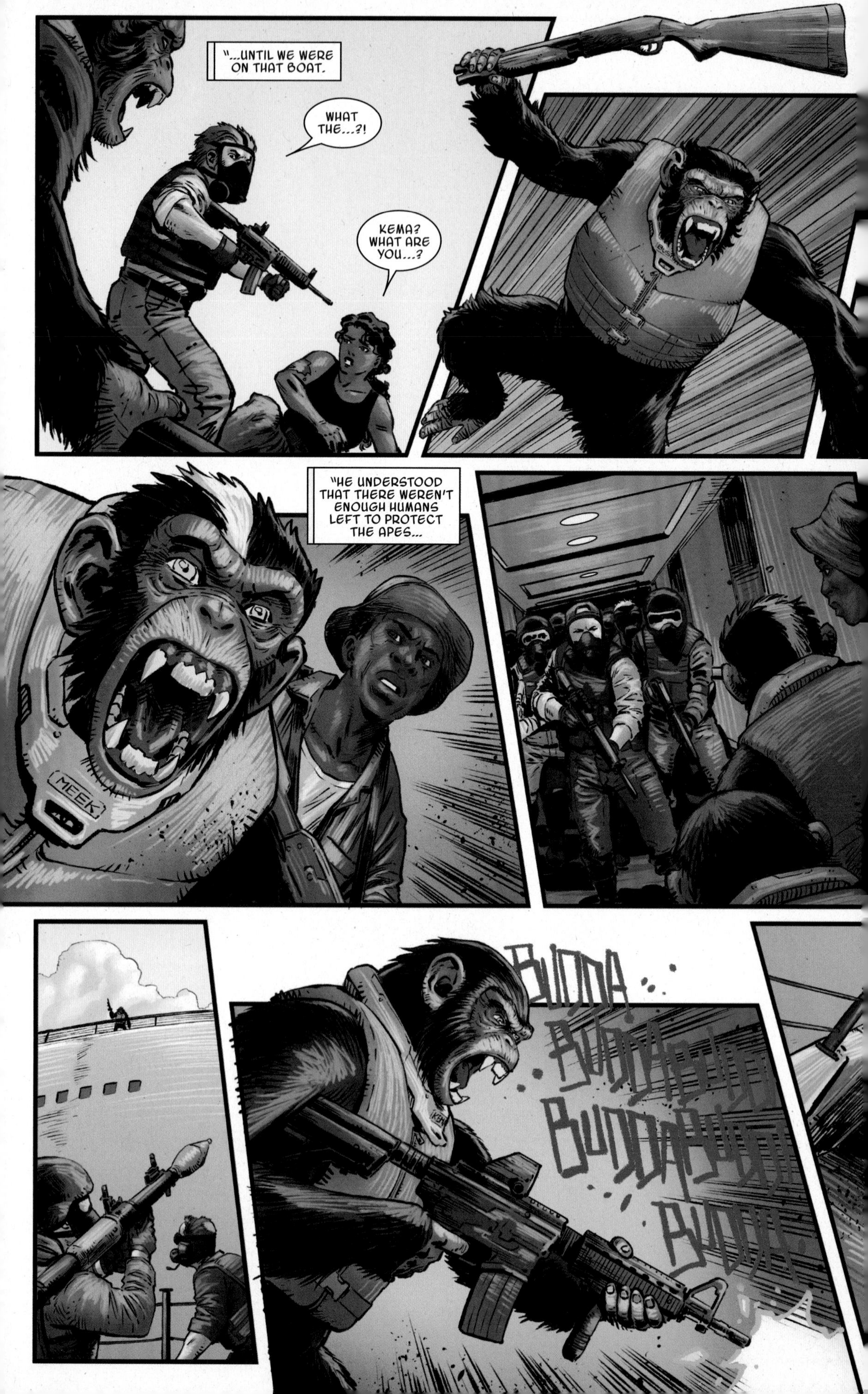
"...UNTIL WE WERE ON THAT BOAT.
WHAT THE...?!
KEMA? WHAT ARE YOU...?
"HE UNDERSTOOD THAT THERE WEREN'T ENOUGH HUMANS LEFT TO PROTECT THE APES...
MEEK
BUDDA

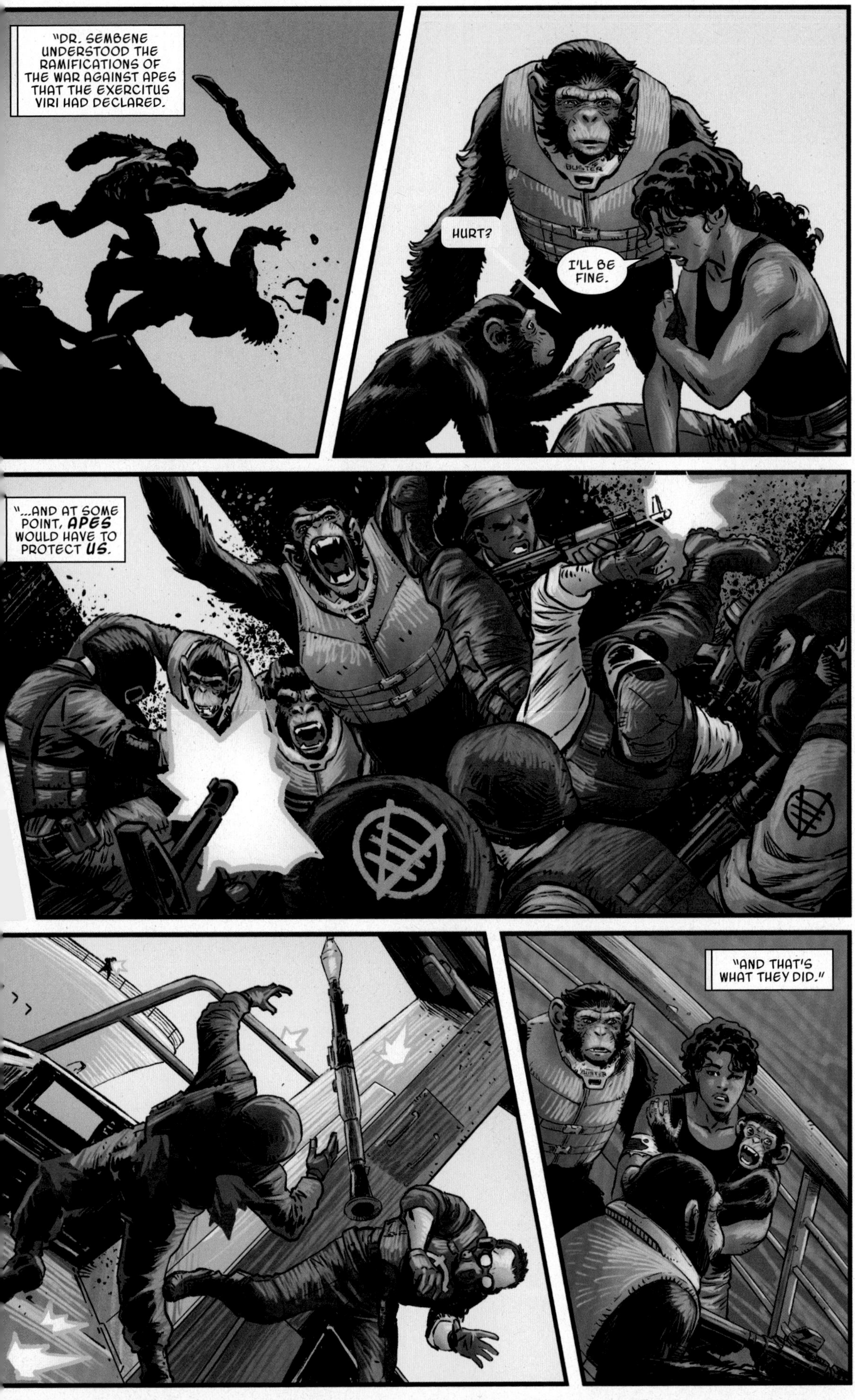
"DR. SEMBENE UNDERSTOOD THE RAMIFICATIONS OF THE WAR AGAINST APES THAT THE EXERCITUS VIRI HAD DECLARED.
HURT?
I'LL BE FINE.
"...AND AT SOME POINT, APES WOULD HAVE TO PROTECT US.
"AND THAT'S WHAT THEY DID."

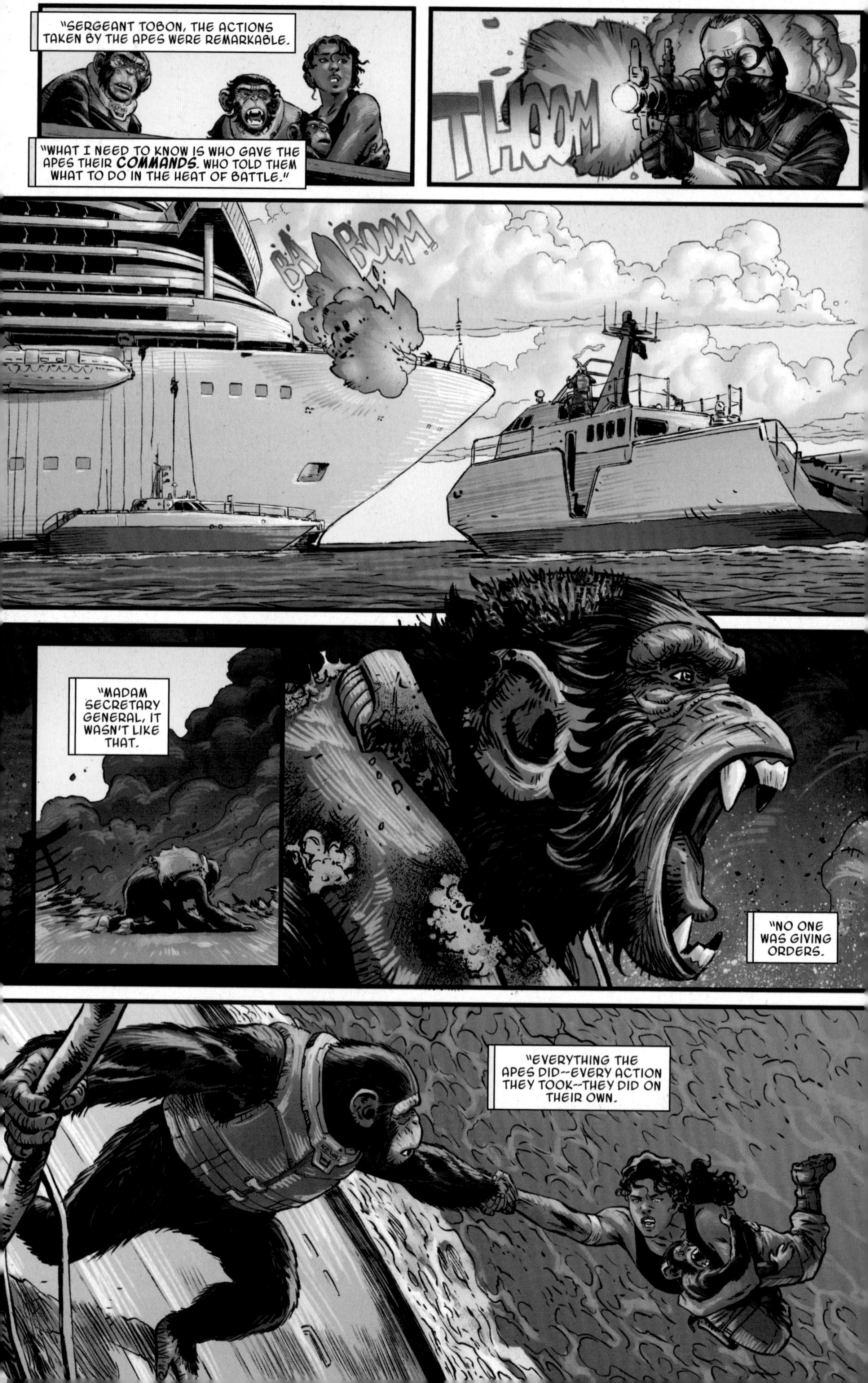
"SERGEANT TOBON, THE ACTIONS TAKEN BY THE APES WERE REMARKABLE.
"WHAT I NEED TO KNOW IS WHO GAVE THE APES THEIR COMMANDS. WHO TOLD THEM WHAT TO DO IN THE HEAT OF BATTLE."
THOOM
BA BOOM!
"MADAM SECRETARY GENERAL, IT WASN'T LIKE THAT.
"NO ONE WAS GIVING ORDERS.
"EVERYTHING THE APES DID--EVERY ACTION THEY TOOK--THEY DID ON THEIR OWN.

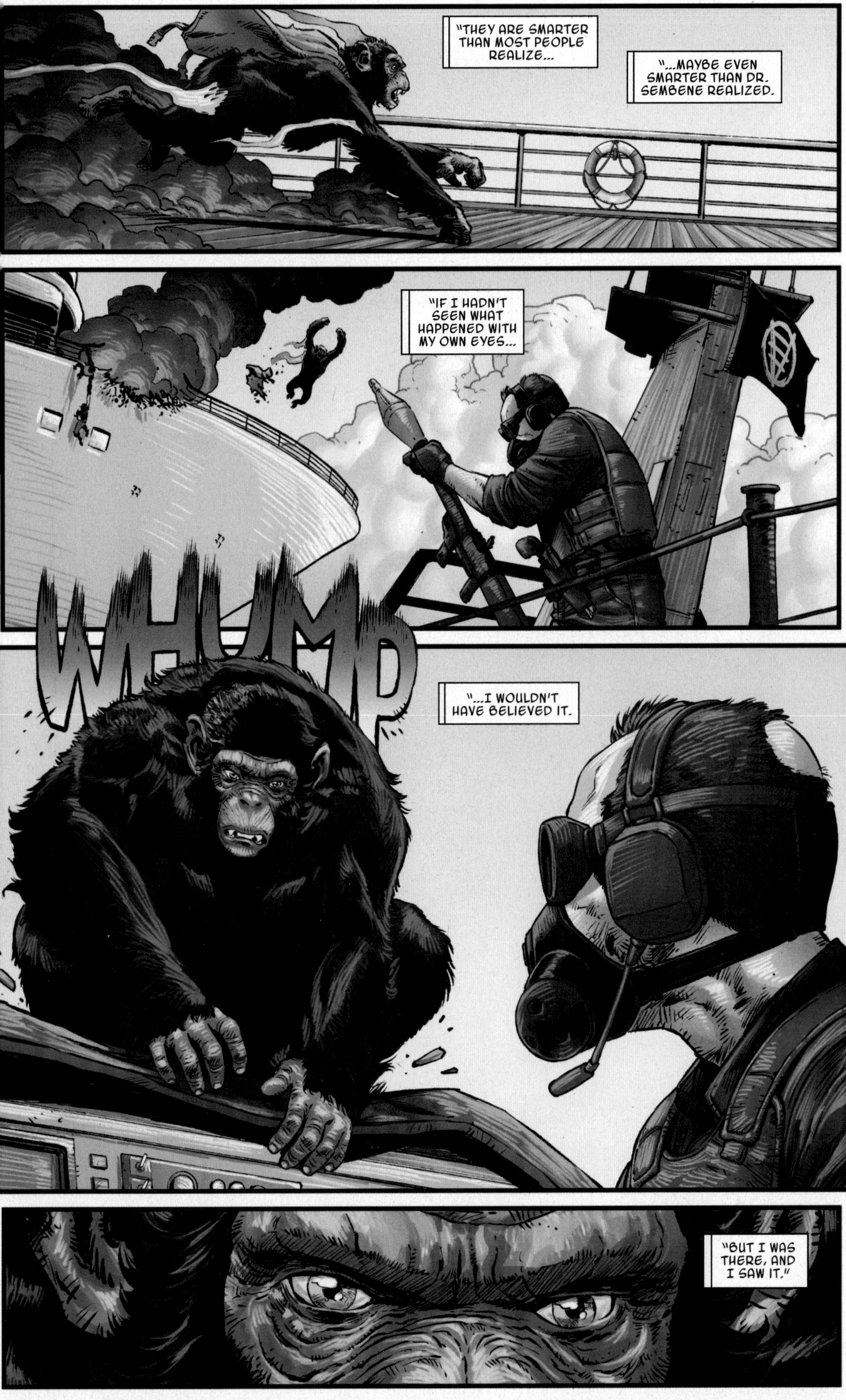
"THEY ARE SMARTER THAN MOST PEOPLE REALIZE...
"...MAYBE EVEN SMARTER THAN DR. SEMBENE REALIZED.
"IF I HADN'T SEEN WHAT HAPPENED WITH MY OWN EYES...
WHUMP
"...I WOULDN'T HAVE BELIEVED IT.
"BUT I WAS THERE, AND I SAW IT."

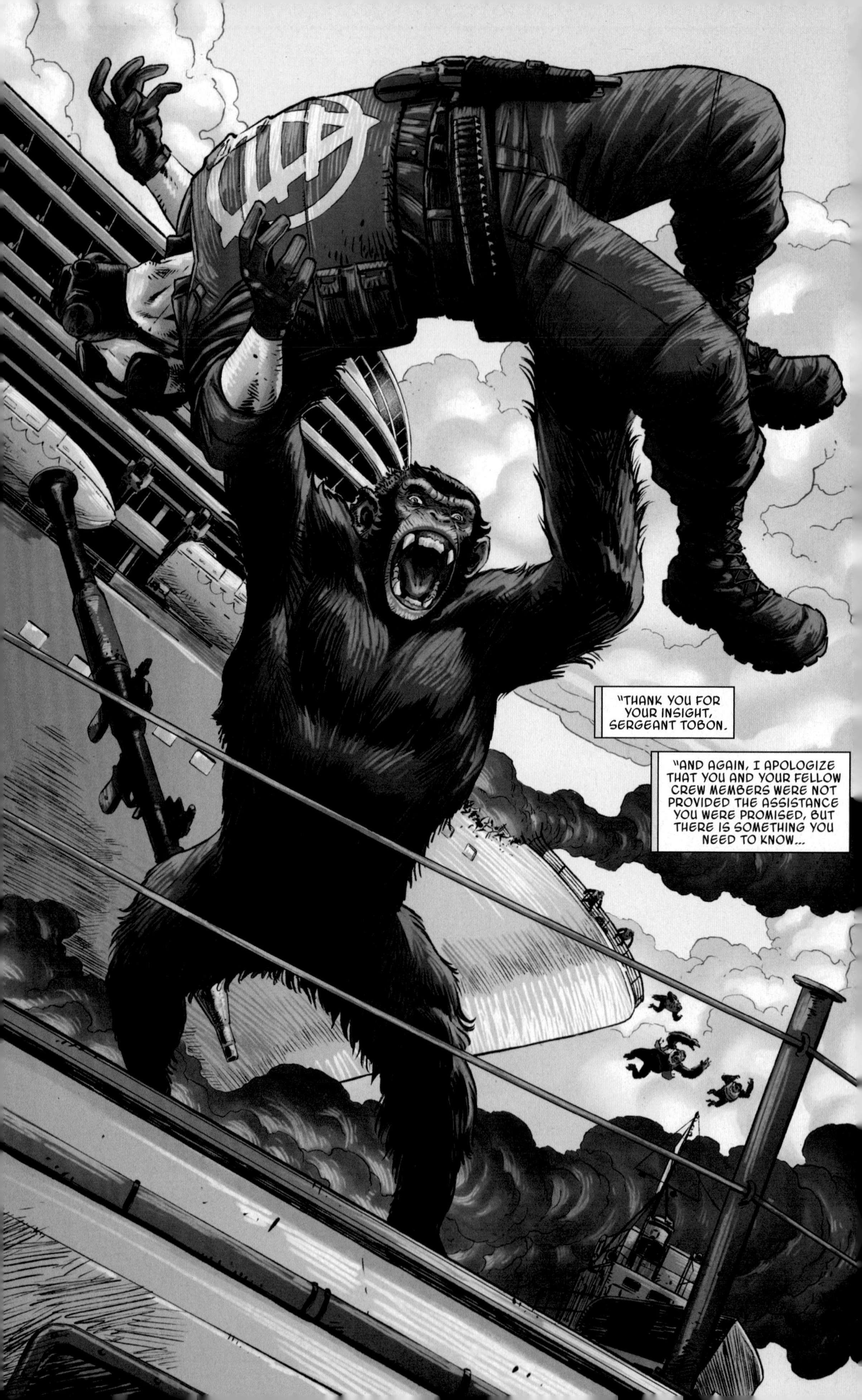
"THANK YOU FOR YOUR INSIGHT, SERGEANT TOBON.
"AND AGAIN, I APOLOGIZE THAT YOU AND YOUR FELLOW CREW MEMBERS WERE NOT PROVIDED THE ASSISTANCE YOU WERE PROMISED, BUT THERE IS SOMETHING YOU NEED TO KNOW...

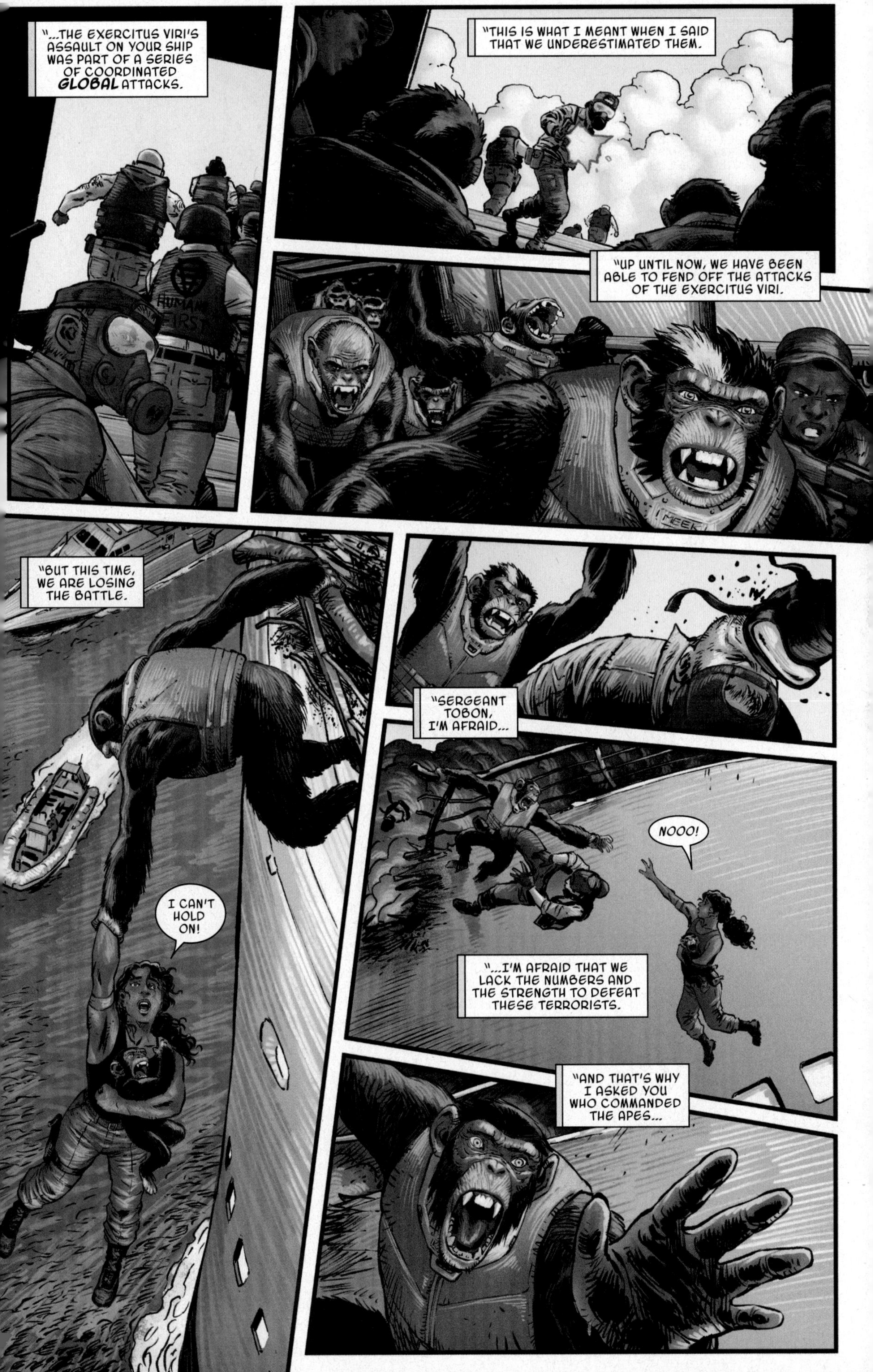
"...THE EXERCITUS VIRI'S ASSAULT ON YOUR SHIP WAS PART OF A SERIES OF COORDINATED GLOBAL ATTACKS.
"THIS IS WHAT I MEANT WHEN I SAID THAT WE UNDERESTIMATED THEM.
HUMAN FIRST
"UP UNTIL NOW, WE HAVE BEEN ABLE TO FEND OFF THE ATTACKS OF THE EXERCITUS VIRI.
"BUT THIS TIME, WE ARE LOSING THE BATTLE.
I CAN'T HOLD ON!
"SERGEANT TOBON, I'M AFRAID...
NOOO!
"...I'M AFRAID THAT WE LACK THE NUMBERS AND THE STRENGTH TO DEFEAT THESE TERRORISTS.
"AND THAT'S WHY I ASKED YOU WHO COMMANDED THE APES...

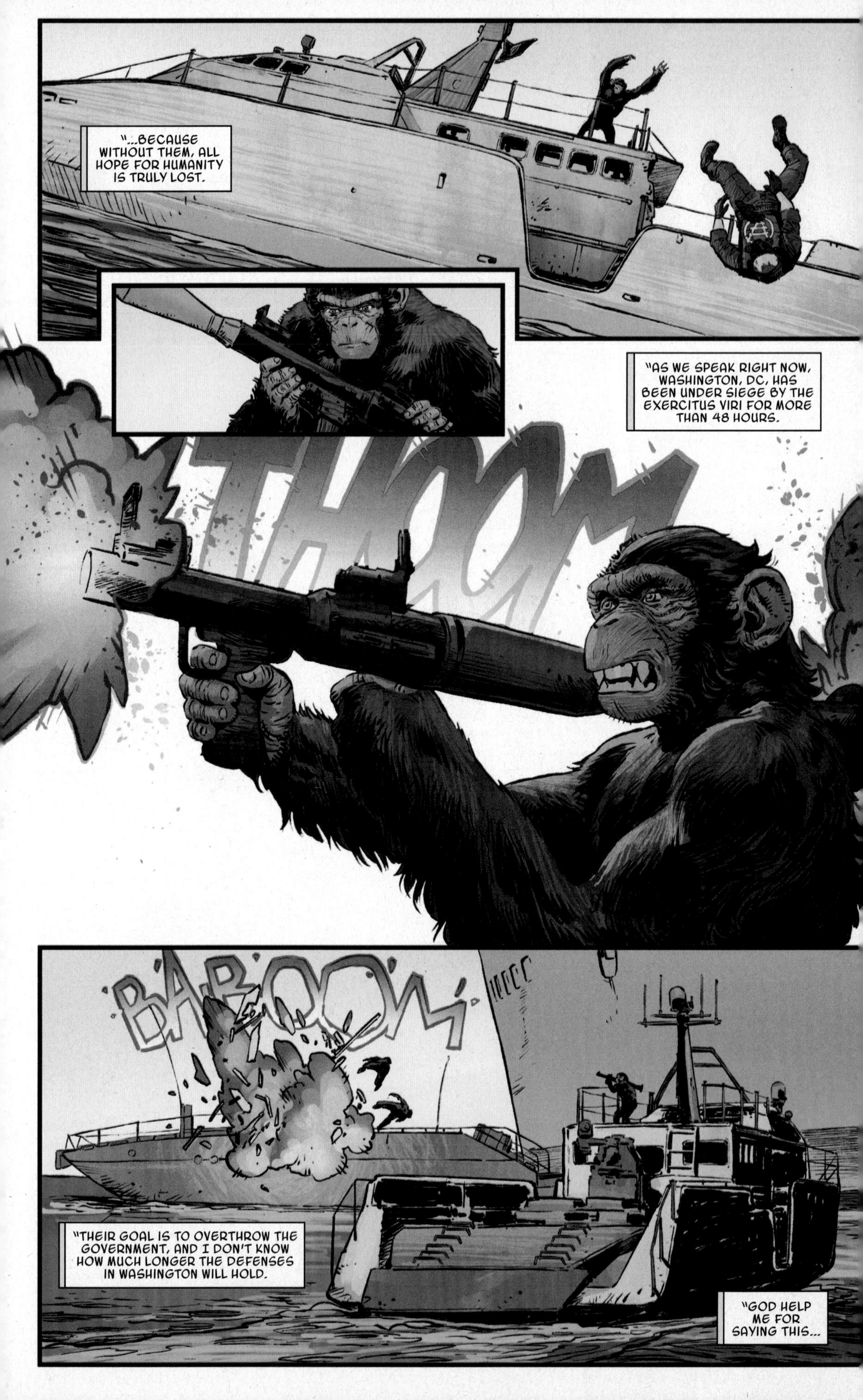
"...BECAUSE WITHOUT THEM, ALL HOPE FOR HUMANITY IS TRULY LOST.
"AS WE SPEAK RIGHT NOW, WASHINGTON, DC, HAS BEEN UNDER SIEGE BY THE EXERCITUS VIRI FOR MORE THAN 48 HOURS.
THOOM
BAROOM
"THEIR GOAL IS TO OVERTHROW THE GOVERNMENT, AND I DON'T KNOW HOW MUCH LONGER THE DEFENSES IN WASHINGTON WILL HOLD.
"GOD HELP ME FOR SAYING THIS...

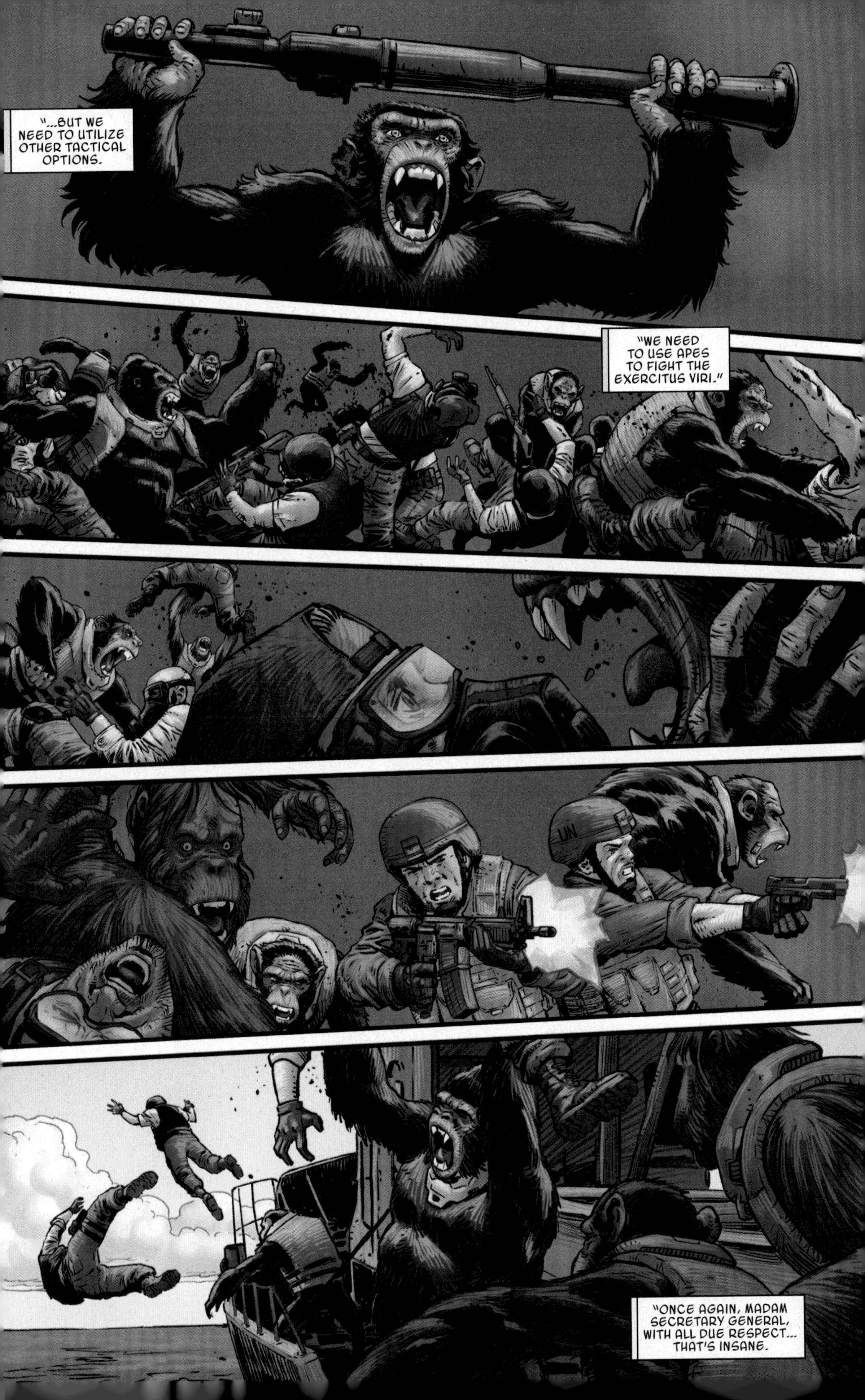
"...BUT WE NEED TO UTILIZE OTHER TACTICAL OPTIONS.
"WE NEED TO USE APES TO FIGHT THE EXERCITUS VIRI."
UN
"ONCE AGAIN, MADAM SECRETARY GENERAL, WITH ALL DUE RESPECT... THAT'S INSANE.

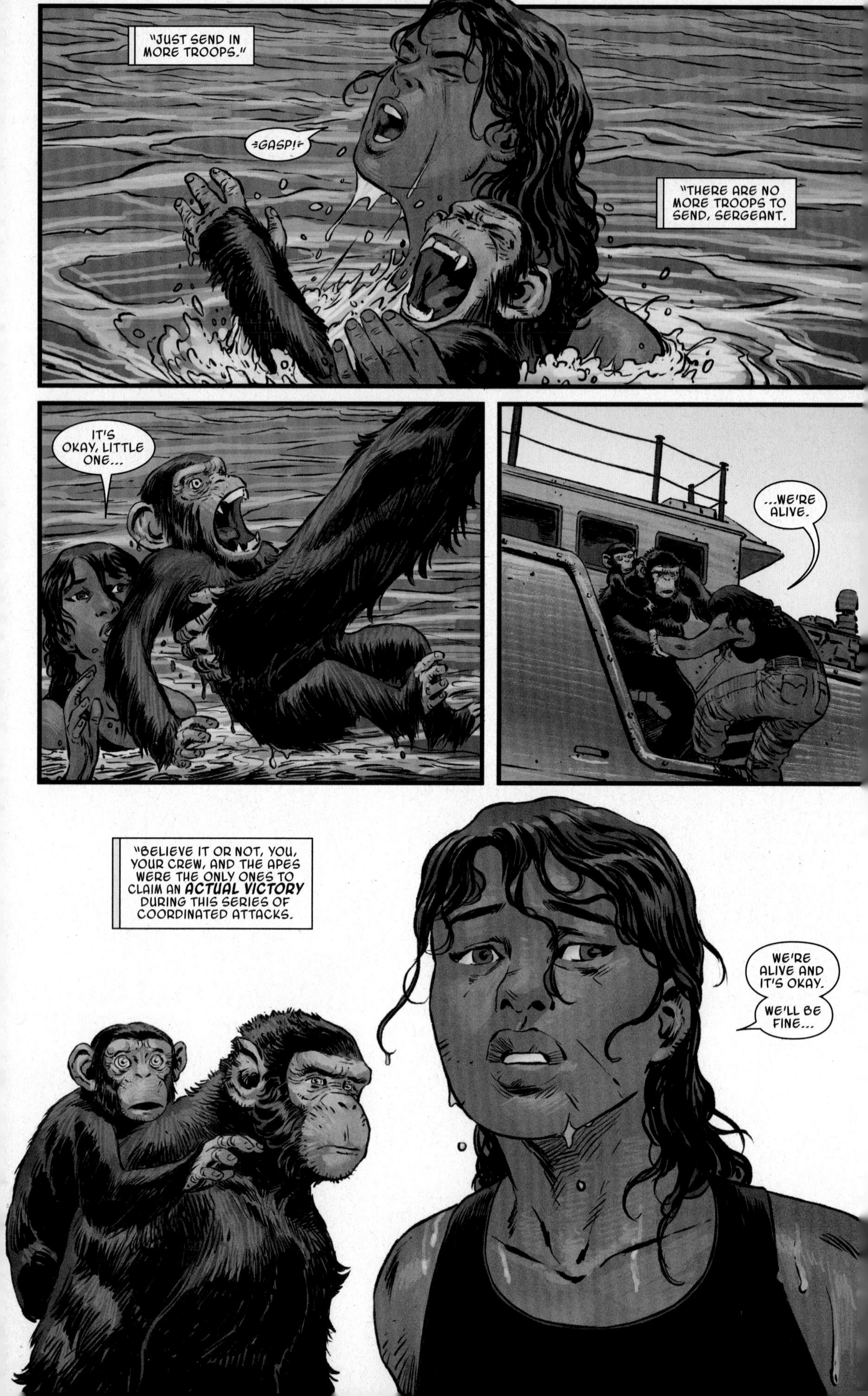
"JUST SEND IN MORE TROOPS."
=GASP!=
"THERE ARE NO MORE TROOPS TO SEND, SERGEANT.
IT'S OKAY, LITTLE ONE...
...WE'RE ALIVE.
"BELIEVE IT OR NOT, YOU, YOUR CREW, AND THE APES WERE THE ONLY ONES TO CLAIM AN ACTUAL VICTORY DURING THIS SERIES OF COORDINATED ATTACKS.
WE'RE ALIVE AND IT'S OKAY.
WE'LL BE FINE...

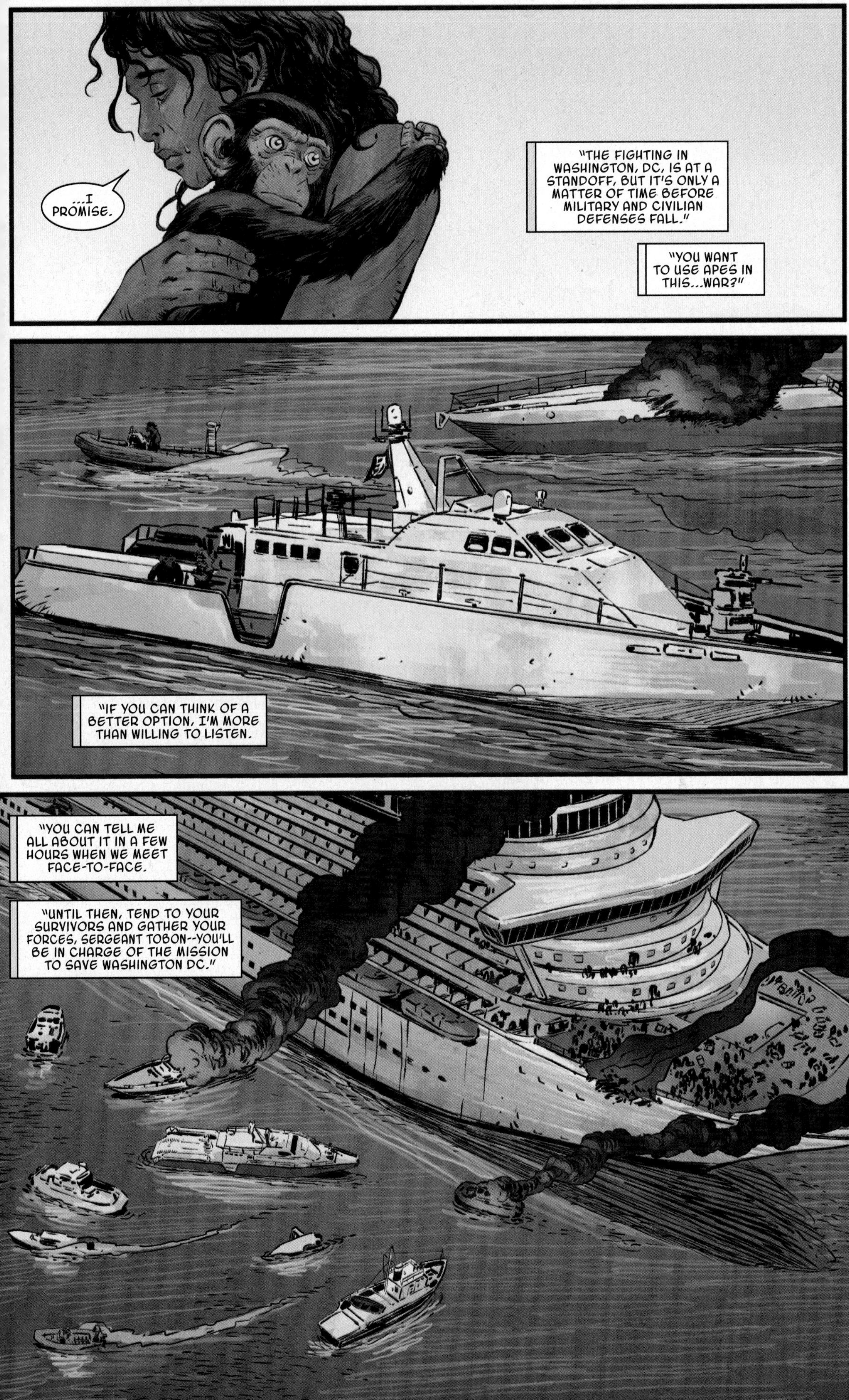
...I PROMISE.
"THE FIGHTING IN WASHINGTON, DC, IS AT A STANDOFF, BUT IT'S ONLY A MATTER OF TIME BEFORE MILITARY AND CIVILIAN DEFENSES FALL."
"YOU WANT TO USE APES IN THIS...WAR?"
"IF YOU CAN THINK OF A BETTER OPTION, I'M MORE THAN WILLING TO LISTEN.
"YOU CAN TELL ME ALL ABOUT IT IN A FEW HOURS WHEN WE MEET FACE-TO-FACE.
"UNTIL THEN, TEND TO YOUR SURVIVORS AND GATHER YOUR FORCES, SERGEANT TOBON--YOU'LL BE IN CHARGE OF THE MISSION TO SAVE WASHINGTON DC."

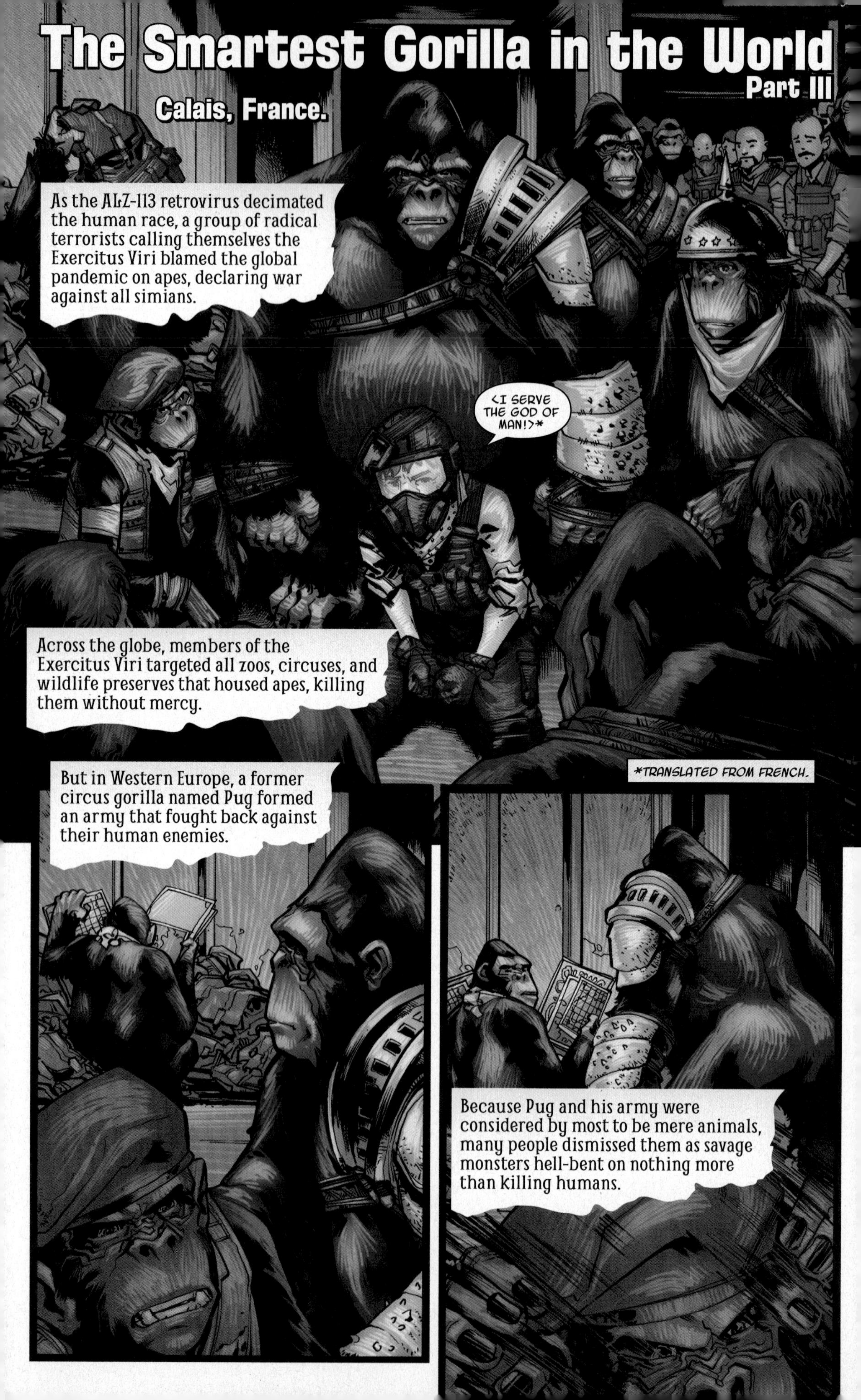
The Smartest Gorilla in the World
Part III
Calais, France.
As the ALZ-113 retrovirus decimated the human race, a group of radical terrorists calling themselves the Exercitus Viri blamed the global pandemic on apes, declaring war against all simians.
<I SERVE THE GOD OF MAN!>*
Across the globe, members of the Exercitus Viri targeted all zoos, circuses, and wildlife preserves that housed apes, killing them without mercy.
*TRANSLATED FROM FRENCH.
But in Western Europe, a former circus gorilla named Pug formed an army that fought back against their human enemies.
Because Pug and his army were considered by most to be mere animals, many people dismissed them as savage monsters hell-bent on nothing more than killing humans.

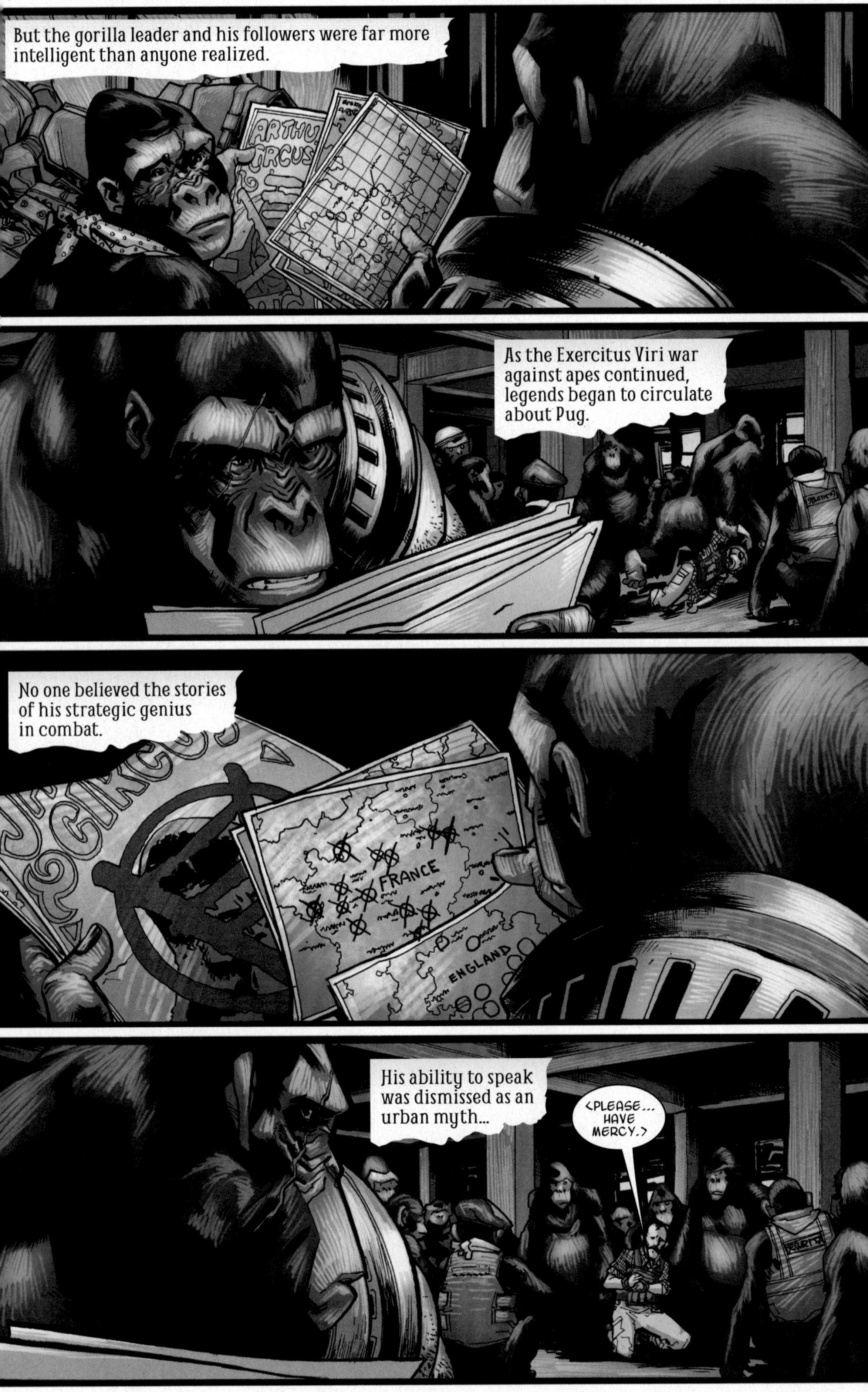
But the gorilla leader and his followers were far more intelligent than anyone realized.
As the Exercitus Viri war against apes continued, legends began to circulate about Pug.
No one believed the stories of his strategic genius in combat.
FRANCE
ENGLAND
His ability to speak was dismissed as an urban myth...
<PLEASE... HAVE MERCY.>

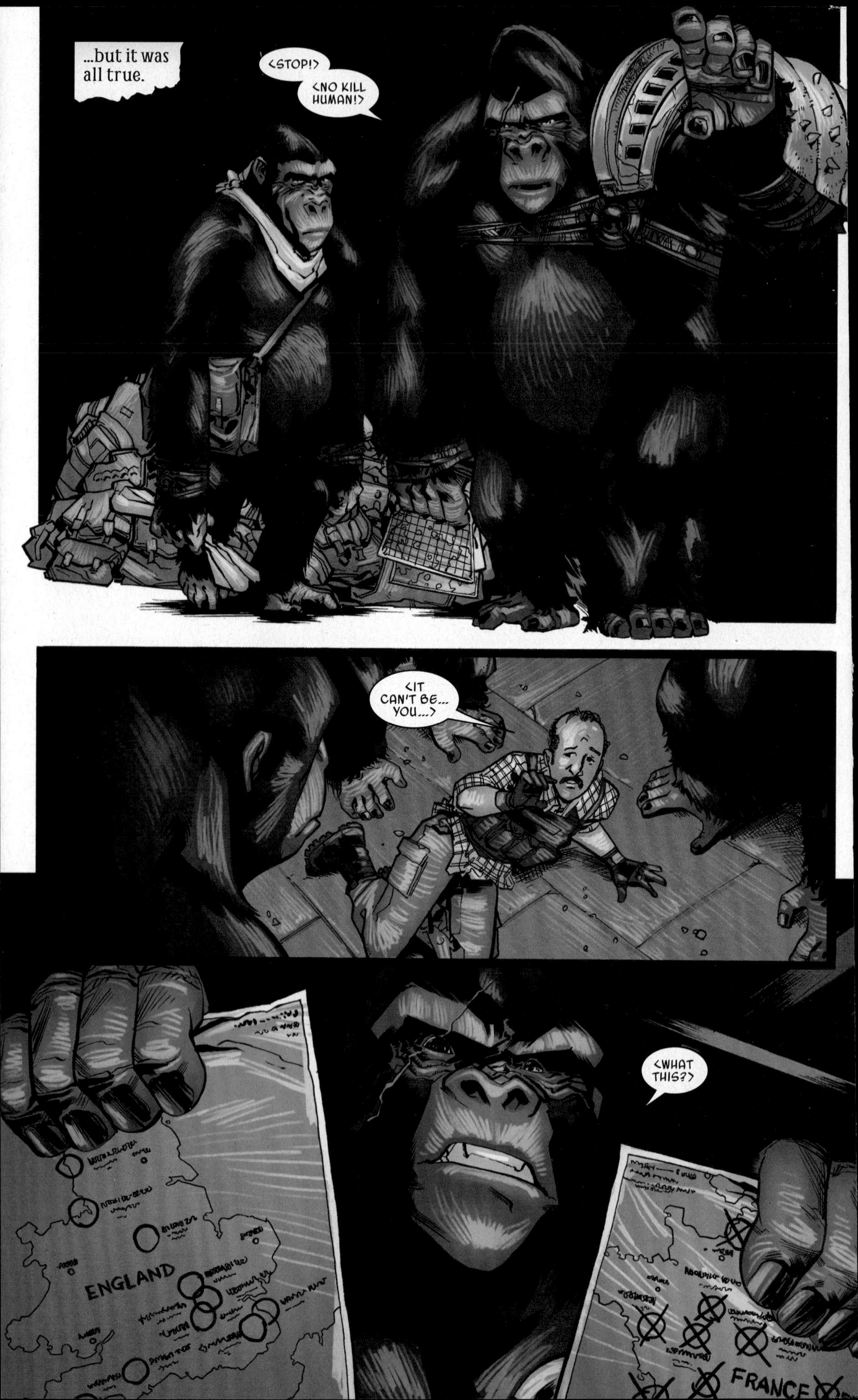
...but it was all true.
<STOP!>
<NO KILL HUMAN!>
<IT CAN'T BE... YOU...>
<WHAT THIS?>
ENGLAND
FRANCE

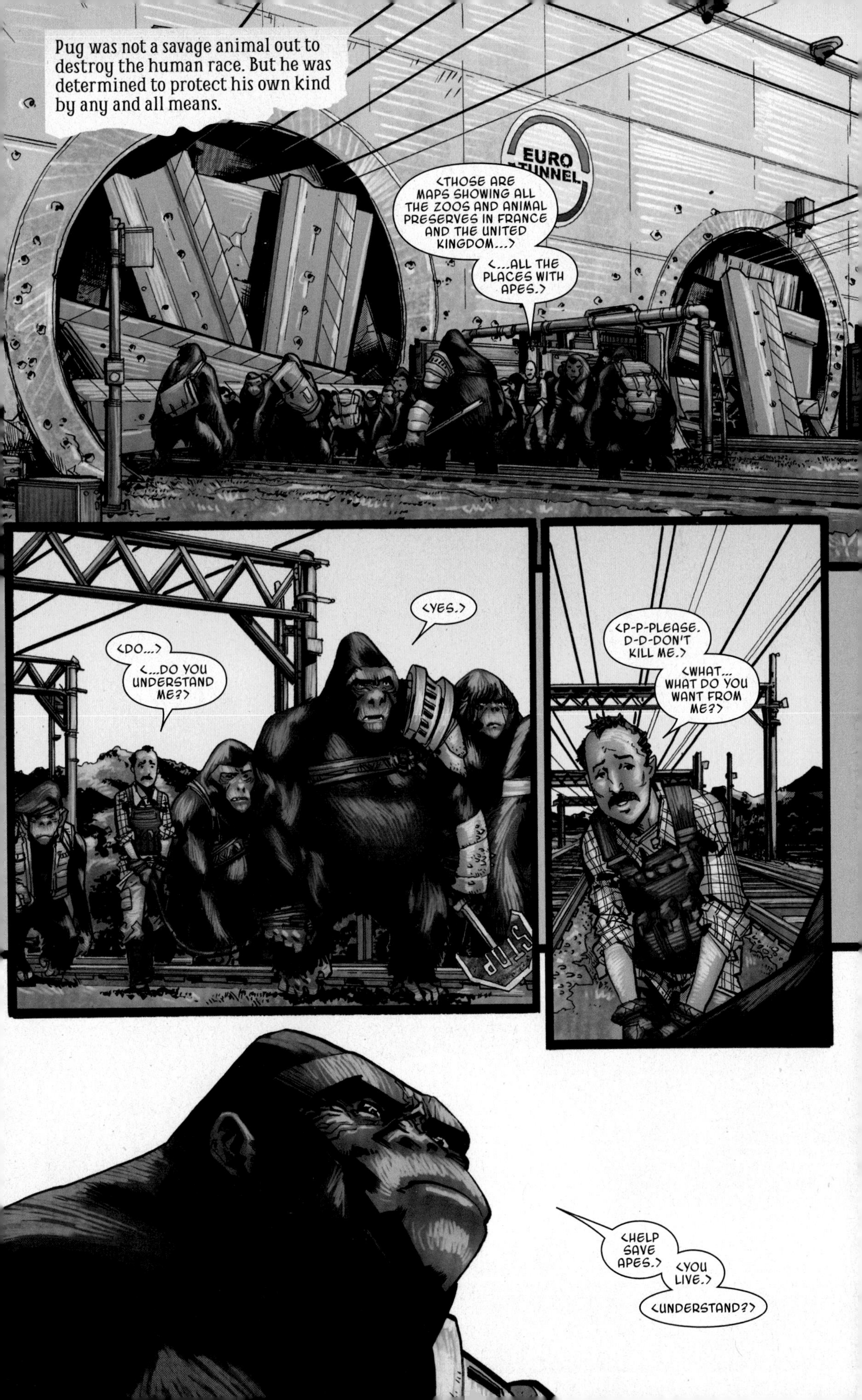
Pug was not a savage animal out to destroy the human race. But he was determined to protect his own kind by any and all means.
EURO TUNNEL
<THOSE ARE MAPS SHOWING ALL THE ZOOS AND ANIMAL PRESERVES IN FRANCE AND THE UNITED KINGDOM...>
<...ALL THE PLACES WITH APES.>
<DO...>
<...DO YOU UNDERSTAND ME?>
<YES.>
<P-P-PLEASE. D-D-DON'T KILL ME.>
<WHAT... WHAT DO YOU WANT FROM ME?>
<HELP SAVE APES.>
<YOU LIVE.>
<UNDERSTAND?>

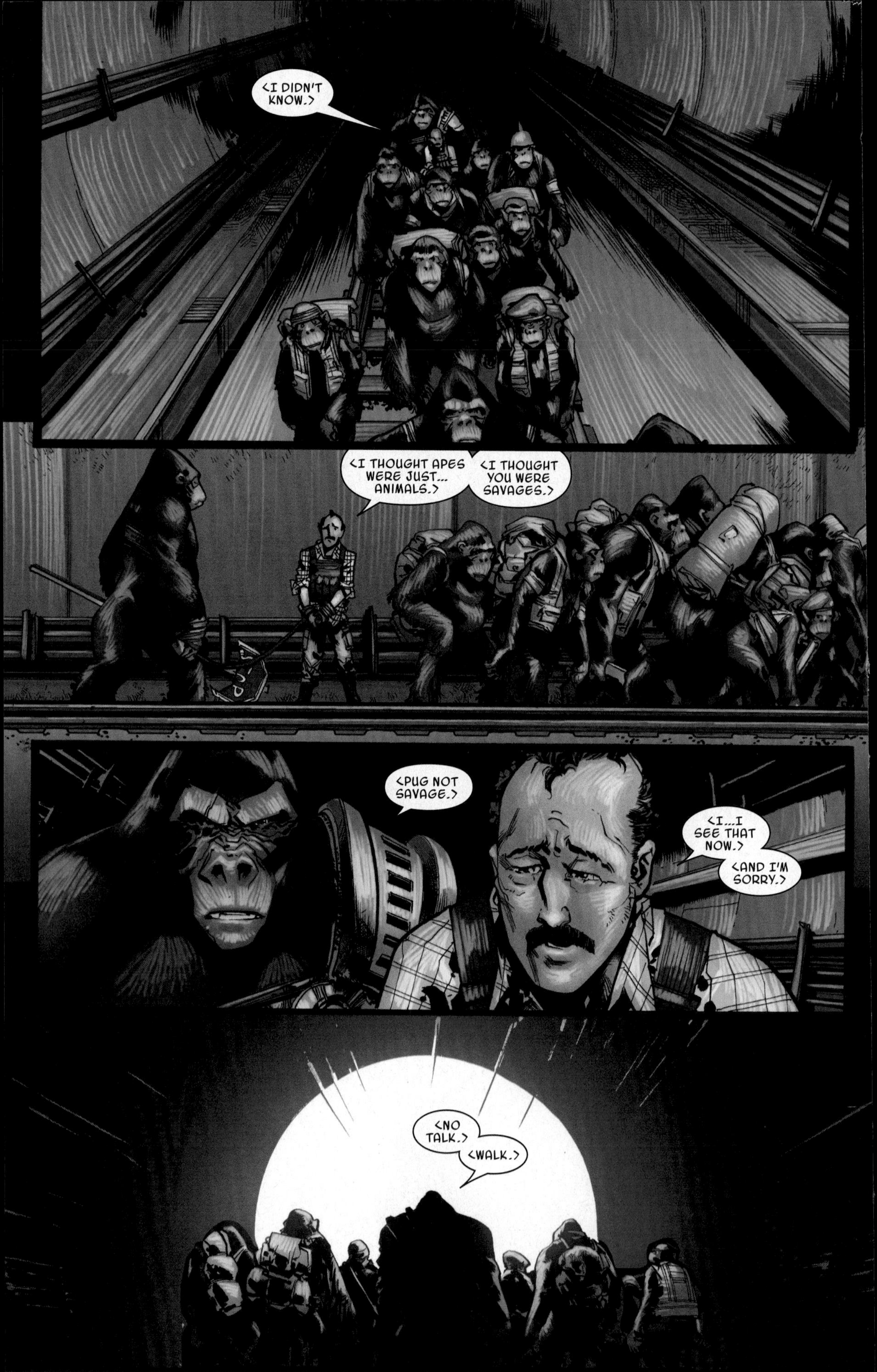
<I DIDN'T KNOW.>
<I THOUGHT APES WERE JUST... ANIMALS.>
<I THOUGHT YOU WERE SAVAGES.>
<PUG NOT SAVAGE.>
<I...I SEE THAT NOW.>
<AND I'M SORRY.>
<NO TALK.>
<WALK.>

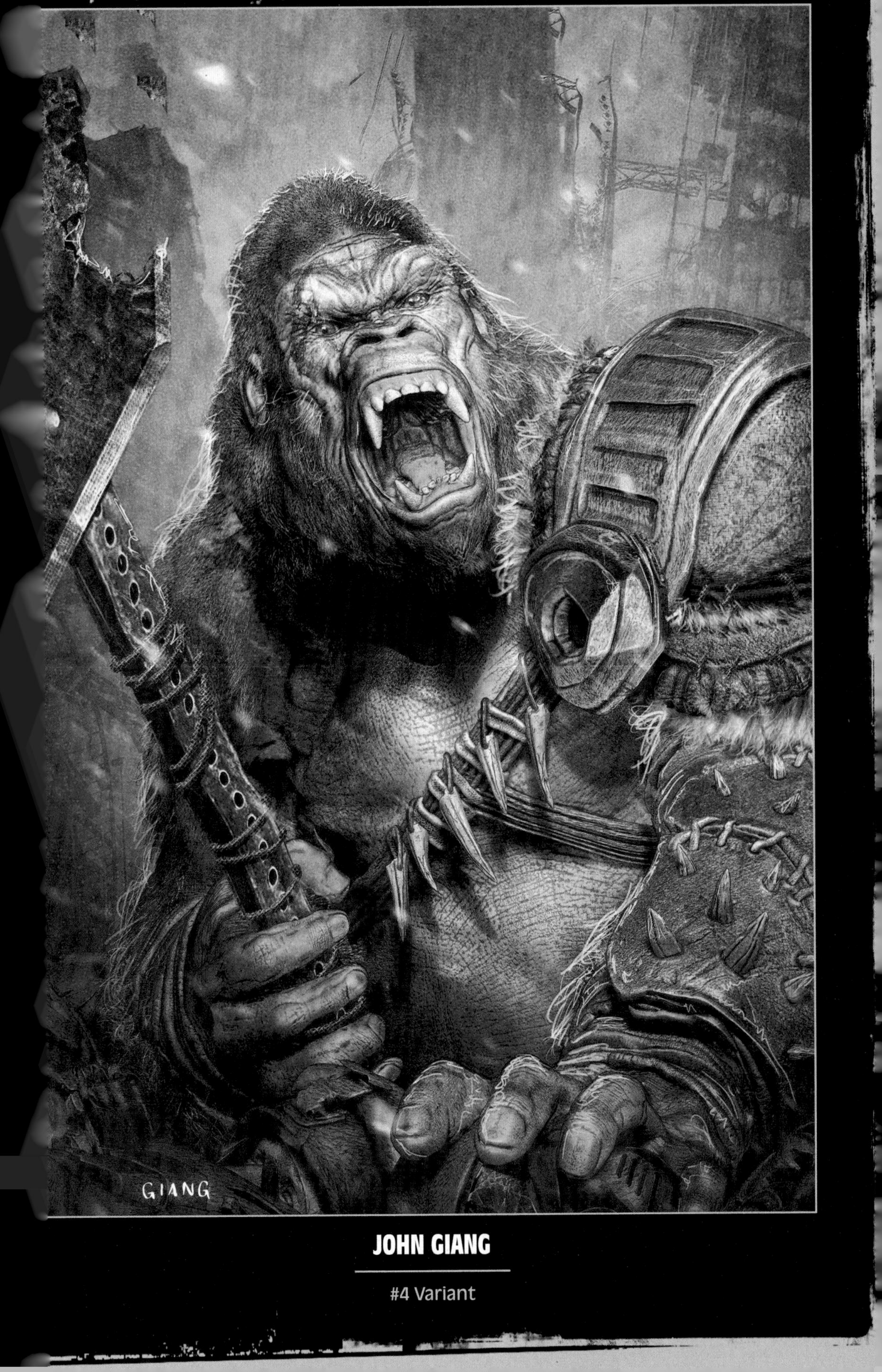
GIANG

JOHN GIANG

#4 Variant

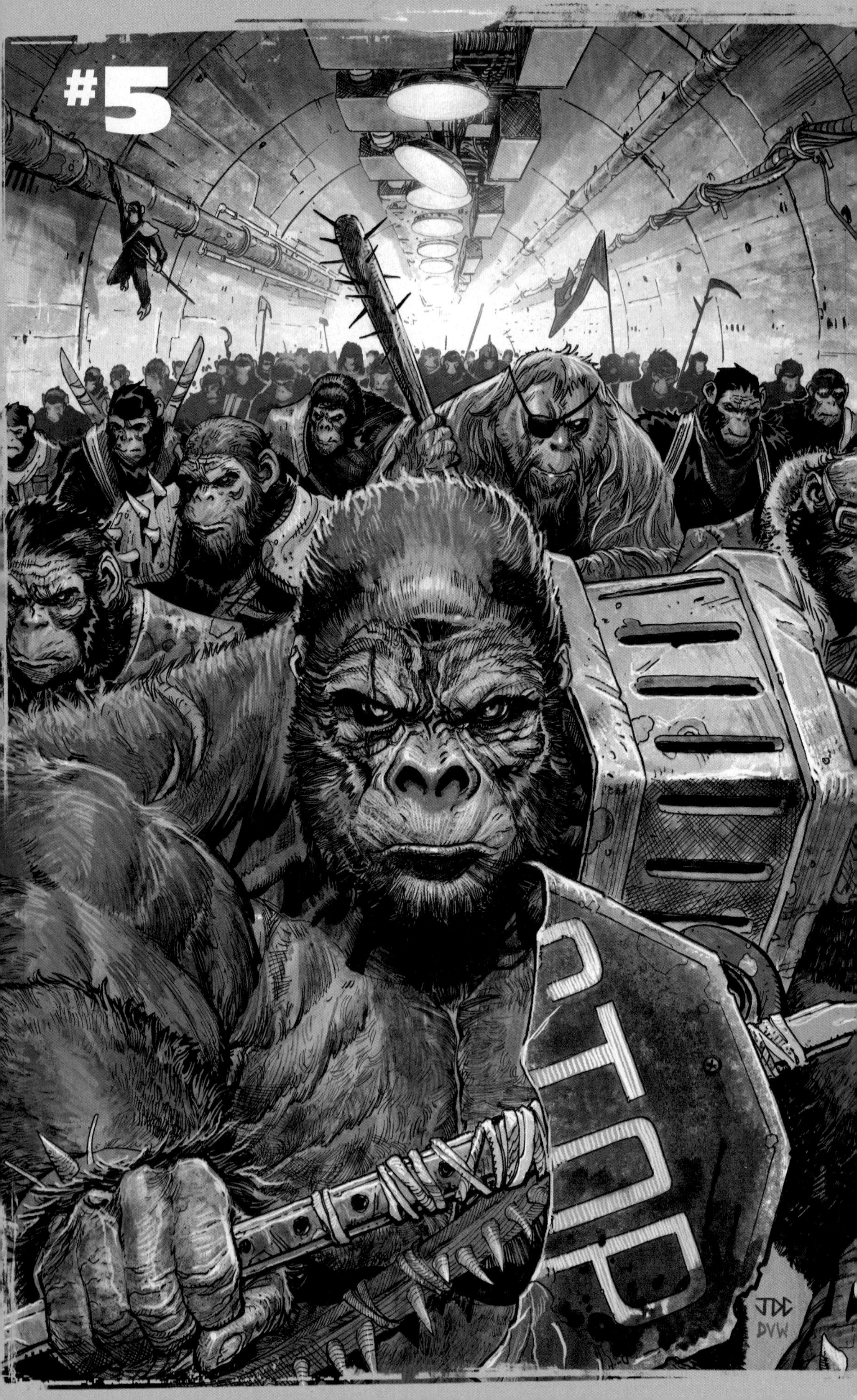
#5

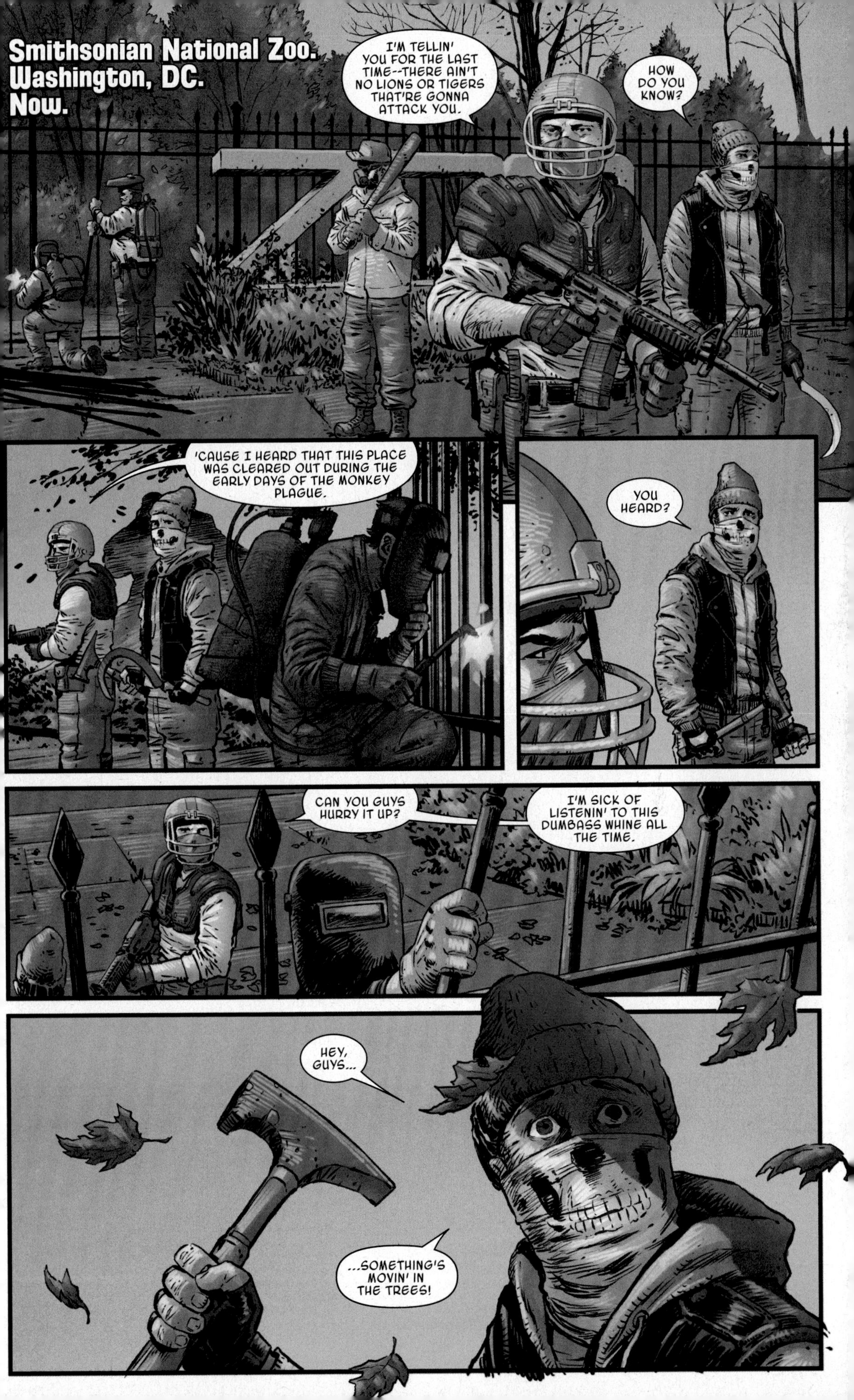
Smithsonian National Zoo.
Washington, DC.
Now.
I'M TELLIN' YOU FOR THE LAST TIME--THERE AIN'T NO LIONS OR TIGERS THAT'RE GONNA ATTACK YOU.
HOW DO YOU KNOW?
'CAUSE I HEARD THAT THIS PLACE WAS CLEARED OUT DURING THE EARLY DAYS OF THE MONKEY PLAGUE.
YOU HEARD?
CAN YOU GUYS HURRY IT UP?
I'M SICK OF LISTENIN' TO THIS DUMBASS WHINE ALL THE TIME.
HEY, GUYS...
...SOMETHING'S MOVIN' IN THE TREES!

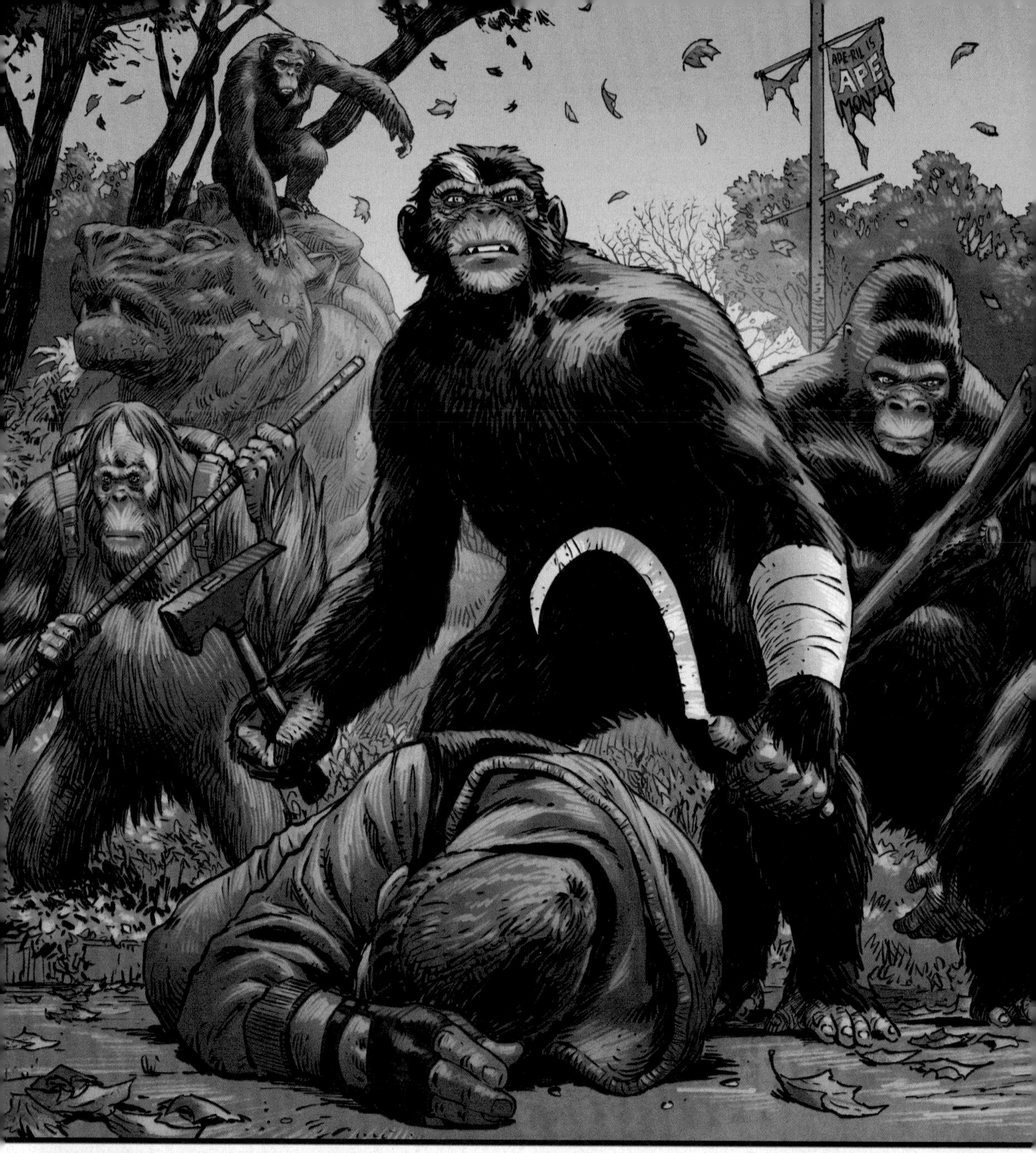
APE-RIL IS
APE

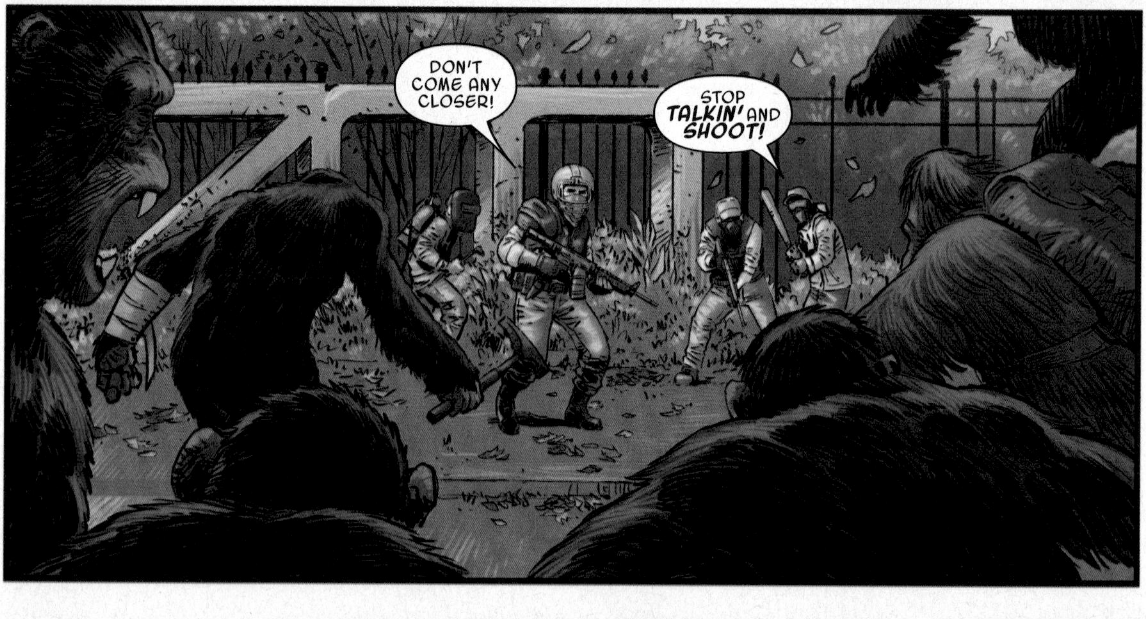
DON'T COME ANY CLOSER!
STOP TALKIN' AND SHOOT!

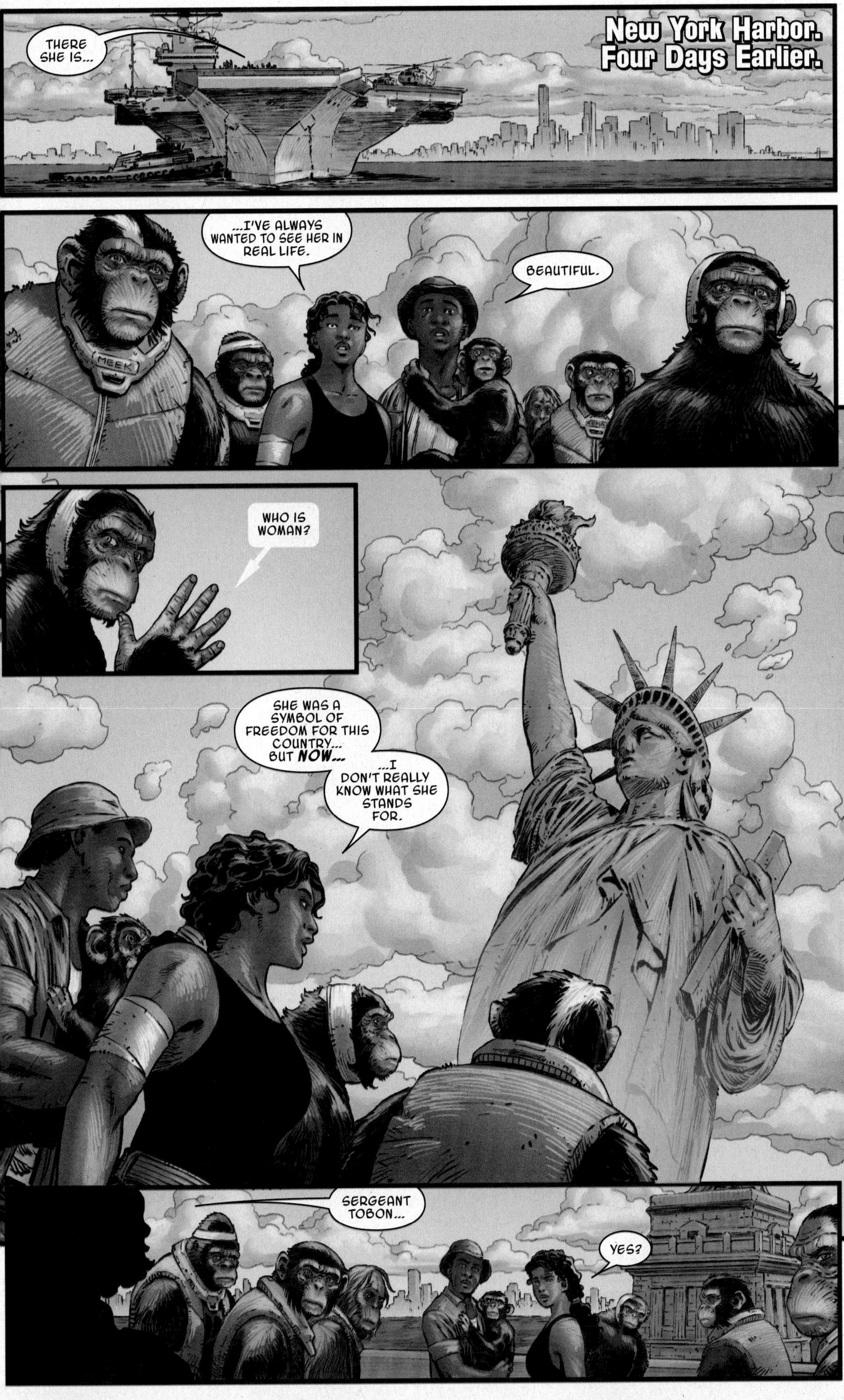
New York Harbor. Four Days Earlier.
THERE SHE IS...
...I'VE ALWAYS WANTED TO SEE HER IN REAL LIFE.
BEAUTIFUL.
WHO IS WOMAN?
SHE WAS A SYMBOL OF FREEDOM FOR THIS COUNTRY... BUT NOW...
...I DON'T REALLY KNOW WHAT SHE STANDS FOR.
SERGEANT TOBON...
YES?

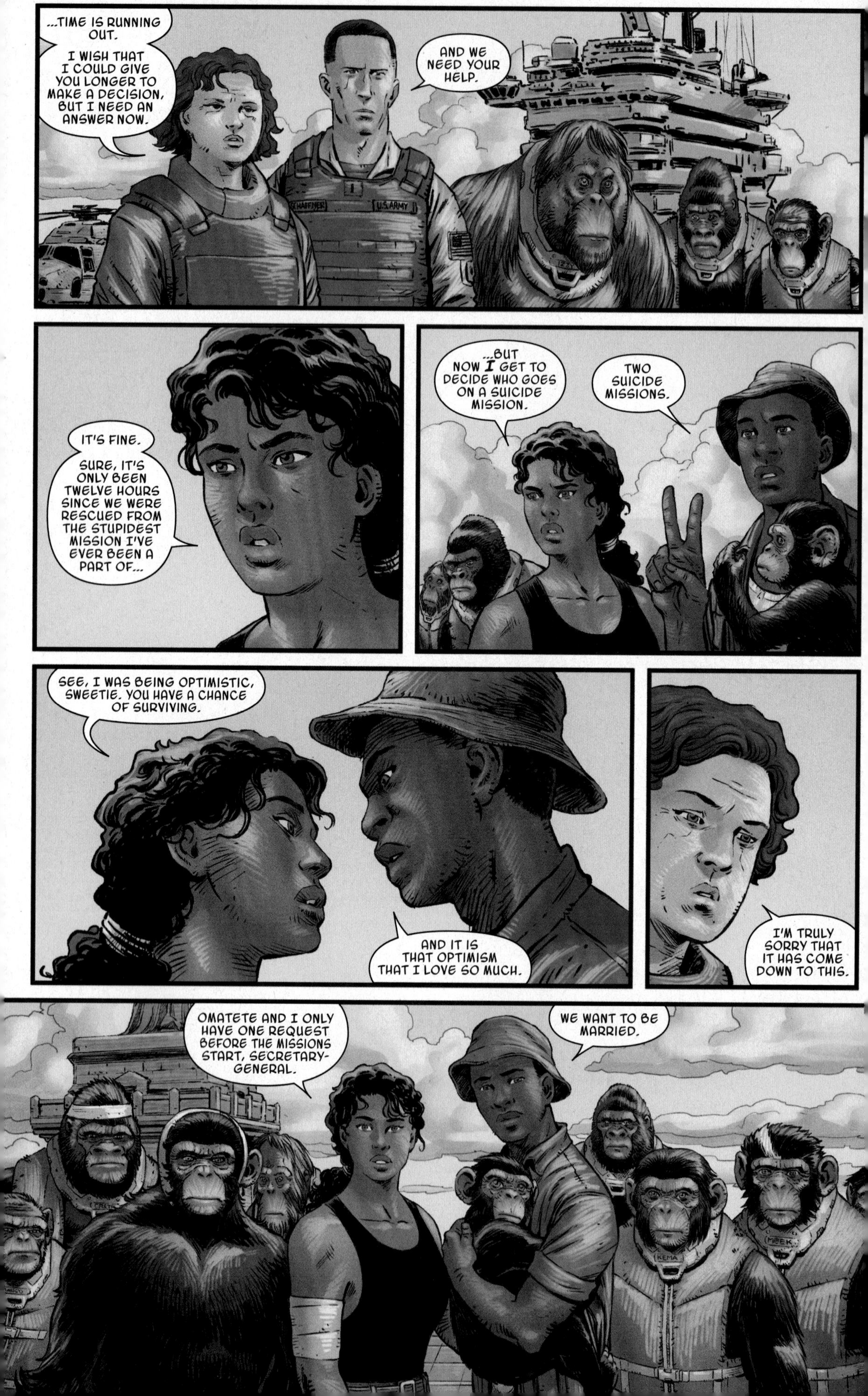
...TIME IS RUNNING OUT.
I WISH THAT I COULD GIVE YOU LONGER TO MAKE A DECISION, BUT I NEED AN ANSWER NOW.
AND WE NEED YOUR HELP.
CHAFFNER
U.S. ARMY
IT'S FINE.
SURE, IT'S ONLY BEEN TWELVE HOURS SINCE WE WERE RESCUED FROM THE STUPIDEST MISSION I'VE EVER BEEN A PART OF...
...BUT NOW I GET TO DECIDE WHO GOES ON A SUICIDE MISSION.
TWO SUICIDE MISSIONS.
SEE, I WAS BEING OPTIMISTIC, SWEETIE. YOU HAVE A CHANCE OF SURVIVING.
AND IT IS THAT OPTIMISM THAT I LOVE SO MUCH.
I'M TRULY SORRY THAT IT HAS COME DOWN TO THIS.
OMATETE AND I ONLY HAVE ONE REQUEST BEFORE THE MISSIONS START, SECRETARY-GENERAL.
WE WANT TO BE MARRIED.

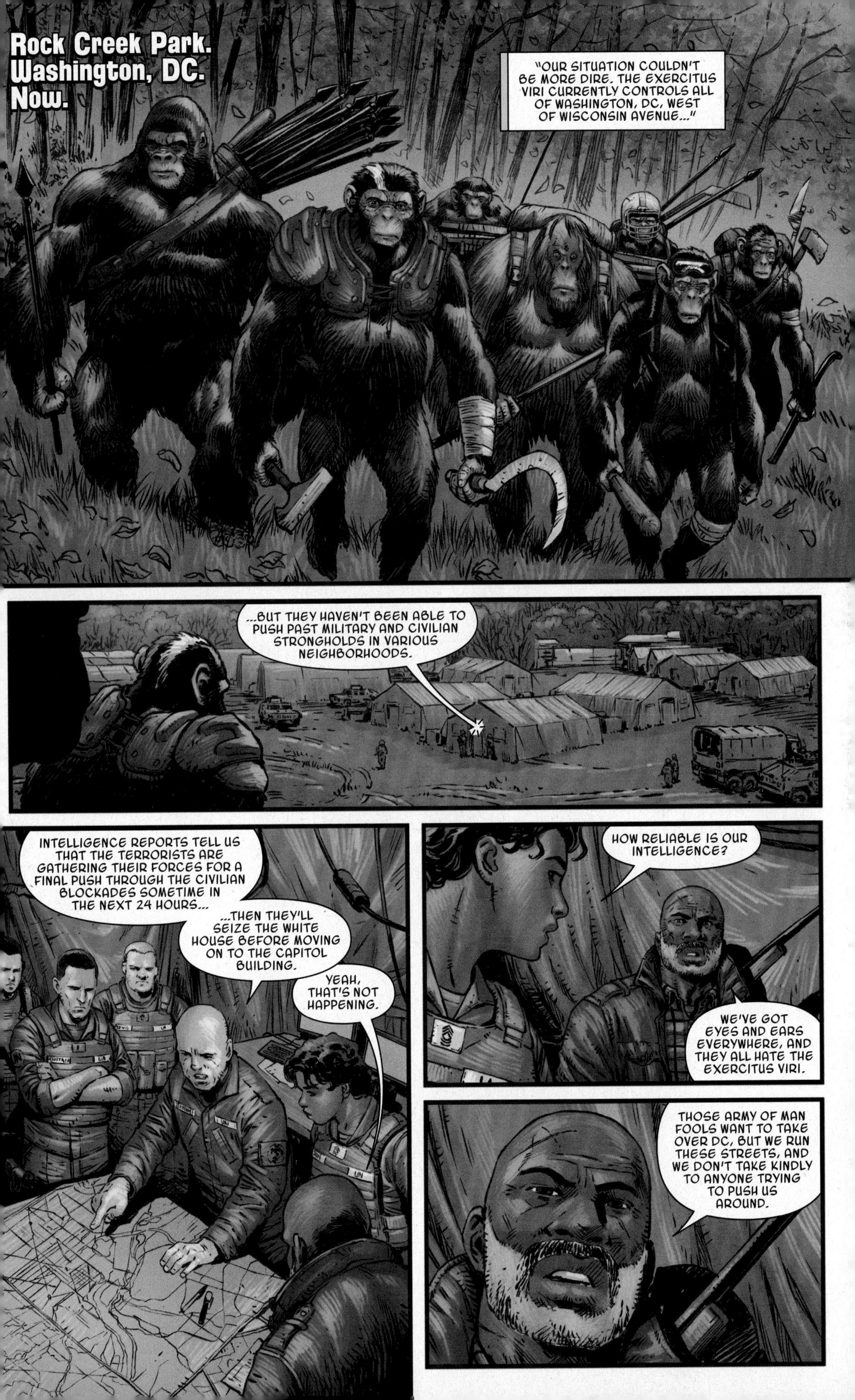
Rock Creek Park.
Washington, DC.
Now.
"OUR SITUATION COULDN'T BE MORE DIRE. THE EXERCITUS VIRI CURRENTLY CONTROLS ALL OF WASHINGTON, DC, WEST OF WISCONSIN AVENUE..."
...BUT THEY HAVEN'T BEEN ABLE TO PUSH PAST MILITARY AND CIVILIAN STRONGHOLDS IN VARIOUS NEIGHBORHOODS.
INTELLIGENCE REPORTS TELL US THAT THE TERRORISTS ARE GATHERING THEIR FORCES FOR A FINAL PUSH THROUGH THE CIVILIAN BLOCKADES SOMETIME IN THE NEXT 24 HOURS...
...THEN THEY'LL SEIZE THE WHITE HOUSE BEFORE MOVING ON TO THE CAPITOL BUILDING.
YEAH, THAT'S NOT HAPPENING.
HOW RELIABLE IS OUR INTELLIGENCE?
WE'VE GOT EYES AND EARS EVERYWHERE, AND THEY ALL HATE THE EXERCITUS VIRI.
THOSE ARMY OF MAN FOOLS WANT TO TAKE OVER DC, BUT WE RUN THESE STREETS, AND WE DON'T TAKE KINDLY TO ANYONE TRYING TO PUSH US AROUND.

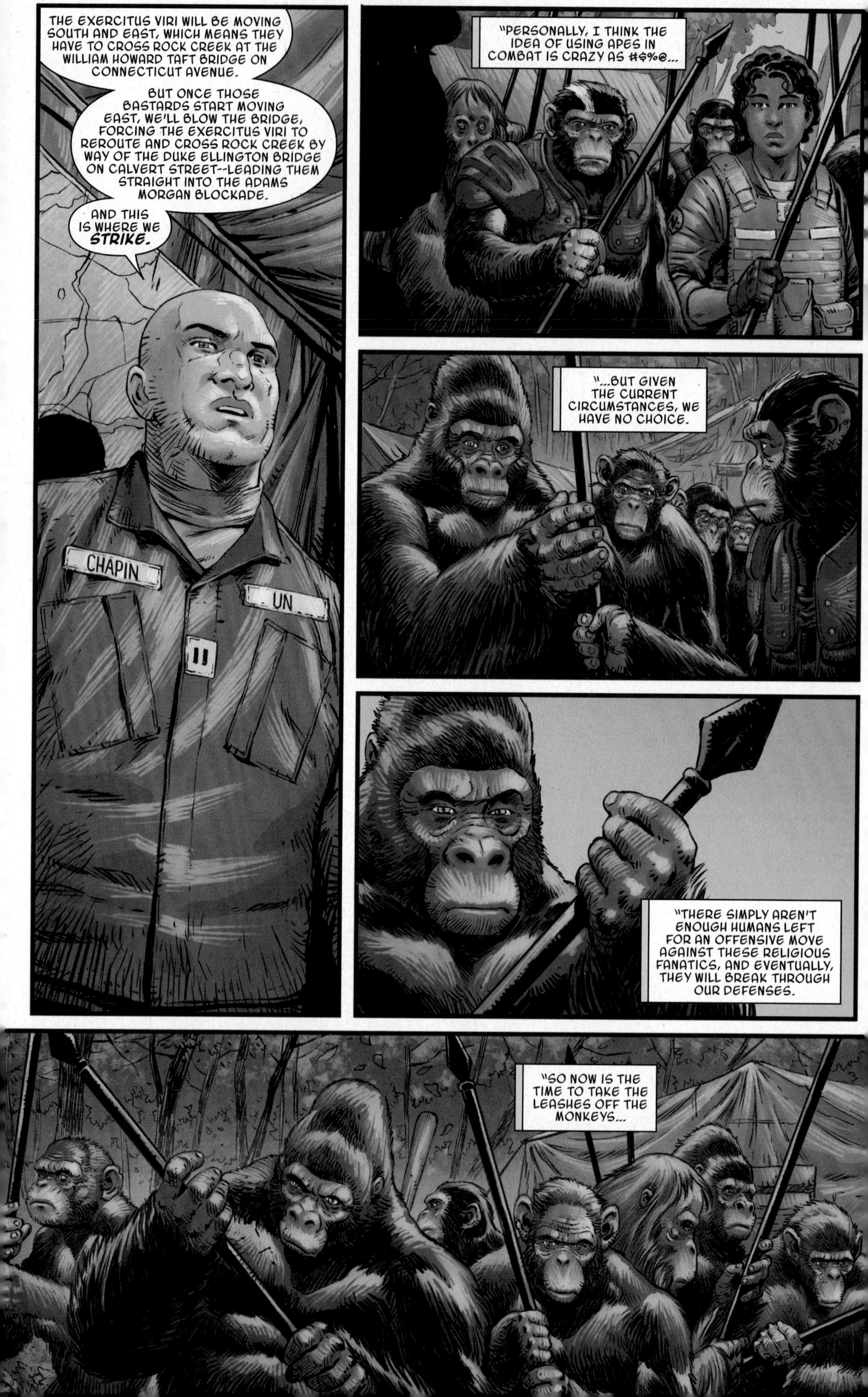

THE EXERCITUS VIRI WILL BE MOVING SOUTH AND EAST, WHICH MEANS THEY HAVE TO CROSS ROCK CREEK AT THE WILLIAM HOWARD TAFT BRIDGE ON CONNECTICUT AVENUE.
BUT ONCE THOSE BASTARDS START MOVING EAST, WE'LL BLOW THE BRIDGE, FORCING THE EXERCITUS VIRI TO REROUTE AND CROSS ROCK CREEK BY WAY OF THE DUKE ELLINGTON BRIDGE ON CALVERT STREET--LEADING THEM STRAIGHT INTO THE ADAMS MORGAN BLOCKADE.
AND THIS IS WHERE WE *STRIKE.*
CHAPIN
UN
"PERSONALLY, I THINK THE IDEA OF USING APES IN COMBAT IS CRAZY AS #$%@...
"...BUT GIVEN THE CURRENT CIRCUMSTANCES, WE HAVE NO CHOICE.
"THERE SIMPLY AREN'T ENOUGH HUMANS LEFT FOR AN OFFENSIVE MOVE AGAINST THESE RELIGIOUS FANATICS, AND EVENTUALLY, THEY WILL BREAK THROUGH OUR DEFENSES.
"SO NOW IS THE TIME TO TAKE THE LEASHES OFF THE MONKEYS...

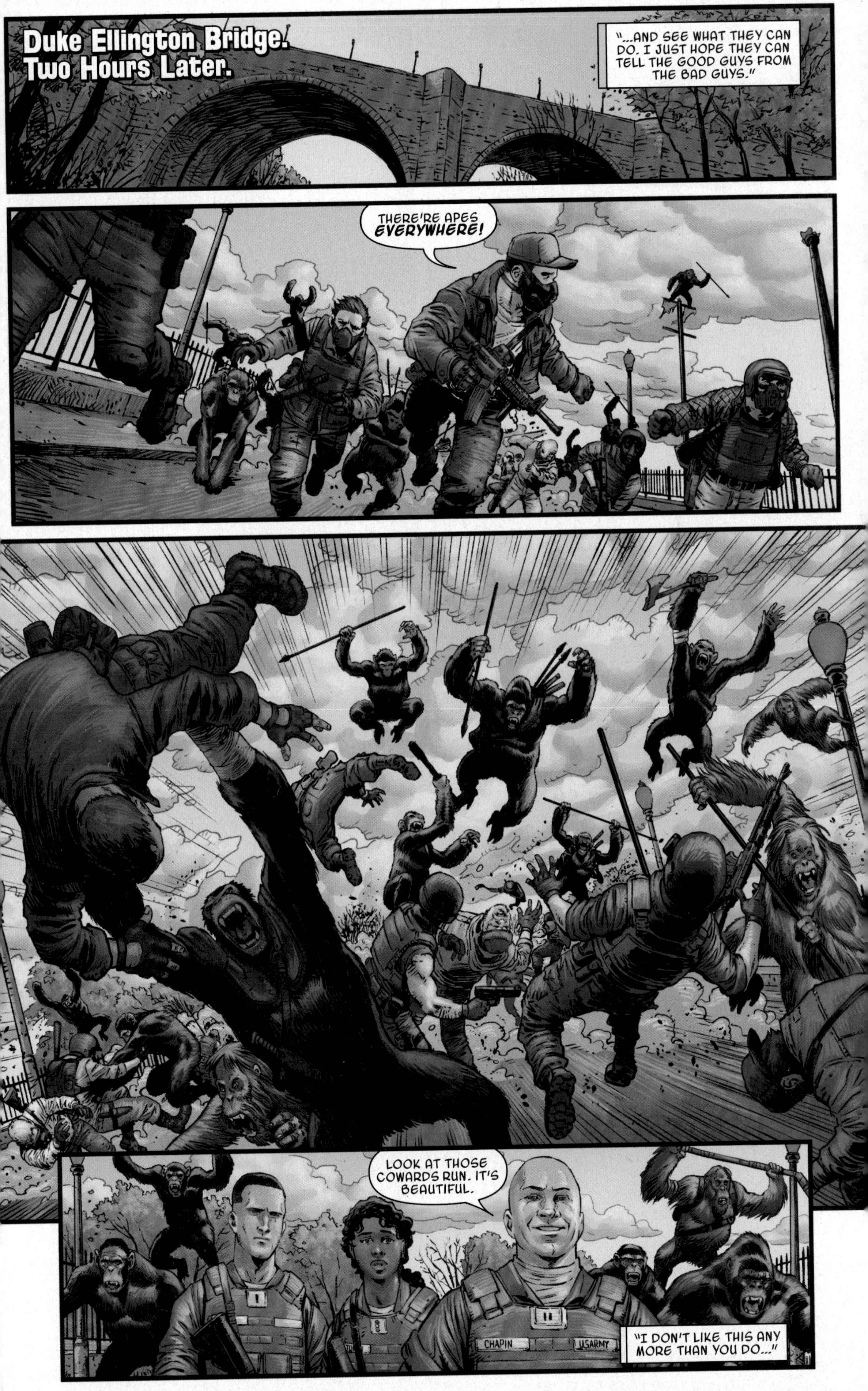
Duke Ellington Bridge. Two Hours Later.
"...AND SEE WHAT THEY CAN DO. I JUST HOPE THEY CAN TELL THE GOOD GUYS FROM THE BAD GUYS."
THERE'RE APES EVERYWHERE!
LOOK AT THOSE COWARDS RUN. IT'S BEAUTIFUL.
CHAPIN
U.S. ARMY
"I DON'T LIKE THIS ANY MORE THAN YOU DO..."

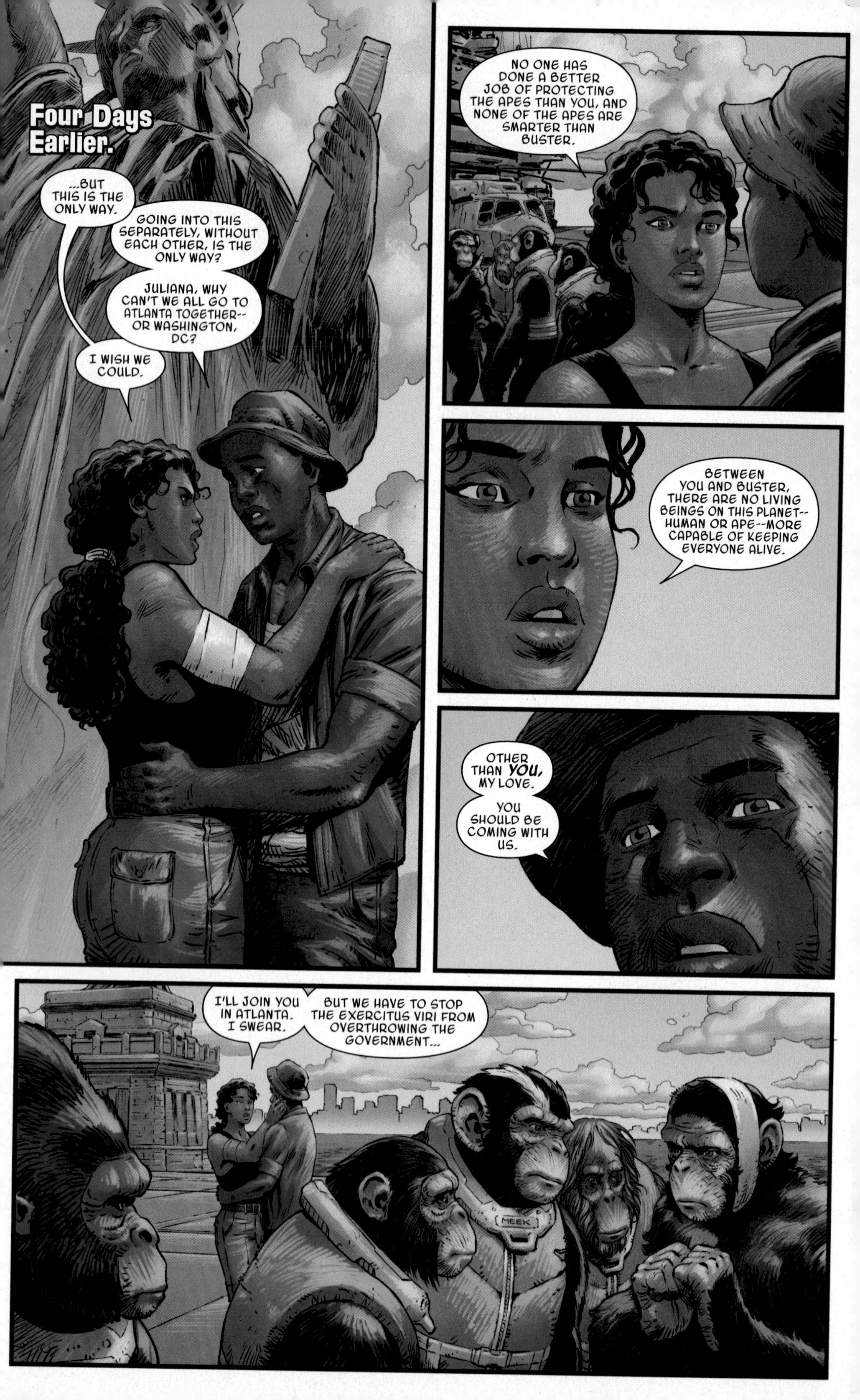
Four Days Earlier.
...BUT THIS IS THE ONLY WAY.
GOING INTO THIS SEPARATELY, WITHOUT EACH OTHER, IS THE ONLY WAY?
JULIANA, WHY CAN'T WE ALL GO TO ATLANTA TOGETHER-- OR WASHINGTON, DC?
I WISH WE COULD.
NO ONE HAS DONE A BETTER JOB OF PROTECTING THE APES THAN YOU, AND NONE OF THE APES ARE SMARTER THAN BUSTER.
BETWEEN YOU AND BUSTER, THERE ARE NO LIVING BEINGS ON THIS PLANET-- HUMAN OR APE--MORE CAPABLE OF KEEPING EVERYONE ALIVE.
OTHER THAN YOU, MY LOVE.
YOU SHOULD BE COMING WITH US.
I'LL JOIN YOU IN ATLANTA. I SWEAR.
BUT WE HAVE TO STOP THE EXERCITUS VIRI FROM OVERTHROWING THE GOVERNMENT...
MEEK

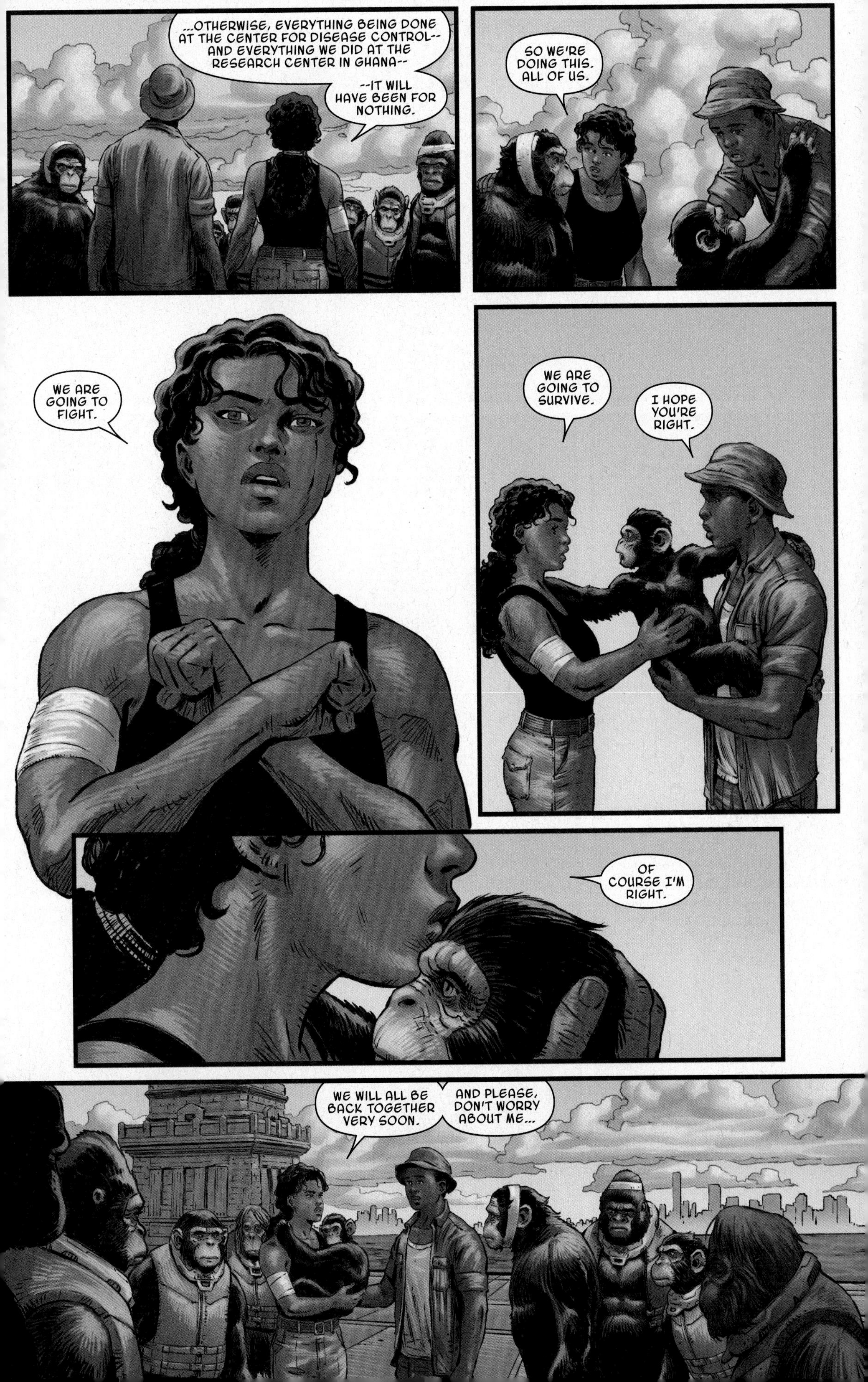
...OTHERWISE, EVERYTHING BEING DONE AT THE CENTER FOR DISEASE CONTROL-- AND EVERYTHING WE DID AT THE RESEARCH CENTER IN GHANA--
--IT WILL HAVE BEEN FOR NOTHING.
SO WE'RE DOING THIS. ALL OF US.
WE ARE GOING TO FIGHT.
WE ARE GOING TO SURVIVE.
I HOPE YOU'RE RIGHT.
OF COURSE I'M RIGHT.
WE WILL ALL BE BACK TOGETHER VERY SOON.
AND PLEASE, DON'T WORRY ABOUT ME...

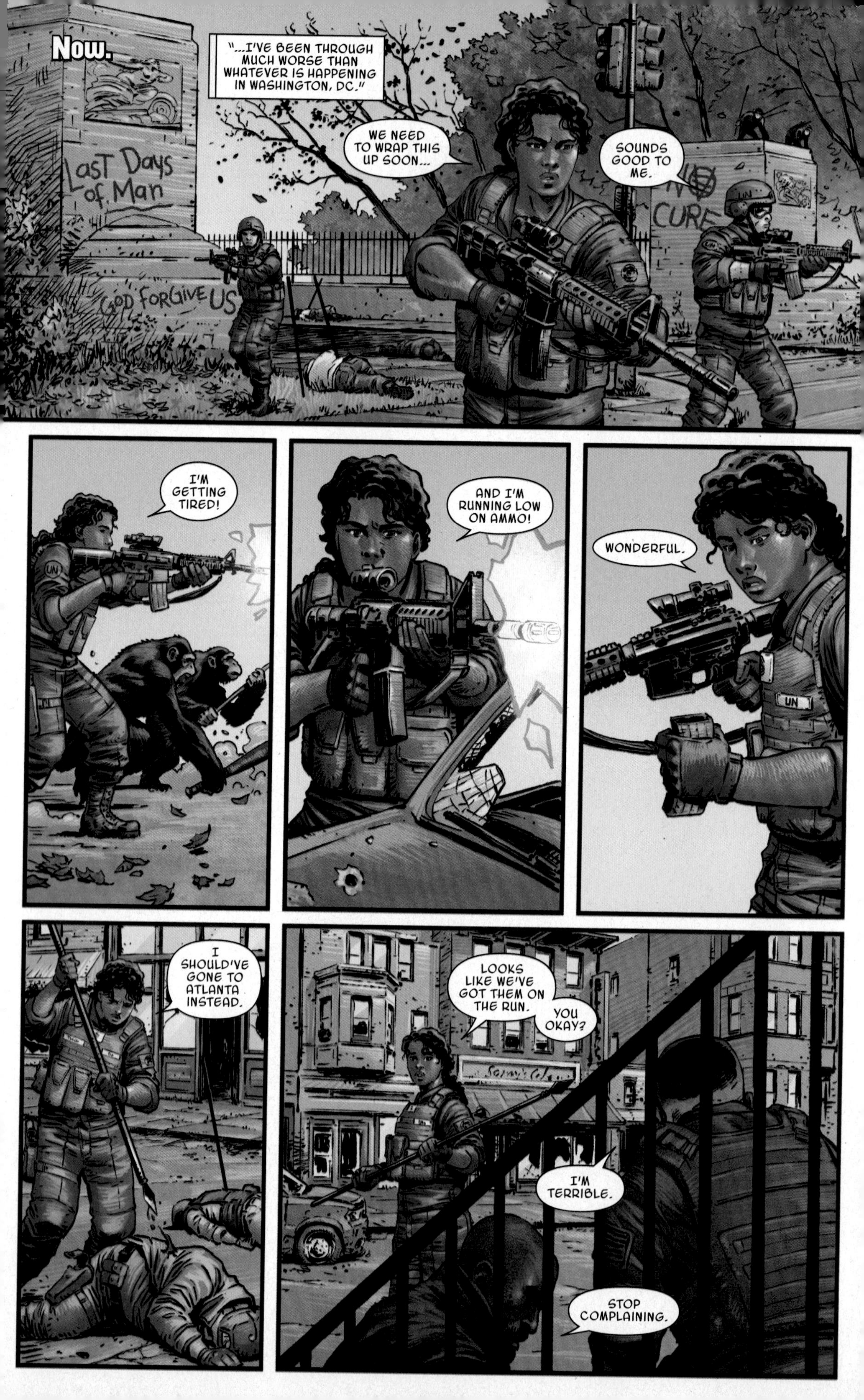
Now.
"...I'VE BEEN THROUGH MUCH WORSE THAN WHATEVER IS HAPPENING IN WASHINGTON, DC."
Last Days of Man
GOD FORGIVE US
NO CURE
WE NEED TO WRAP THIS UP SOON...
SOUNDS GOOD TO ME.
UN
I'M GETTING TIRED!
AND I'M RUNNING LOW ON AMMO!
WONDERFUL.
UN
I SHOULD'VE GONE TO ATLANTA INSTEAD.
LOOKS LIKE WE'VE GOT THEM ON THE RUN.
YOU OKAY?
I'M TERRIBLE.
STOP COMPLAINING.

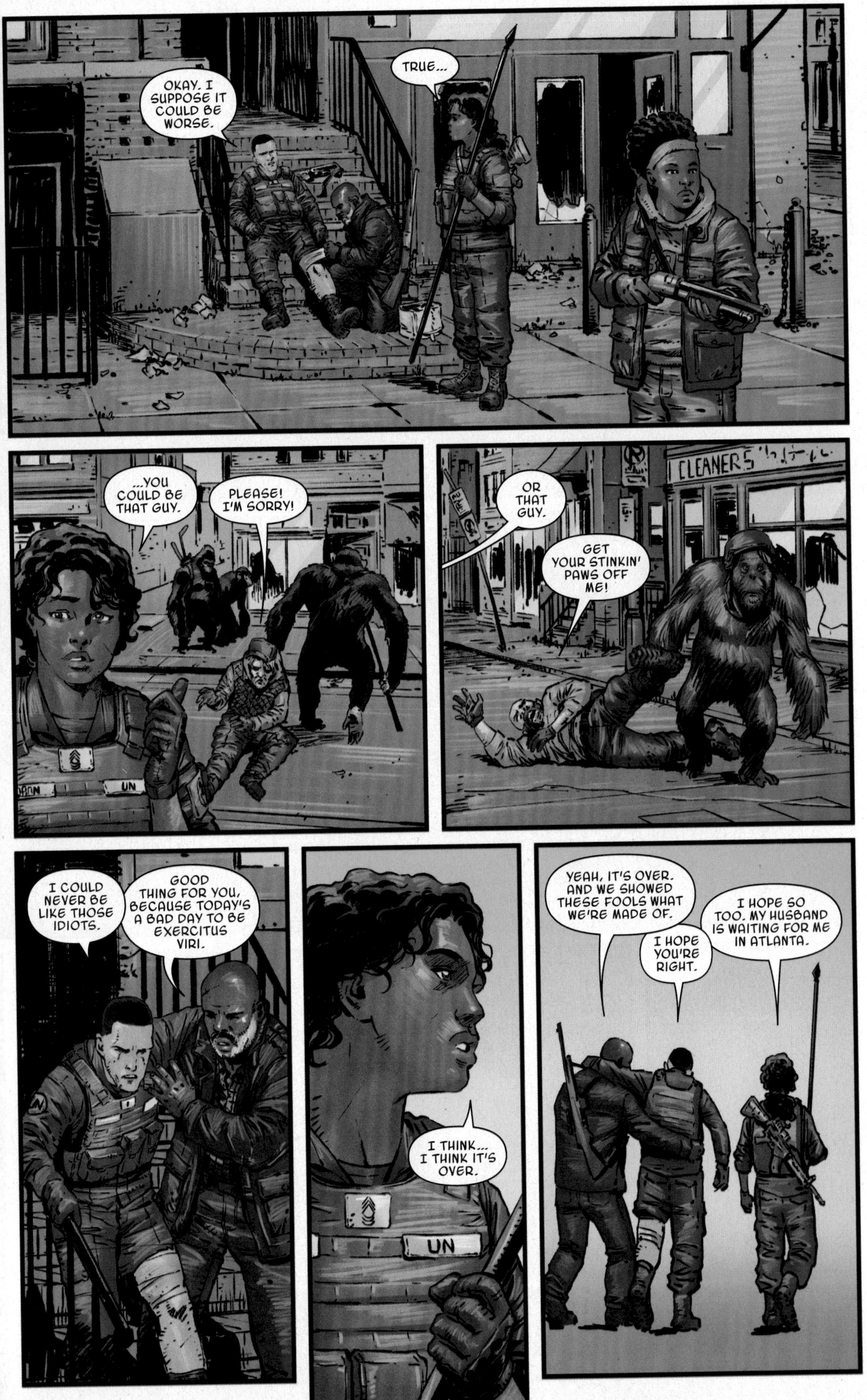
OKAY. I SUPPOSE IT COULD BE WORSE.
TRUE...
...YOU COULD BE THAT GUY.
PLEASE! I'M SORRY!
OR THAT GUY.
CLEANERS
GET YOUR STINKIN' PAWS OFF ME!
UN
I COULD NEVER BE LIKE THOSE IDIOTS.
GOOD THING FOR YOU, BECAUSE TODAY'S A BAD DAY TO BE EXERCITUS VIRI.
I THINK... I THINK IT'S OVER.
UN
YEAH, IT'S OVER. AND WE SHOWED THESE FOOLS WHAT WE'RE MADE OF.
I HOPE YOU'RE RIGHT.
I HOPE SO TOO. MY HUSBAND IS WAITING FOR ME IN ATLANTA.

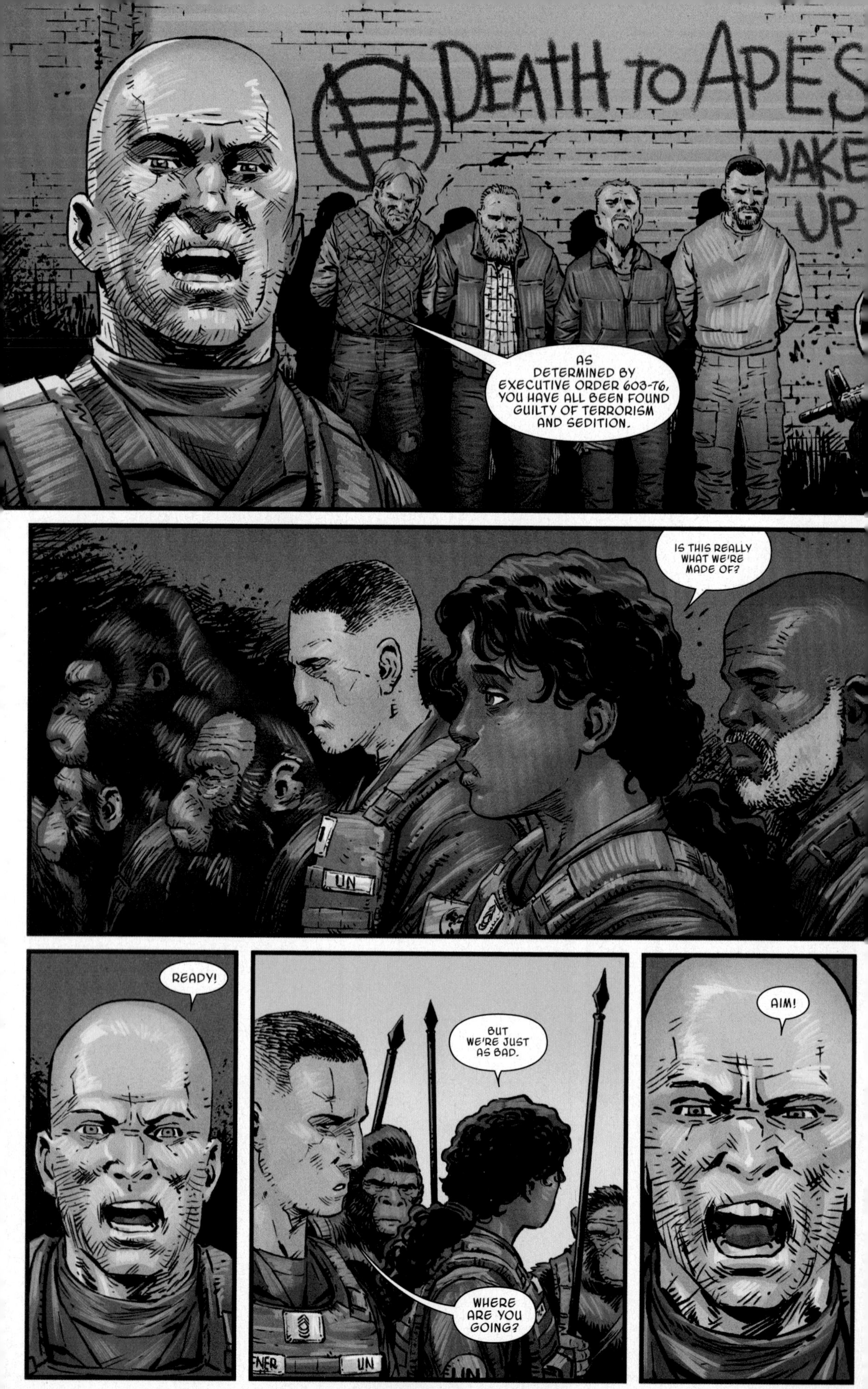
DEATH TO APES
WAKE UP
AS DETERMINED BY EXECUTIVE ORDER 603-76, YOU HAVE ALL BEEN FOUND GUILTY OF TERRORISM AND SEDITION.
IS THIS REALLY WHAT WE'RE MADE OF?
UN
READY!
BUT WE'RE JUST AS BAD.
WHERE ARE YOU GOING?
UN
AIM!

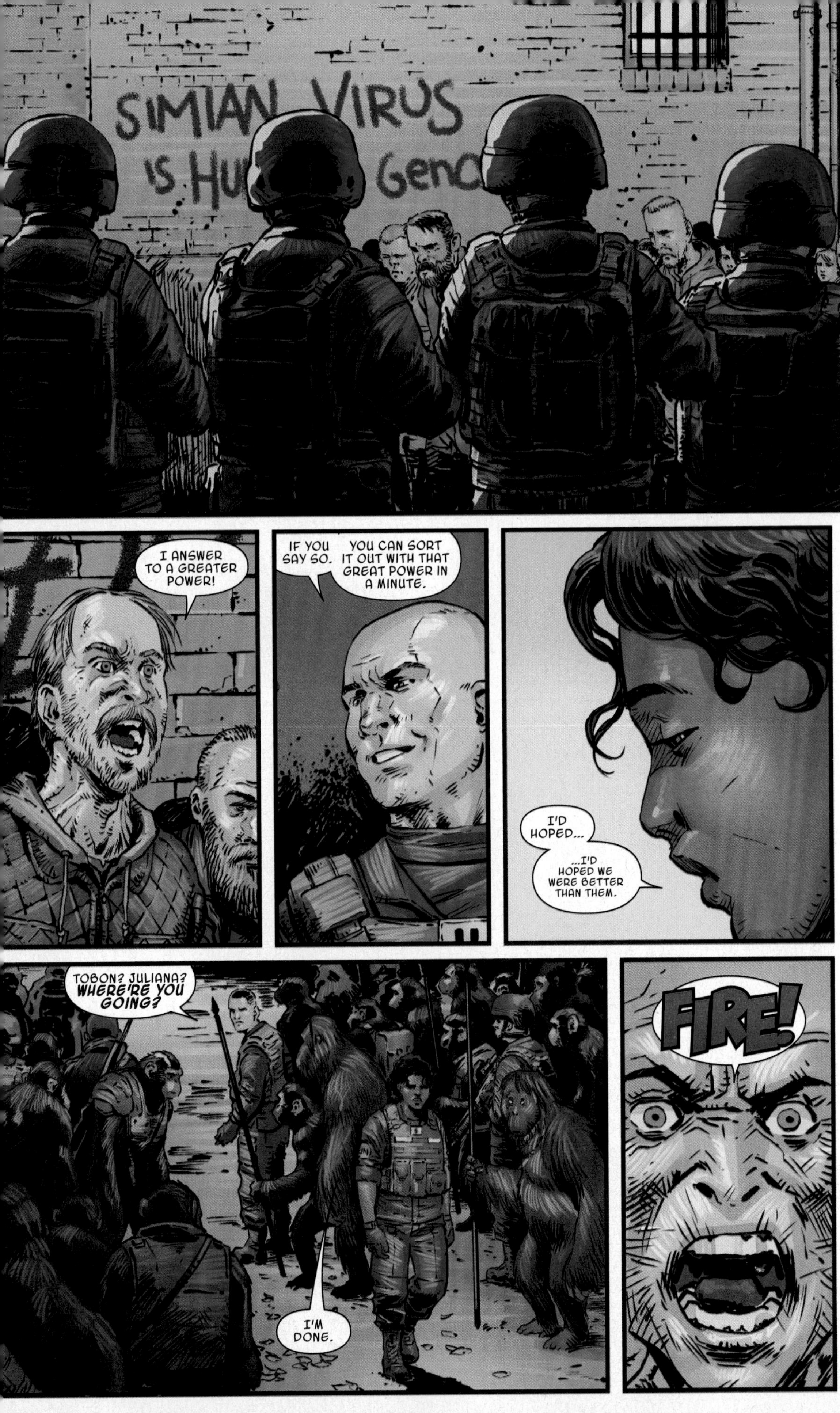

SIMIAN VIRUS
IS HU GENC
I ANSWER TO A GREATER POWER!
IF YOU SAY SO.
YOU CAN SORT IT OUT WITH THAT GREAT POWER IN A MINUTE.
I'D HOPED...
...I'D HOPED WE WERE BETTER THAN THEM.
TOBON? JULIANA? WHERE'RE YOU GOING?
I'M DONE.
FIRE!

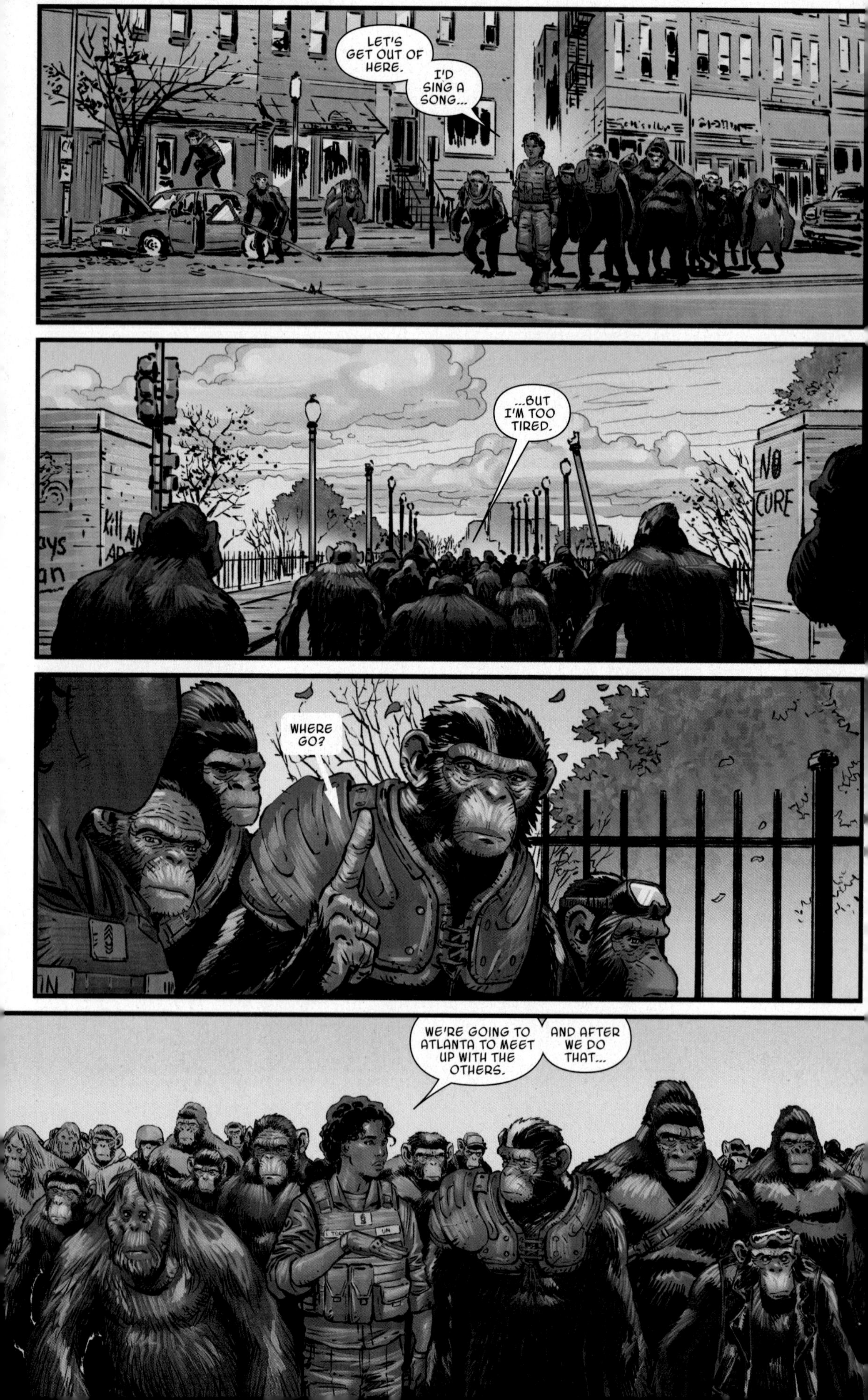
LET'S GET OUT OF HERE.
I'D SING A SONG...
...BUT I'M TOO TIRED.
NO CURE
WHERE GO?
WE'RE GOING TO ATLANTA TO MEET UP WITH THE OTHERS.
AND AFTER WE DO THAT...

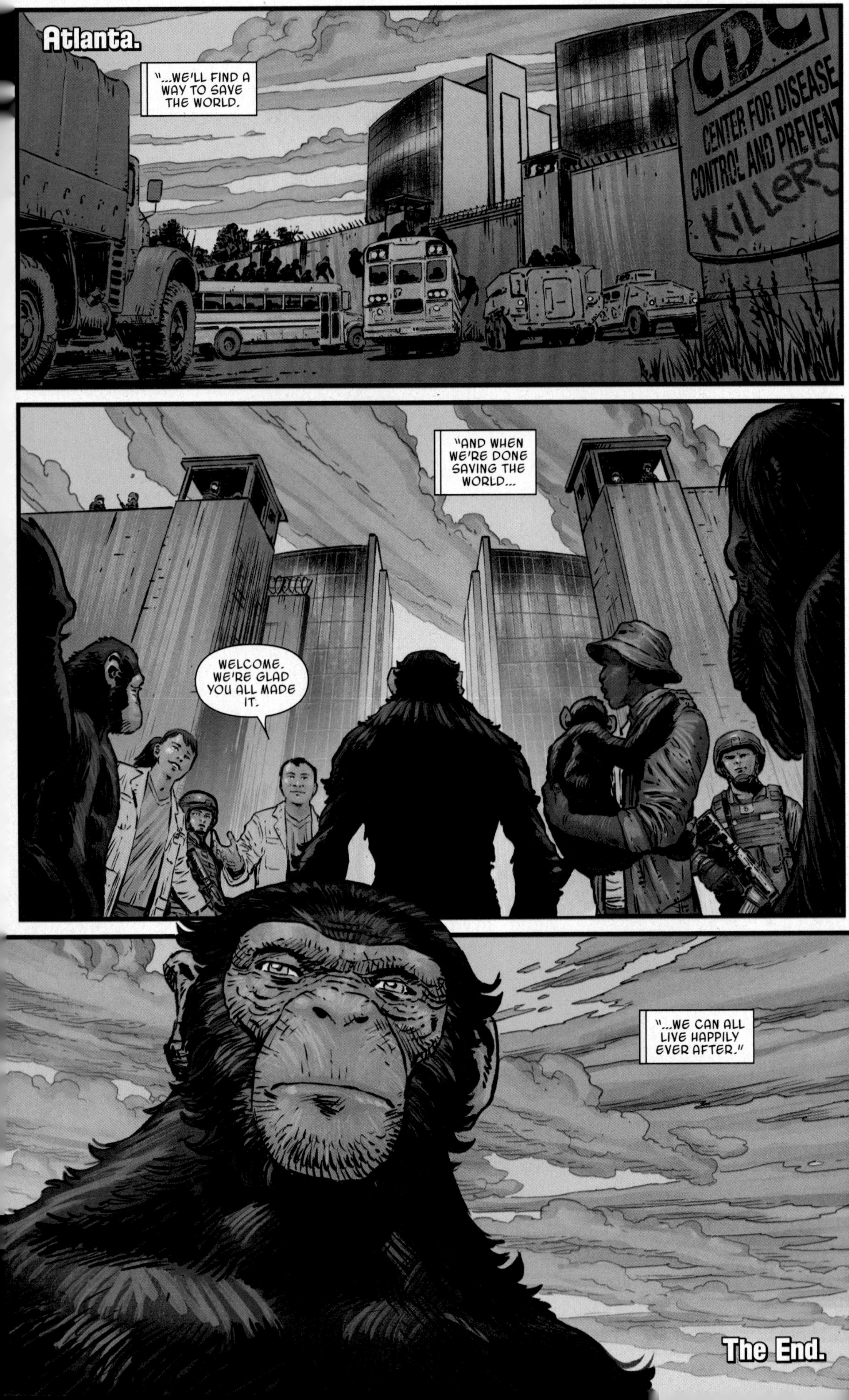

Atlanta.
"...WE'LL FIND A WAY TO SAVE THE WORLD.
CDC
CENTER FOR DISEASE
CONTROL AND PREVENT
KILLERS
"AND WHEN WE'RE DONE SAVING THE WORLD...
WELCOME. WE'RE GLAD YOU ALL MADE IT.
"...WE CAN ALL LIVE HAPPILY EVER AFTER."
The End.

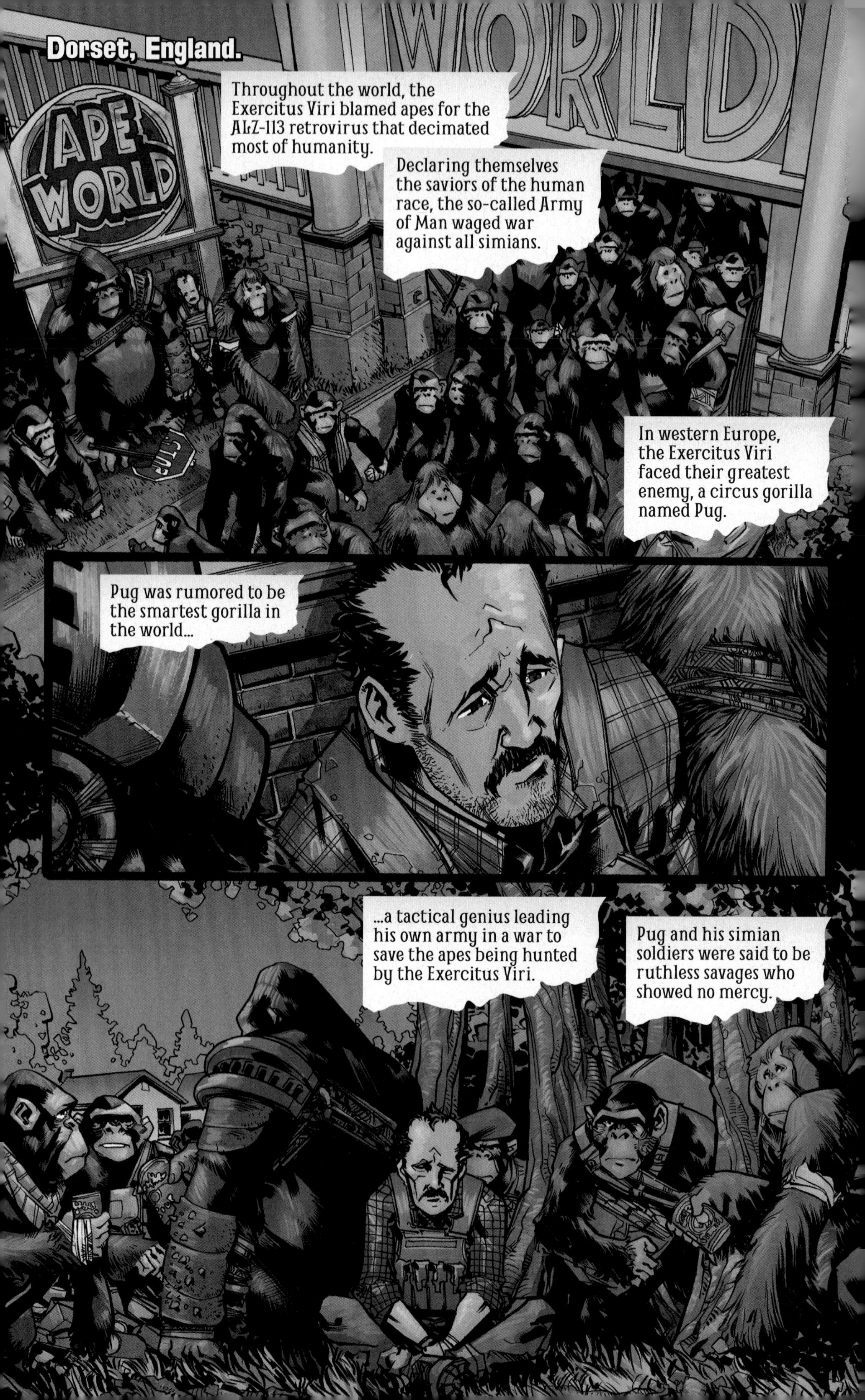
Dorset, England.
APE WORLD
WORLD
Throughout the world, the Exercitus Viri blamed apes for the ALZ-113 retrovirus that decimated most of humanity.
Declaring themselves the saviors of the human race, the so-called Army of Man waged war against all simians.
STOP
In western Europe, the Exercitus Viri faced their greatest enemy, a circus gorilla named Pug.
Pug was rumored to be the smartest gorilla in the world...
...a tactical genius leading his own army in a war to save the apes being hunted by the Exercitus Viri.
Pug and his simian soldiers were said to be ruthless savages who showed no mercy.

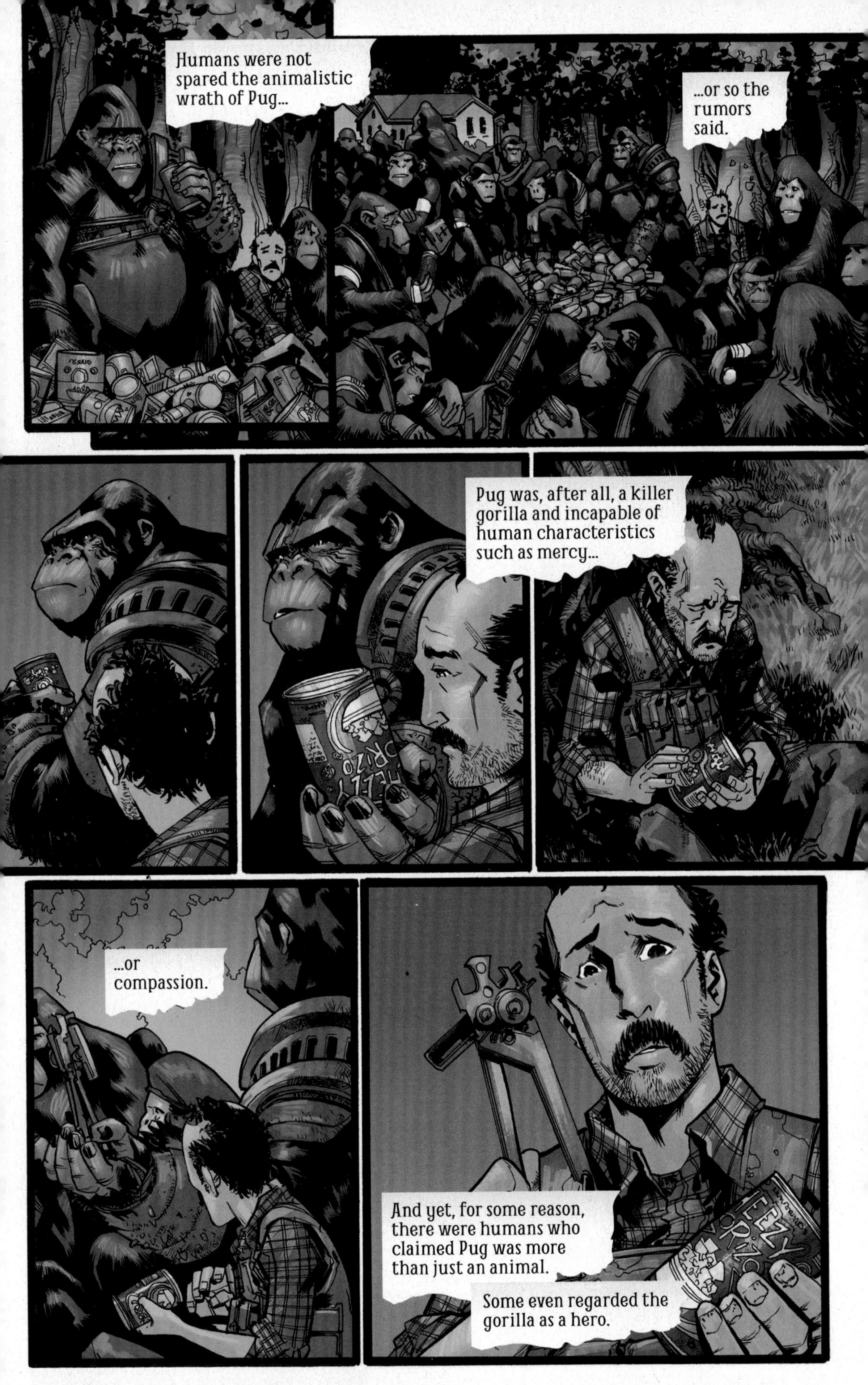

Humans were not spared the animalistic wrath of Pug...
...or so the rumors said.
Pug was, after all, a killer gorilla and incapable of human characteristics such as mercy...
...or compassion.
And yet, for some reason, there were humans who claimed Pug was more than just an animal.
Some even regarded the gorilla as a hero.

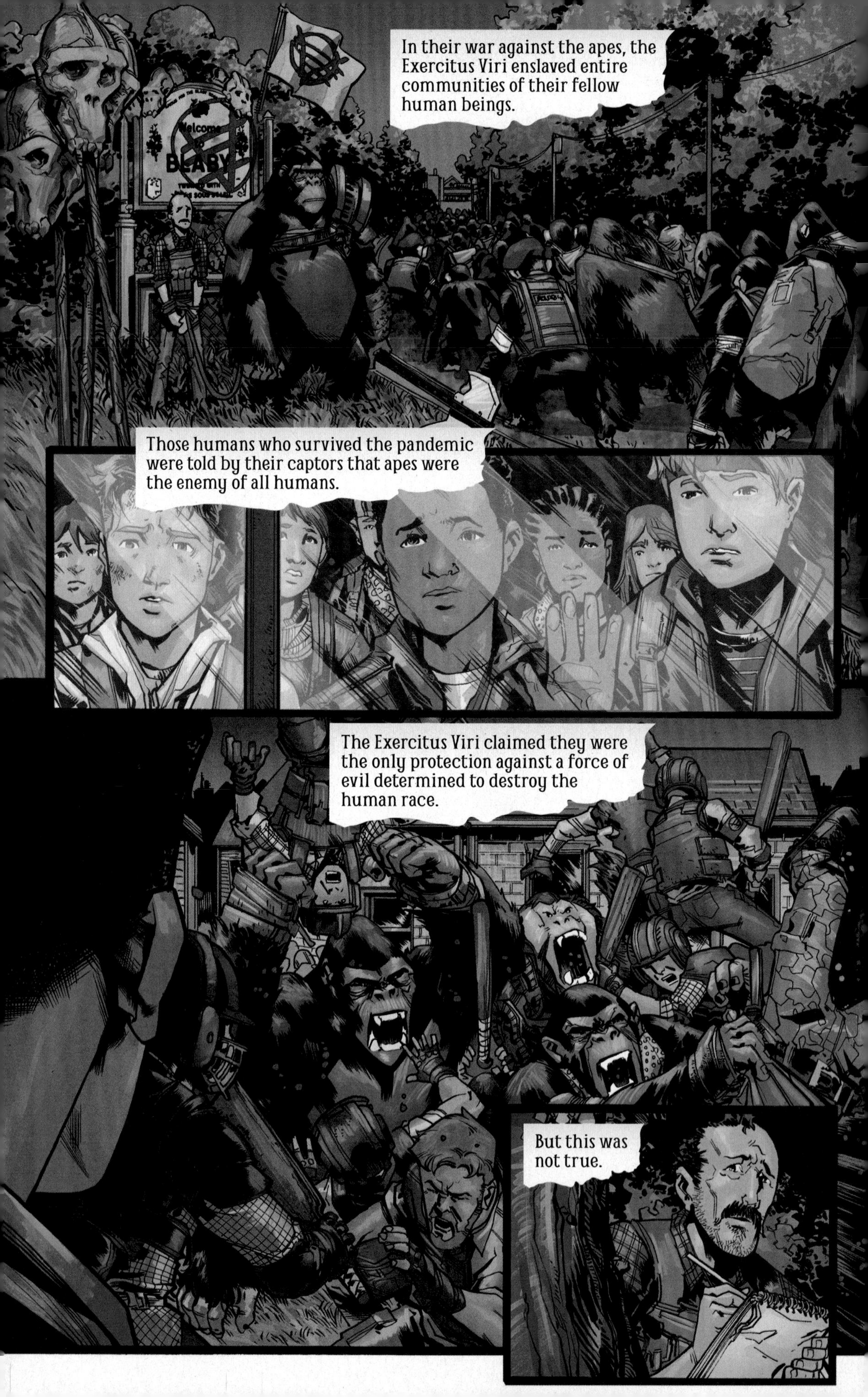
In their war against the apes, the Exercitus Viri enslaved entire communities of their fellow human beings.
Those humans who survived the pandemic were told by their captors that apes were the enemy of all humans.
The Exercitus Viri claimed they were the only protection against a force of evil determined to destroy the human race.
But this was not true.

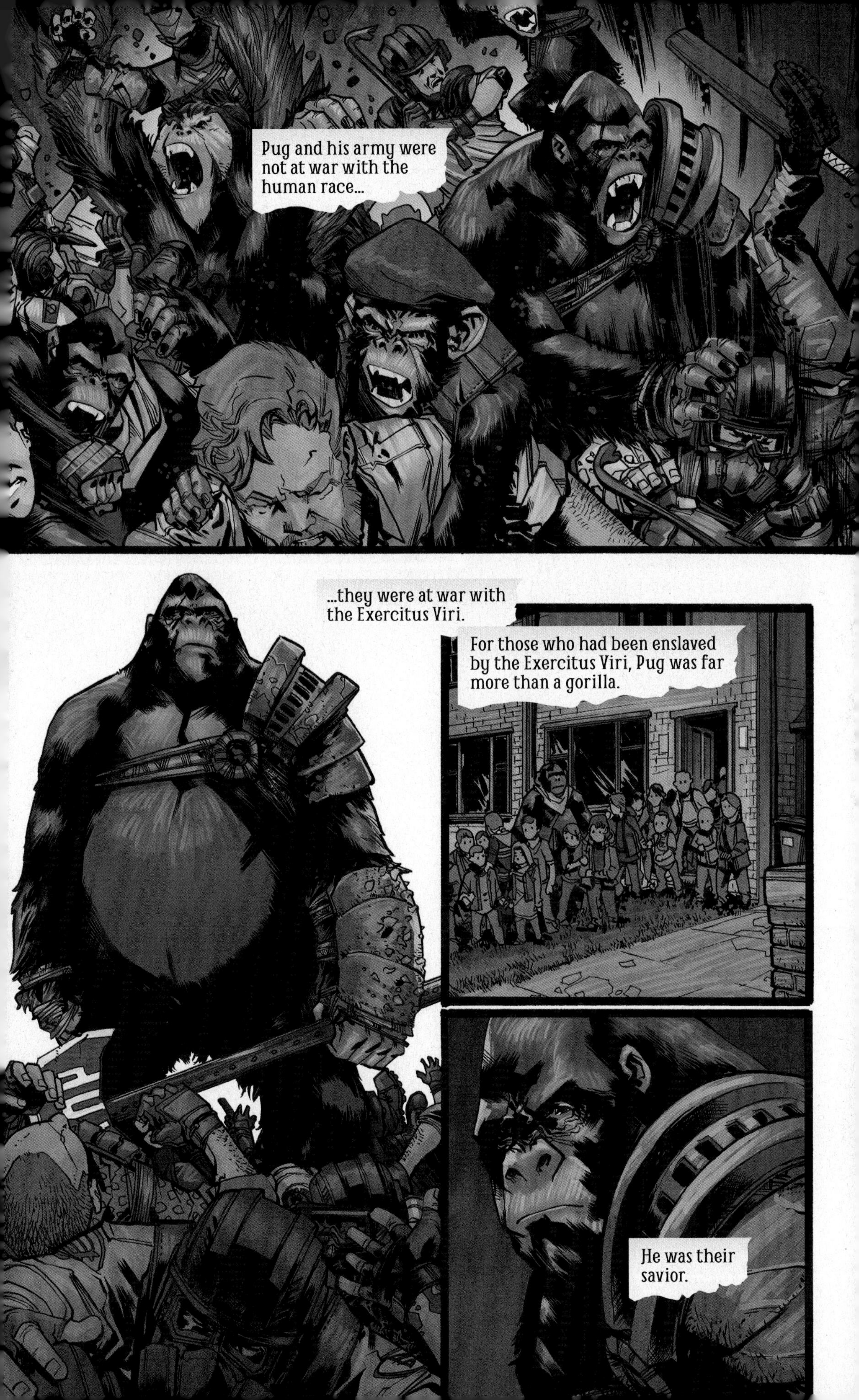
Pug and his army were not at war with the human race...
...they were at war with the Exercitus Viri.
For those who had been enslaved by the Exercitus Viri, Pug was far more than a gorilla.
He was their savior.

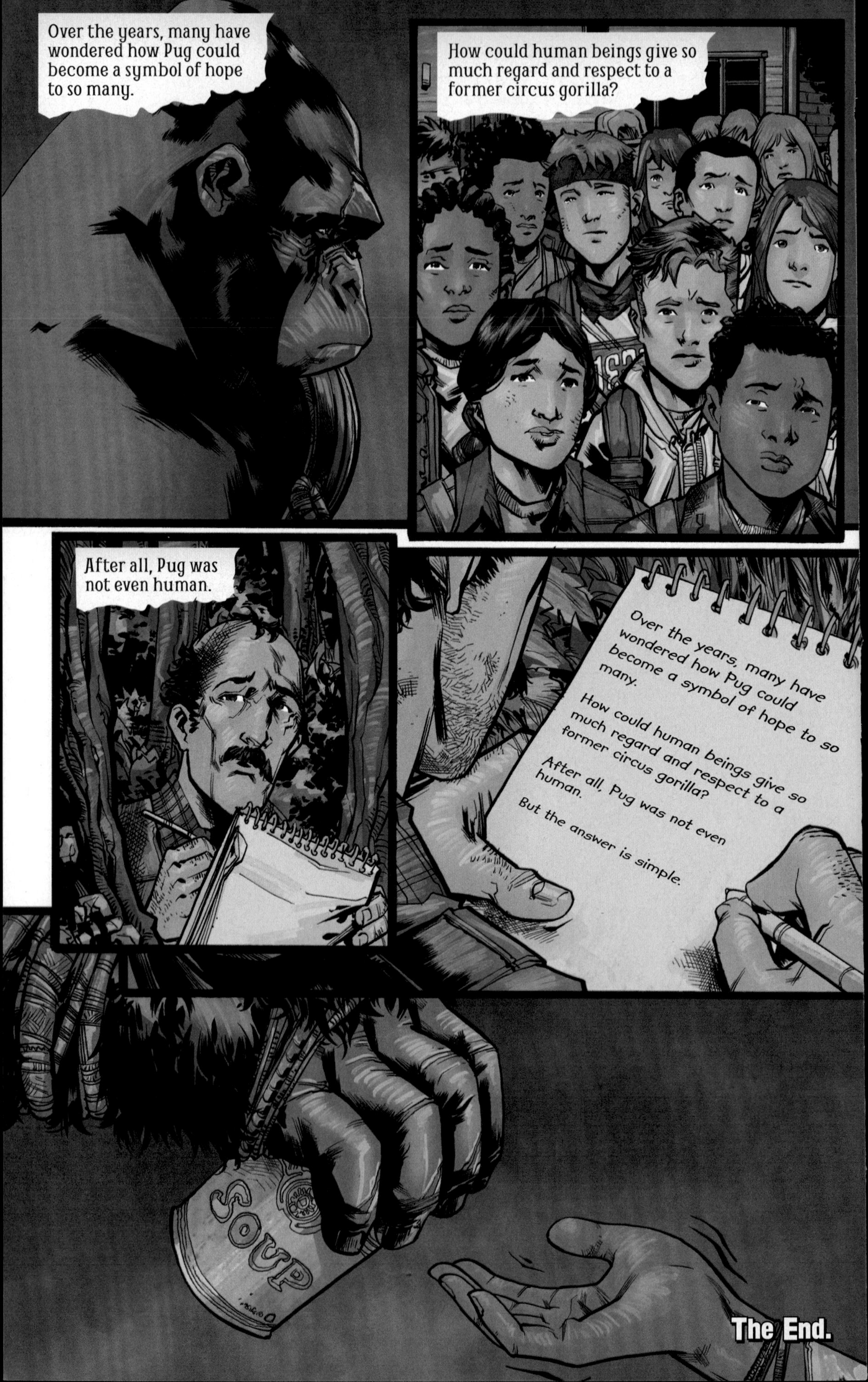

Over the years, many have wondered how Pug could become a symbol of hope to so many.
How could human beings give so much regard and respect to a former circus gorilla?
After all, Pug was not even human.
Over the years, many have wondered how Pug could become a symbol of hope to so many.
How could human beings give so much regard and respect to a former circus gorilla?
After all, Pug was not even human.
But the answer is simple.
SOUP
The End.

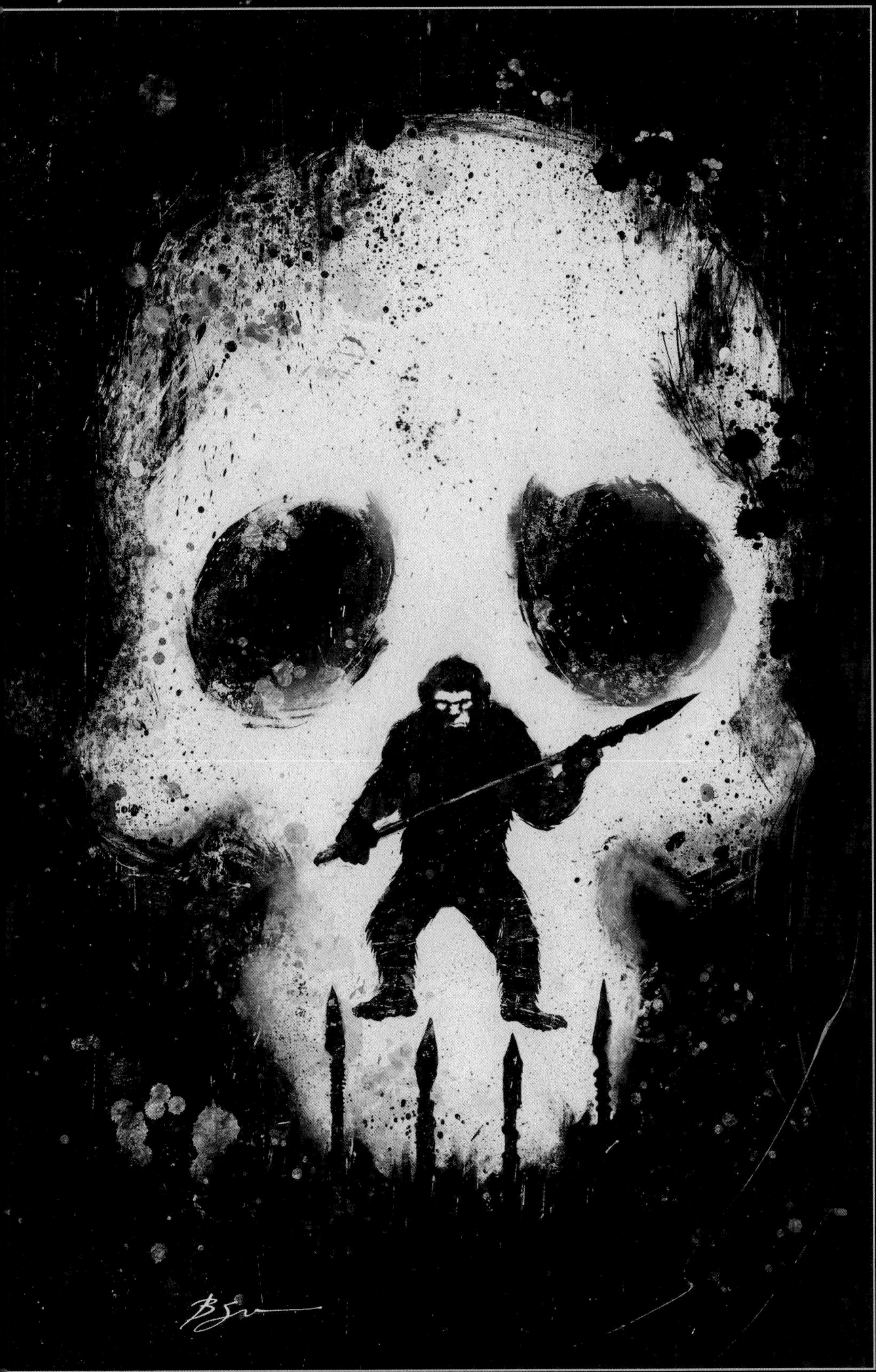

BENJAMIN SU

#3 Variant

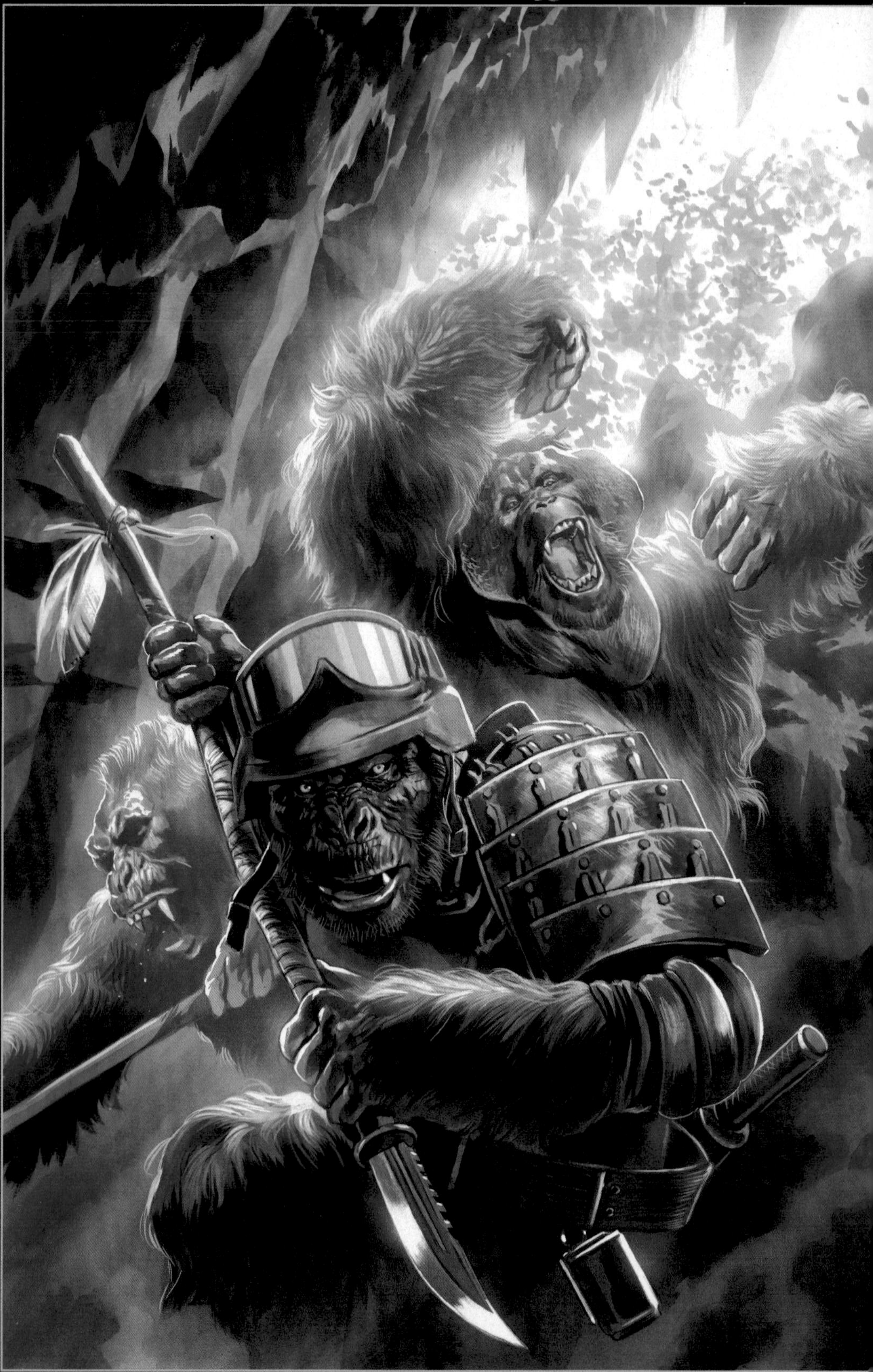

FELIPE MASSAFERA

#5 Variant

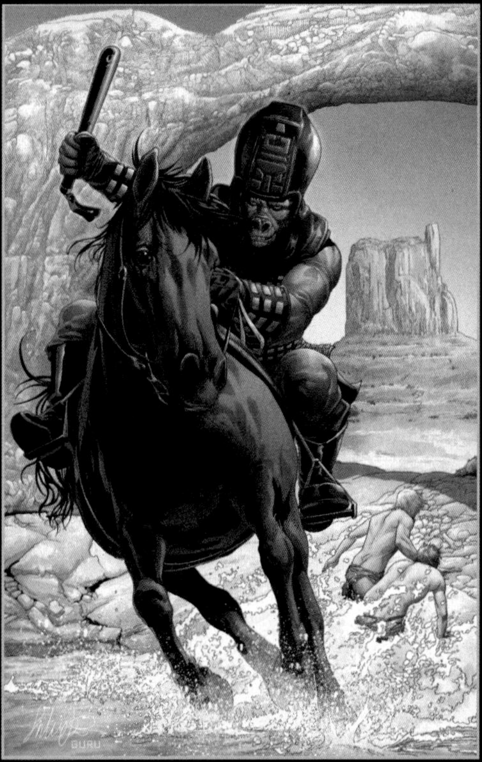
NAUCK

SALVADOR LARROCA & GURU-eFX

#1 Variant

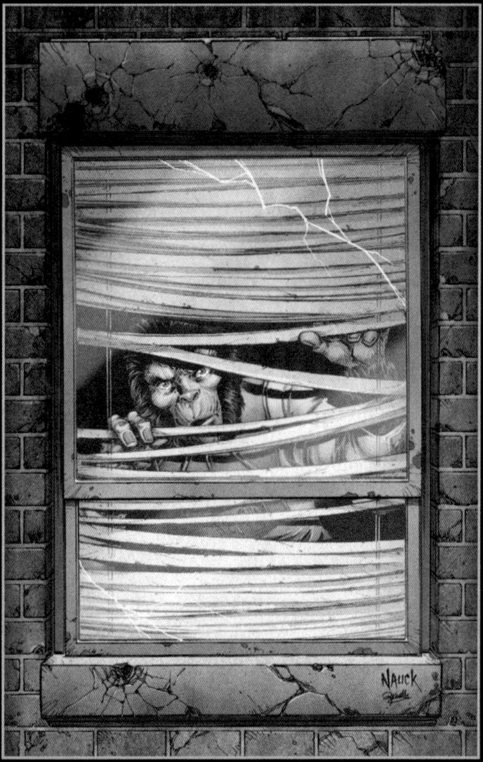

TODD NAUCK & RACHELLE ROSENBERG

#1 Variant

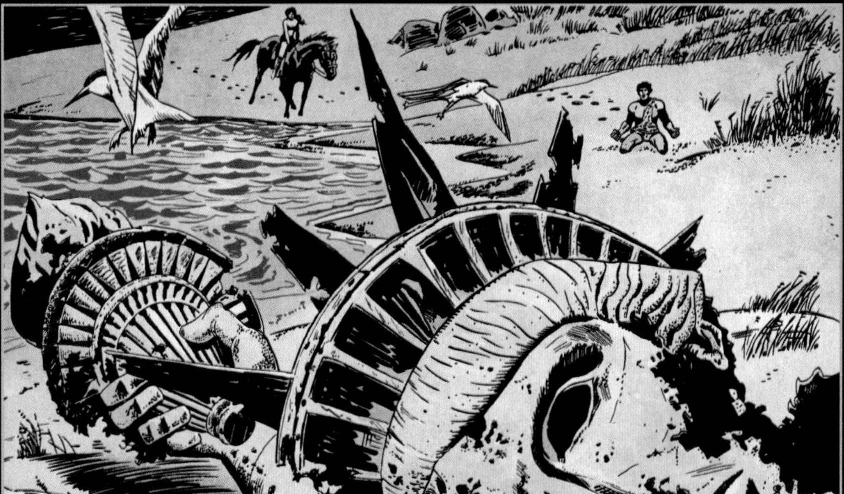

GEORGE TUSKA, MIKE ESPOSITO, TONY MORTELLARO & MATHEUS LOPES

#1 Remastered Variant

LOGAN LUBERA & **ISRAEL SILVA**

#1 Variant

MIKE McKONE & **RACHELLE ROSENBERG**

#1 Variant

RAFAEL ALBUQUERQUE

#2 Variant

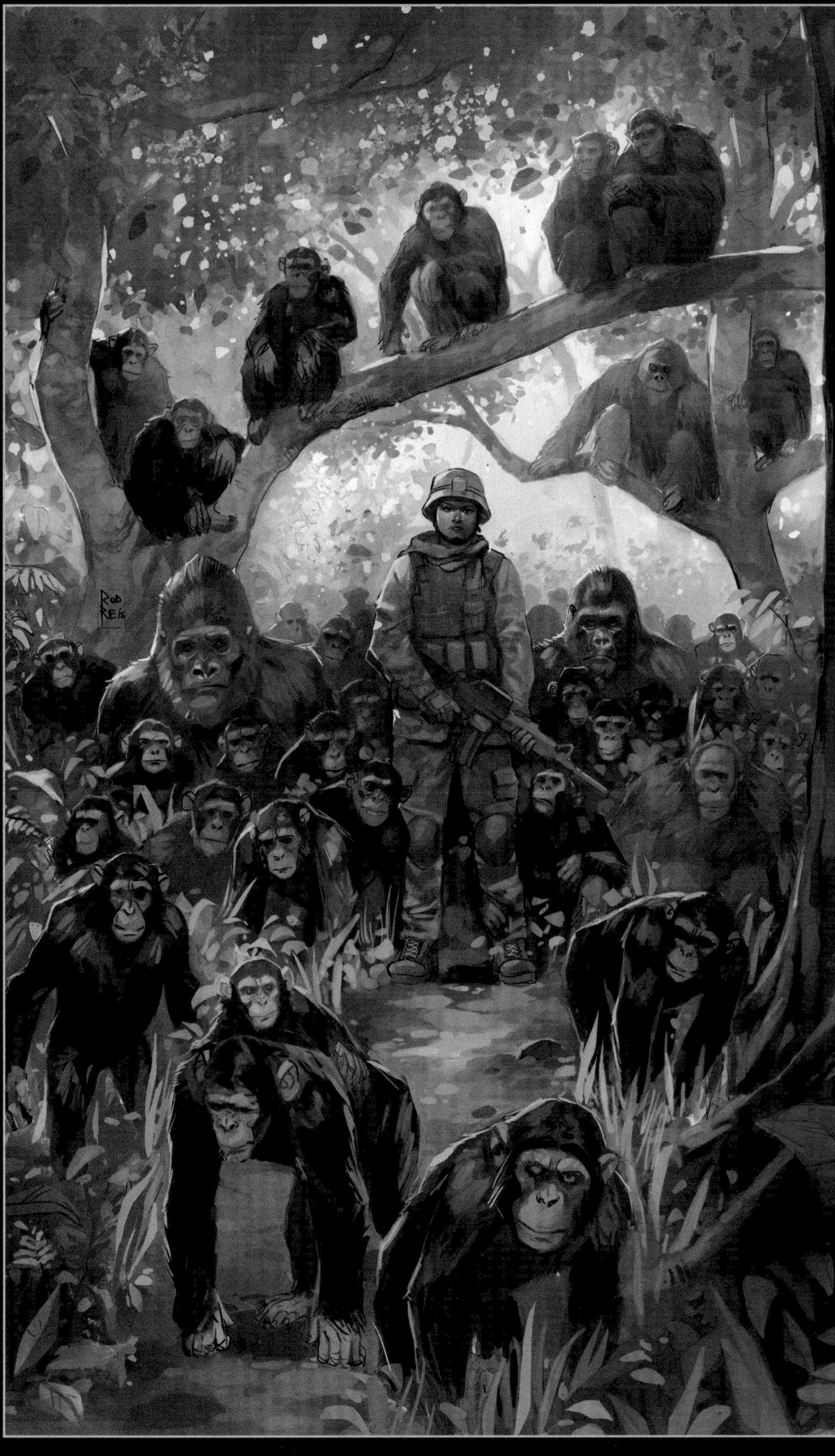
ROD REIS

ROD REIS

#2 Variant

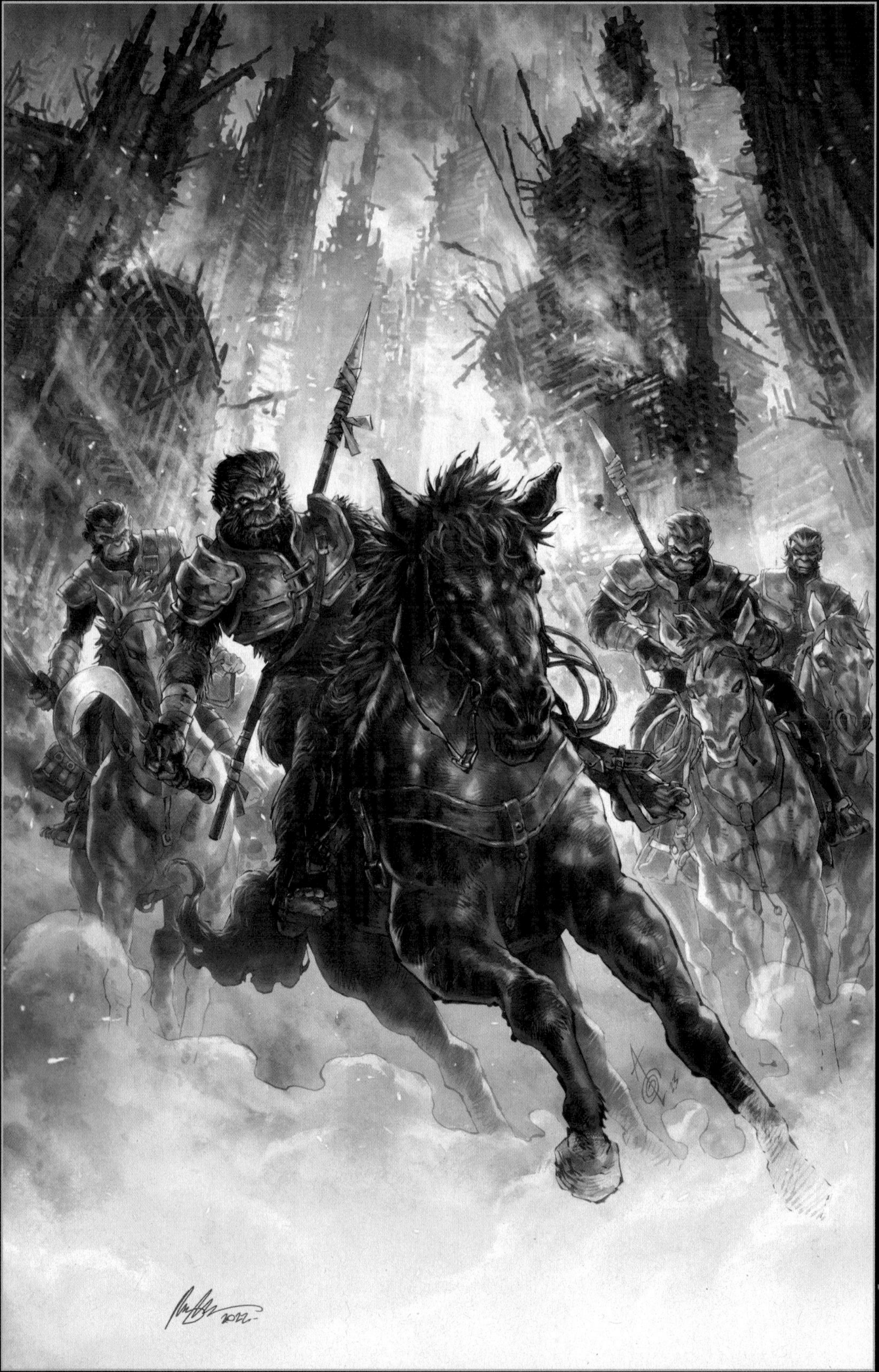

ALAN QUAH

#3 Variant